An Ordinary City

Justin B. Hollander

An Ordinary City

Planning for Growth and Decline in New Bedford, Massachusetts

Justin B. Hollander
Tufts University
Medford, Massachusetts, USA

ISBN 978-3-319-60704-7   ISBN 978-3-319-60705-4 (eBook)
DOI 10.1007/978-3-319-60705-4

Library of Congress Control Number: 2017946744

© The Editor(s) (if applicable) and The Author(s) 2018
This work is subject to copyright. All rights are solely and exclusively licensed by the Publisher, whether the whole or part of the material is concerned, specifically the rights of translation, reprinting, reuse of illustrations, recitation, broadcasting, reproduction on microfilms or in any other physical way, and transmission or information storage and retrieval, electronic adaptation, computer software, or by similar or dissimilar methodology now known or hereafter developed.
The use of general descriptive names, registered names, trademarks, service marks, etc. in this publication does not imply, even in the absence of a specific statement, that such names are exempt from the relevant protective laws and regulations and therefore free for general use.
The publisher, the authors and the editors are safe to assume that the advice and information in this book are believed to be true and accurate at the date of publication. Neither the publisher nor the authors or the editors give a warranty, express or implied, with respect to the material contained herein or for any errors or omissions that may have been made. The publisher remains neutral with regard to jurisdictional claims in published maps and institutional affiliations.

Cover illustration: Photo by David W. Siu / licensed under CC-BY 2.0

Printed on acid-free paper

This Palgrave Macmillan imprint is published by Springer Nature
The registered company is Springer International Publishing AG
The registered company address is: Gewerbestrasse 11, 6330 Cham, Switzerland

Acknowledgments

This book owes much to the support and encouragement of a broad network of friends, colleagues, and family members. First, there are my colleagues in the Department of Urban and Environmental Policy and Planning (UEP) at Tufts University: Julian Agyeman, Rachel Bratt, Mary Davis, Michael Flanary, Laurie Goldman, Rob Hollister, Lorlene Hoyt, Fran Jacobs, James Jennings, Shelly Krimsky, Penn Loh, Maria Nicolau, Barbara Parmenter, Ann Rappaport, Shomon Shamsuddin, Sumeeta Srinivasan, Jon Witten, and Weiping Wu. Beyond UEP, I also enjoyed great support from colleagues across the Tufts campus; special thanks go to Bob Cook, Jackie Dejean, Andrew McClellan, Durwood Marshall, Susan Morrison, Monica Pontes, Kent Portney, Donna Tyson, and Jeff Zabel. Graduate and undergraduate students at Tufts provided invaluable research assistance on this book, including Anna Krane, Alex Kostura, Erin Kizer, Lindsey Wright, Dan Zinder, Dan Runfola, Hanaa Rohman, Eliza Whiteman, Renee Guo, Alyssa Rosen Saunders, Sarah Spicer, Shuning Wang, Hanna Carr, Claudia Aliff, Ka Lum "Judy" Fung, Lorenzo Siemann, Max Lalanne, and McKayla Dunfey. I am also deeply indebted to the scores of local officials, community leaders, and engaged residents who participated in this research.

Early versions of this research were presented and benefited from constructive feedback at the Department of Urban Studies and Planning Lecture Series (MIT), Massachusetts Association of Planning Directors Monthly Luncheon Series, Community & Regional Planning Program (Iowa State University), UMass Creative Economy Lecture Series, Department of Landscape Architecture and Urban Planning Lecture

Series (Texas A&M University), Department of Urban Affairs and Planning Spring Lecture Series (Virginia Tech), Connecting for Change Annual Conference (Marion Institute), Schaeffer Family Seminar Series (College of the Holy Cross), Annual Academic Meeting of the Danske Landinspektørforening (The Danish Association of Chartered Surveyors), and Return of the American City: Redeeming the American Dream Symposium (University of Michigan School of Law). And during guest lectures in several courses, including Niall Kirkwood's Brownfields Practicum at the Graduate School of Design, Harvard University, Cathy Stanton's Global Cities course, and a colloquium session in the Department of Urban and Environmental Policy and Planning at Tufts.

The research for this book was partially supported through grants from the Government of Quebec, the Lincoln Institute of Land Policy, and the Tufts Faculty Research Awards Committee.

Special thanks go to the librarians at the New Bedford Public Library, Jay Avila at Spinner Publications, Bob Engler at SEB, Anne Louro of the City of New Bedford, and Jennifer Smith. Thanks also go to Susan Schulman and Rolf Pendall for their early feedback, Jeremy Németh for his willingness to share our collaborations more broadly, and to the acquisition, editing, production and marketing team at Palgrave, especially Rachel Krause Daniel for her interest and support of this project.

Most of all I offer my deepest appreciation to my family for helping make this book a reality.

Contents

1	Introduction	1
2	Planning for Growth and Decline in America: A Concise History	15
3	Theories of Smart Shrinkage and Smart Growth	39
4	How Much Change Is Too Much: A Look at the Numbers	63
5	The Legacy of Change: Depopulation and Growth's Impact on New Bedford Today	87
6	After the Hurricane: Government Responses to Employment and Population Decline, 1929–1975	101
7	Coming to Terms with Change: Contemporary Policy Responses	123
8	Urban Absorption	151

9 Conclusion	189
Appendix A	197
Appendix B	205
Appendix C	209
Appendix D	213
Bibliography	215
Index	231

LIST OF FIGURES

Fig. 1.1	New Bedford population, 1920–2010	8
Fig. 1.2	New Bedford employment, 1930–2010	9
Fig. 4.1	Locus map of New Bedford	64
Fig. 4.2	Map of New Bedford	66
Fig. 4.3	Population by the decade, 1970–2015	81
Fig. 4.4	Percentage population change, 1970–2015	82
Fig. 4.5	Reverse tract model	83
Fig. 6.1	South terminal before urban renewal project, c. 1965	108
Fig. 6.2	South terminal after urban renewal project, c. 1967	109
Fig. 6.3	Sketch of the proposed united front housing project	112
Fig. 6.4	Figure-ground drawings of South Central neighborhood 1924–1975	115
Fig. 6.5	Figure-ground drawings of Bullard Street neighborhood 1924–1975	116
Fig. 6.6	Figure-ground drawings of Cove Street neighborhood 1924–1975	117
Fig. 6.7	Cove Street lot	118
Fig. 8.1	Figure-ground drawings of South Central neighborhood 1924–2010	153
Fig. 8.2	Figure-ground drawings of Bullard Street neighborhood 1924–2010	154
Fig. 8.3	Figure-ground drawings of Cove Street neighborhood 1924–2010	155
Fig. 8.4	Map indicating Cove Street parcels	156
Fig. 8.5	South Central vacant lot	173
Fig. 8.6	South Central vacant lot	174
Fig. 8.7	South Central vacant lot	175

Fig. 8.8	South Central bus lot	176
Fig. 8.9	Cove Street garden	177
Fig. 8.10	Cove Street vacant lot	178
Fig. 8.11	Cove Street vacant lot	179
Fig. 8.12	South Central garden	180
Fig. 8.13	South Central parking lot	181
Fig. 8.14	South Central garden	182
Fig. A.1	Map of cities included in typicality analysis	198
Fig. A.2	Mahalanobis distances for 144 cities, 1970	203
Fig. A.3	Mahalanobis distances for 144 cities, 1970	204

LIST OF TABLES

Table 1.1	Population and employment levels in New Bedford, 1920–2010	5
Table 4.1	City-wide demographic data, New Bedford, 1970–2010	68
Table 4.2	City-wide demographic and housing data, New Bedford, 1970–2010	69
Table 4.3	North End (Bullard Street) demographic data	69
Table 4.4	North End (Bullard Street) demographic and housing data	70
Table 4.5	Cove Street demographic data	71
Table 4.6	Cove Street demographic and housing data	72
Table 4.7	South End demographic data	73
Table 4.8	South End demographic and housing data	76
Table 4.9	Occupied housing density in city of New Bedford, 1970–2000	84
Table 4.10	Occupied housing density for three study neighborhoods, 1970–2010	84
Table 7.1	New Bedford reports	126
Table 7.2	Policy emphasis	128
Table 7.3	Reasons for policies	131
Table 7.4	Word counts	136
Table 8.1	Cove Street neighborhood	158
Table 8.2	North End neighborhood	161
Table 8.3	South Central neighborhood	166
Table 8.4	Lot summary	172
Table 8.5	Lot uses	172
Table 8.6	Summary of results—Cove Street title searches	183

Table A.1	Variables used in typicality analysis	199
Table B.1	Reports used in content analysis	205
Table C.1	Themes used in latent content analysis	209
Table D.1	Keywords used in manifest content analysis	213

CHAPTER 1

Introduction

How and why do cities change? How should cities change? These are questions that great minds have grappled with since the most prominent architect and engineer of Ancient Rome, Vitruvius, strolled the *cardo* and the *decumanus*—the main streets of his city—on his way to meet with contemporaries in the forum.

This book seeks to slice off more focused research questions under those broader themes and contribute answers through an in-depth case study of New Bedford, Massachusetts. The urban studies literature is rich with general answers to urban change questions, but much less is understood about the nature of change in places facing depopulation and distress.

By many measures, New Bedford is a great city. But for much of the last century, it has also faced shrinkage in terms of jobs, and population and income levels. How can this be if growth is what makes a city great? Western culture tends to measure greatness in terms of expansion, development, and wealth. How can a city be great when these elements are in decline?

The New Bedford story—its rapid nineteenth-century rise as a global whale oil capital to its twenty-first century celebrity for a robust stock of abandoned housing, crime, and unemployment—is not a unique one. While the nearby Boston region exploded in population, from 3.9 million in 1970 to 4.6 million in 2012, New Bedford dropped from 101,777 to 94,929 people. The factors that make New Bedford great, then, are not completely obvious.

Decline or "shrinking" does tend to wreak havoc on a city. Decline extracts wealth from a place, leaving behind vast levels of poverty, criminality, and social change. New Bedford is no different. Losing jobs has meant fewer people, emptying out once much more populated streets and neighborhoods. But this phenomenon of *change* happens everywhere. The world is always changing, and cities are constantly cycling in and out of growth and decline—if not citywide, then certainly at the scale of neighborhoods and blocks. What matters, and really makes a difference, is how that *change* is managed. Looking closely at just one rather typical city helps to elucidate that change management.

Zoning—still the primary local land-use regulation—originated at the beginning of the twentieth century and was aimed to manage the ill effects of growth. In fact, the entire urban planning and local government development apparatus is built around managing growth: subdivision control regulation, design review boards, development impact fees, and so on. When I interviewed a Phoenix planner several years ago about what his office was working on during the Great Recession, when growth ground to a halt, he said they were getting ready for the next round of growth. When I asked him how the Phoenix's planning office was working to manage decline, he said that they weren't. The city was overwhelmed with tens of thousands of vacant homes, but the answer was that the planning office did not do that kind of work. Other cities have attempted to manage decline, but most, like Phoenix, manage only growth.

Cities have been, historically, a lot less adept at managing decline than managing growth. Through both historical and contemporary viewpoints, this book seeks to examine this very conundrum. How does a city manage its shrinkage? Who does, and who ought to do, the managing? What does well-managed decline mean for the people who live in a shrinking place? What does it mean for the physical form of neighborhoods when streets, parks, and institutions like schools and hospitals decline?

How does local government respond to this shrinkage? Within cities, what does the city planning function do relative to shrinkage? What can it do? Can public policy and planning make a difference in managing the change that comes with decline?

By looking closely at one city—New Bedford—I offer in this book the beginnings of answers to those questions. This memoir of an ordinary city paints New Bedford's story in a way that shows both the special qualities of a small coastal, postindustrial city in New England and how the process of decline and growth affect what is, by most measures, an average city.¹

New Bedford really represents an entire category of cities that escape mainstream urban studies' more customary attention to global cities (e.g., New York), booming cities (Atlanta), and shrinking cities (Flint). New Bedford-style ordinary cities don't belong in those categories as they neither grow nor decline drastically. In their inconspicuousness, however, they account for the vast majority of cities in the USA.

San Francisco has grown spectacularly in recent years, yet nearby cities including San Mateo, Richmond, and Daly City all grew less than 1% (California Department of Finance 2015). States and the federal government in the USA pay attention to the problems of the headliner cities, like the New York State billion-dollar investment in the dramatically shrinking city of Buffalo. But in tens of thousands of cities across the globe, the quotidian task of running a city without any appreciable growth or decline is left unstudied. In New England, for example, among the 168 cities and towns with a population of 20,000 or higher in 2010, only 33 grew by more than 1% per year since 1980 (booming cities). Twenty-four experienced a net loss (shrinking cities), but the wide majority, 111 cities, were in between—not really growing or shrinking. These middle-of-the-road cities are not topping any "best of" or "worst of" list of cities, though the challenges that local officials face are daunting. They have both the real estate and gentrification pressures of new development in some areas, while they experience the difficulties of depopulation and disinvestment in other areas. Such schizophrenia within a single city can be particularly hard to manage and effectively plan for.

My own research has used the easy, dichotomous growth-decline categorization to understand the problems of depopulation, disinvestment, and abandonment, but sometimes those categories are muddied in reality. One of my earliest research projects took me to a devastated neighborhood in Youngstown, Ohio, replete with abandoned buildings and overgrown lots. Through a mix of qualitative and quantitative research, I was able to say something meaningful about how the city changed when jobs and people started to leave. In retrospect, the problem with my initial conclusions was that some Youngstown neighborhoods are now thriving. The active investment going on in the downtown of the city meant that calling Youngstown a shrinking city was oversimplification. In this book, I seek to remedy that weakness of categorization by acknowledging that even in emptied-out cities, there is some growth. Similarly, as I've witnessed in my research into the Sun Belt region of the USA, there is decline even in growing cities.

For a little context on New Bedford, I offer here a quick tour of the demographic shifts in the surrounding New England landscape. New Bedford's population decline began in the 1930s; but by 1950, nearby Boston and Providence also began to witness precipitous drops in their own populations, as did scores of similarly situated postindustrial cities in New England and throughout the Rust belt, like Hartford (Connecticut), Portland (Maine), Buffalo (New York), Scranton (Pennsylvania), Cleveland (Ohio), Gary (Indiana), and many, many more (see Table 1.1).

While New Bedford continued to struggle, by 1980 demographics had shifted all around it. The larger Eastern Massachusetts region[2] added more than one-million inhabitants, from 3.5 million in 1980 to 4.6 million in 2012 (U.S. Census 2014; Hobbs and Stoops 2002), led by a steady growth in both Boston and Providence's population. Today, the Eastern Massachusetts growth machine continues to churn out new housing, shopping centers, and office parks. But New Bedford never "turned itself around" and instead remains small, home to some 95,000 people. It takes some digging to figure out how and why New Bedford paradoxically continues to thrive in unorthodox ways.

The end of the nineteenth century saw the rapid rise of the whaling business and the increase of New Bedford's locational advantage and its employment levels, population, and number of housing units. Those elements suffered, with decline in jobs and a drop in population, when a number of events combined to make New Bedford less appealing to industry. But housing units do not disappear, like people and jobs do, in a shrinking city. In fact, housing is quite durable, and even when demand evaporates, the wood and metal and brick typically stay put. Homes are often abandoned in shrinking cities and become a scourge on their neighborhoods.

To be more precise, people do not just leave a place as the winds of locational advantage shift. Some individuals and families stay put when they lose their jobs and their employment outlook diminishes. Some people have such strong attachment to a place that they are reluctant to follow their jobs out of the area and instead chose to live close to relatives and friends, where they are able to visit family cemeteries and support their community. In this age of *Bowling Alone*, such die-hards are rare, but not in New Bedford.[3] One lifelong resident and community activist in

Table 1.1 Population and employment levels in New Bedford, 1920–2010

	1920	1930	1940	1950	1960	1970	1980	1990	2000	2010
New Bedford total population	121,217	112,597	110,341	109,189	102,477	101,777	98,478	99,922	93,768	95,072
New Bedford total employment	—	52,124	40,400	46,421	41,771	41,090	44,891	39,663	39,758	41,649
% pop fall from last decade	—	−7%	−2%	−1%	−6%	−1%	−3%	1%	−6%	1%
% employ fall from last decade	—	—	−22%	15%	−10%	−2%	9%	−12%	0%	5%
Sources						Total employed in Civilian labor force		Total employed (16 yrs+) in Civilian labor force	Total employed (16 yrs+) in Civilian labor force	Total employed (16 yrs+) in Civilian labor force
		Table 14, Gainfully Occupied Males and Females, 10 years and over, by Color and Nativity, for Cities of 100,000 or more: 1930. United States. Bureau of the Census. Title Fifteenth census of the United States: 1930. Abstract of the Fifteenth census of the United States. Publication Info. Washington, U. S. Govt. Print. Off., 1933	U.S. Bureau of the Census. *County Data Book, 1947*. (A Supplement to the Statistical Abstract of the United States.) U.S. Government Printing Office, Washington, DC, 1947. p. 194–195	U.S. Bureau of the Census. *County and City Data Book, 1956*. (A Statistical Abstract Supplement.) U.S. Government Printing Office, Washington, DC, 1957. p. 441	U.S. Bureau of the Census. *County and City Data Book, 1967*. (A Statistical Abstract Supplement.) U.S. Government Printing Office, Washington, DC, 1967. p. 163 and p. 591	U.S. Bureau of the Census. *County and City Data Book, 1972*. (A Statistical Abstract Supplement.) U.S. Government Printing Office, Washington, DC, 1973. p. 224 and 702	U.S. Bureau of the Census. *County and City Data Book, 1983*. (A Statistical Abstract Supplement.) U.S. Government Printing Office, Washington, DC, 1983. p. 256, 262, 266 and 724	U.S. Bureau of the Census. *County and City Data Book, 1994*. (A Statistical Abstract Supplement.) U.S. Government Printing Office, Washington, DC, 1994. p. 256, 264 and p. 746 754	U.S. Bureau of the Census. *County and City Data Book, 2002*. (A Statistical Abstract Supplement.) U.S. Government Printing Office, Washington, DC, 2002. p. 995, 999; AND U.S. Bureau of the Census. *County and City Data Book, 200*. (A Statistical Abstract Supplement.) U.S. Government Printing Office, Washington, DC, 1994	U.S. Census Bureau, 2007–2011 American Community Survey. http://quickfacts.census.gov/qfd/states/25/25005.html Accessed April 3, 2013

Notes: Statistical abstracts from 1892–1910 include imports, exports, public school, metals, ag, population only, gold, silver, debts; U.S. census website doesn't appear to make any data pre-1998 available; 1930 and earlier, there's no Country and Data book only statistical abstracts with state as smallest unit; 1970 and after census starts using "labor force" and "civilian" workforce instead of employment"

New Bedford, who was the only one of all her high school friends to stay behind, explained:

> For those of us who stayed, there's hope; you know it's gonna get better. You have family, friends. I could live anywhere in the country, I'm a military brat, but I want to live here. As bad as it gets or seems to the outside world, it's good here.

But as Lucy and Philips (2000) showed in their study of shrinking suburbs, most people are always on the go. In metropolitan areas, 50% of all household relocate every five years. Places need to remain attractive to outsiders to continually replace those outmigrants. As Lucy and Philips explain, the places that cannot replace outmigrants experience a net loss in population and begin to experience decline in housing and rental prices. Falling prices and further population loss will mean high vacancy levels and housing abandonment problems. That process clearly played out in New Bedford. But something else occurred in the city that adds to the theory of decline by showing how one place absorbed that shrinkage. It is important to emphasize here that New Bedford is not an especially unique city, whether it be in its physical change or in the way city leaders intervened. In many ways, the stories that will unfold in the following chapters are common throughout the Rust Belt. What I have done in this book is to dive deeply into the details and specifics of one ordinary place and ask the question, "How did one city manage shrinkage and change?" This approach differs from a broader multi-case study approach (which I have employed in previous research) and allows for greater depth. By picking New Bedford and studying its story, I can offer to city planners and community leaders lessons from this process so that they may better plan in the future for economic decline in their own communities.

While economists often speak of changing locational advantage in explaining decline, the New Bedford's experience over the last century has been about more than just a shift in locational preferences. A whole array of social problems have appeared in the city. Many are regularly attributed to economic challenges—such as high crime, gang activity, teen pregnancy, and family dislocation—but not necessarily all. No matter how troubled the city may appear today, a vivid glimpse of what some see as the city's high water mark—circa 1880, when the city was proudly labeled the whaling capital of the world—can be visited through the pages of Herman Melville's *Moby Dick*. The early chapters of Melville's classic, which are set in New Bedford, recount in detail the extreme wealth and prosperity that the city once enjoyed:

> The town itself is perhaps the dearest place to live in, in all New England. It is a land of oil, true enough: but not like Canaan; a land, also, of corn and wine. The streets do not run with milk; nor in the spring-time do they pave them with fresh eggs. Yet, in spite of this, nowhere in all America will you find more patrician-like houses; parks and gardens more opulent, than in New Bedford. (Melville 1988, p. 37)

At the same time, Melville shows us the city's underbelly, a district in the city that is empty, dark, and frightening:

> Such dreary streets! blocks of blackness, not houses, on either hand, and here and there a candle, like a candle moving about in a tomb. At this hour of the night, of the last day of the week, that quarter of the town proved all but deserted. But presently, I came to a smoky light proceeding from a low, wide, building, the door of which stood invitingly open. It had a careless look, as if it were meant for the uses of the public; so, entering, the first thing I did was the stumble over an ash-box in the porch. Ha! thought I, ha, as the flying particles almost choked me, are these ashes from that destroyed city, Gomorrah? (Melville 1988, p. 10)

Perhaps the problems of today are not dissimilar to the challenges faced by New Bedford during its zenith. But one of the main differences today is the change in the city's physical presence that occurred when its economic conditions suffered. New Bedford became visually unattractive. Esthetically, the city lost its luster. Its grand and historic buildings became eyesores due to lack of proper maintenance and occupancy. Why? By 1940, there were just 40,400 jobs—a huge fall-off from the 52,124 documented positions in 1930. The city's population hit a high of 121,217 in 1920 and quickly began to drop in subsequent years, a 10% decrease in residents over three decades (see Figs. 1.1 and 1.2). As people left, the city's built environment did not magically contract—there were simply too many buildings for a shrinking city. The city of Youngstown, Ohio, which faces similar shrinkage, was likened to "a size-40 man wearing a size-40 suit" in its "2010 Vision" plan. Unfortunately, it's an apt description for New Bedford as well.

City leadership cannot be blamed for focusing on the physical effects of decline, because that was something that New Bedford had never experienced before. Social problems, crime, and depravity have always been

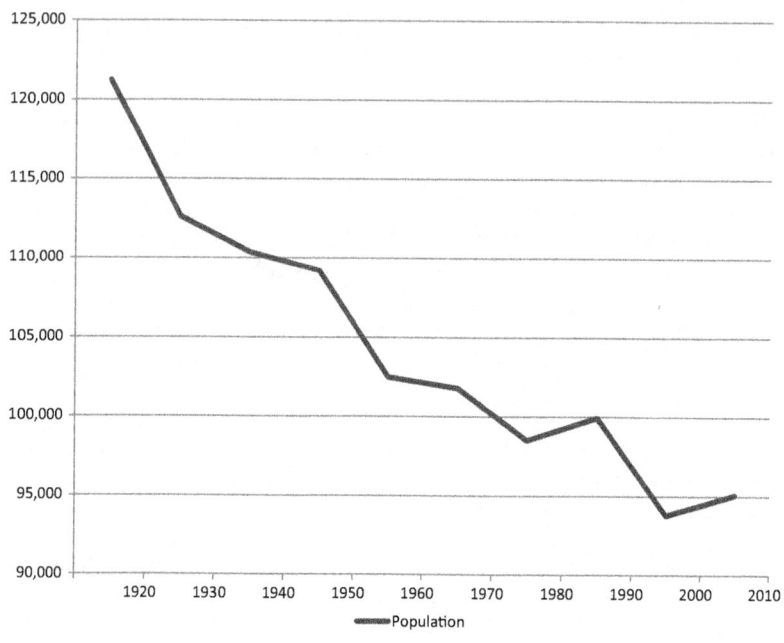

Fig. 1.1 New Bedford population, 1920–2010

around. But with jobs and people starting to leave, the problem of the city's physical deterioration became a new focus.

Located in southeastern Massachusetts, less than 60 miles from Boston, New Bedford was a great industrial center of the nineteenth century and has struggled ever since. The last whaling ship left the city's harbor only 75 years after the publication of *Moby Dick*, and its departure marked the beginning of the city's inexorable slide (Wolfbein 1944). This one-industry town suffered greatly when oil reserves were discovered in Pennsylvania and the market for whale blubber vanished. But the city's attachment to the sea persists even today. The traditions of whaling and maritime trades continue to be a part of the city's heritage, most clearly demonstrated in its *working* waterfront.[4] Despite the difficulties caused by widespread unemployment after the crash of the whaling industry, plans were in the works by the middle of the nineteenth century to invent a replacement business for the city. Many individuals and families grew

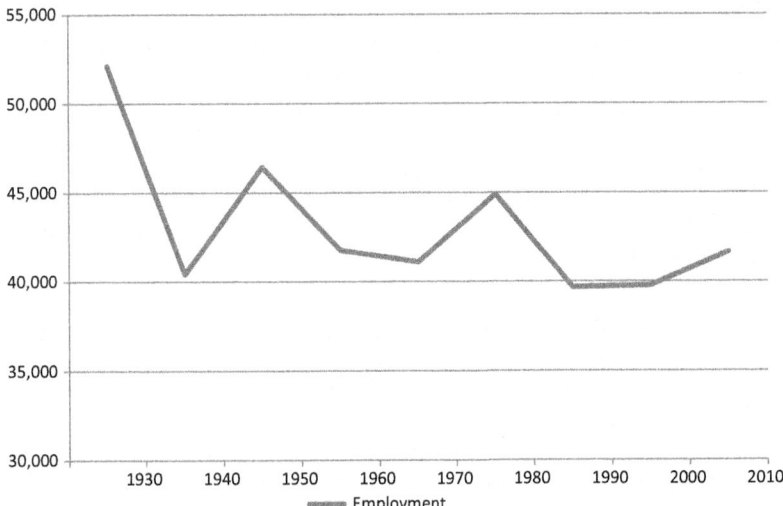

Fig. 1.2 New Bedford employment, 1930–2010

wealthy during the height of whaling and invested those savings in cotton textile mills. The first cotton mill in New Bedford was erected in 1846, and by 1932 there were 42, which meant that "the city had become the center of the manufacture of fine cotton goods in the United States" (Wolfbein 1944). In fact, between 1907 and 1928, an 88% of all capital investments in the city were made in the cotton industry (Voyer et al. 2000, p. 358).

In the same way that the bottom fell out of whaling, the cotton market eventually crashed, and by the end of the Great Depression the lack of industrial diversity was quite apparent. In New Bedford, "it is probable that at least 60,000 persons, or one-half of the entire population were directly and immediately affected by the collapse in cotton textiles" (Wolfbein 1944, p. 107). New Bedford's experience paralleled a broad shift underway throughout New England. Barkin (1981) calculated that there were 357 mills in the region in 1919, down to 259 in 1929, 161 in 1939, and only 64 by 1963. This economic devastation translated quickly to community devastation because "community life [had] to a large extent centered on mill employment" (Bureau of Labor Statistics, as quoted in Hartford 1996, p. 99).

Hartford (1996) conveys the tragedy of these closings through the intimate account of Raymount Dupont, a New Bedford native whose working life spanned the tumultuous twentieth century:

> [Dupont's] textile career had begun at New Bedford's Wamsutta until December 1926, when he quit to become a peg boy at the Nashawena mills. Two decades and ten job changes later, he would be back at Nashawena. On two other occasions, mill closings had forced him to seek new employment. (Hartford 1996, p. 99)

The decimated community sought to fight against this widespread unemployment and consequential poverty, but the massive hurricane of 1938 caused even greater damage, and new, sustained growth has been elusive ever since.

Acclaimed creative non-fiction author Rory Nugent spent 17 years living in New Bedford and wrote the book *Down at the Docks* in 2009. The book tells the stories of a half-dozen real New Bedfordians, with names changed to protect anonymity. They are an unsavory bunch, in part attempting to live up to the bad reputation of New Bedford fishermen, which is summed up to Nugent by a long-time dockworker as "First, they lie; next they rob you; afterwards they screw your daughters; last, before they leave, they hook all the kids in town on dope" (Nugent 2009, 165).

But Nugent looked beyond the surface, finding astute insight among these New Bedfordians:

> As the electronic age blossomed, the city withered, losing tens of thousands of jobs, none of which Mako [one of Nugent's characters] expects to reappear. That leaves fishing as the only vital industry left in town, but he cautions, fishing could go belly-up at any time.... All he's sure of: fishermen are on the wrong side of tomorrow, same as mill workers used to be. (Nugent 2009, p. 79)

Not all of Nugent's subjects were so gloomy:

> [Another resident] calls New Bedford a rust bucket of a town that's sinking at the mooring. Going deeper and deeper into the muck all the time. Because of this, seconds pass as fucking hours for a whole lot of folk, she says, adding, It's all slo-mo when you're hurting and this city's hurting some—bad. Bleeding jobs like crazy. (Nugent 2009, p. 30)

Nugent's own analysis of New Bedford history centers around the one-two punch of the Great Depression and the hurricane of 1938. One of his subjects, Pink, confirms the findings of historians, echoing the sentiment that "the hurricane also emptied many people of the last thing they owned, hope" (p. 139).

What followed was a major outmigration, where just about anyone who could leave New Bedford did. Another of Nugent's real-life characters has never met anyone with money, unless they were a drug dealer, "shady lawyer," or "a couple people who hit the Lotto" (p. 206). As Nugent puts it:

> The old aristocracy had decamped by the late 1960s, unnerved by local race riots and put off by the rising power of the middle class in city affairs. They moved to the burbs or out of state, and today the only palpable evidence of swells ever having lived in New Bedford is their old mansions. Some were converted for use as apartments or offices for lawyers and doctors and dentists; a few ... were bought by drug dealers; and others were abandoned and left to rot, becoming kindling for arsonists. (p. 206)

Amid all this decline and depression, city officials sought to remake the city in the 1960s through urban renewal programs. An unusual facet of this story is that a small band of historic preservationists were able to successfully utilize federal urban renewal monies for historic preservation. This group, the Waterfront Historic Area League (WHALE), asked, "How can we save our city's heritage from death by neglect and the tyranny of the bulldozer?" (McCabe and Thomas 1995, p. 10). WHALE believed that "the rehabilitation of the waterfront could raise the spirits of the whole city" (McCabe and Thomas 1995, p. 25).

The efforts of WHALE eventually led to the 1996 designation of the New Bedford Whaling National Historic Park covering 34 acres at the heart of the city's historic center. The effort led directly to the restoration of 33 buildings and, indirectly, a revival of the adjacent waterfront area (Gittell 1989).

The urban renewal, historic preservation, and federal park designation have all combined to make downtown New Bedford a truly vibrant place today. Indeed, the city was profiled in an "Escapes" section of *The New York Times*, which said that "Tough times and a rough reputation is how the city is generally perceived regionally. ... Truth is, though, New Bedford has plenty of history, architecture, and small museums to fill a weekend" (Schneider 2006, p. 3).

Somewhere between postindustrial wasteland and tourist destination, New Bedford is many things to many people, and for urbanists it is a wholly generalizable laboratory to study the ways that cities adjust to decline, past and present. Whether you visit to enjoy the city's gorgeous parks and harbor views, to work in the bustling fishing and processing industries, or just to get a good price on an apartment (the average residents pays $771 per month for rent, compared to $1320 per month in Boston, according to the 2015 U.S. Census), New Bedford has many amenities along with its numerous aforementioned drawbacks. The city's annual Working Waterfronts Festival welcomes thousands to America's largest commercial fishing port, with games, special events, and locally caught seafood. Several art and historical museums, along with the National Park in the city's core, make the city a cultural hub for the region. With both the good and the bad, the city remains quite typical of much of urban America, making it a useful spot to study the great city planning questions of today.

The remainder of the book is organized around a central thesis: the lessons of New Bedford's growth and decline matter because all outcomes have not been positive and these results mirror the historical tendencies of many similarly situated cities throughout New England and the Midwest. The city has experienced a bumpy demographic ride of population gain, loss, and gain again. As industry came and went, the city's shrinkage has not been even. Throughout the past nine decades, New Bedford has struggled to manage change, resulting in both success and failure. The city has not witnessed the extreme depopulation of places like Buffalo, New York (which has lost more than 50% of its population since 1950). Instead, it represents a more typical profile of an American city today, witnessing some severe population contraction, then decades of ups and downs (Beauregard 2009). A city like that is not easy to plan for. The legacy of major economic collapse and the exit of large segments of the population can be difficult to overcome. For New Bedford, the calamity began around the time of the Great Depression; for many other US cities, it started in earnest in the 1950s or 1970s. But the lessons from this book are about how the physical form of New Bedford adapted to these fits and starts, how vacancy was managed, and where the concept of "smart shrinkage" plays in.

As may already be apparent, my writing style blends conventional academic discourse with more casual and inviting prose, in some cases bordering on journalistic. In a break from past practices, much of contemporary scholarly writing tends to be a hybrid of first person, memoir, authoritative, detached, and even theatrical (see Sheldon Krimsky's *Stem Cell Dialogues*, Columbia University Press [2016]). In part inspired by Herman Melville in his classically hybrid *Moby Dick*, this book includes a bricolage of styles, some intimate and personal, some detached and academic. For different sections of the book, I chose the style that best fits the material, honing that approach to fit the unique purpose and aims of each section.

The two chapters (Chaps. 2 and 3) that follow ground the lessons of New Bedford's changing physical form in the historical, theoretical, and empirical literature—introducing concepts and ideas that will be returned to throughout the book. In Chap. 4, I describe and analyze the current physical conditions in New Bedford, drawing on extensive field research. Chapter 5 provides evidence to support the notion that both growth and depopulation have been actively managed, and describes the impact that change has had on the quality of life for residents based on interviews and focus groups. Chapter 6 takes a step back to review the key historical events that led to the present conditions in New Bedford, with particular attention to how government authorities responded to the early decades of depopulation.

Chapter 7 expands the attention to government action, looking closely at what New Bedford has done over the last decade to respond to simultaneously mounting growth and decline. Chapter 8 introduces a new conceptual model for thinking about quality of life in these very ordinary cities and applies that model through innovative mapping and field observation in three New Bedford neighborhoods. The book concludes by showing how the lessons of New Bedford's stormy history, and contemporary approaches, might be applied to similarly situated cities.

Notes

1. See Appendix A where I draw on dozens of socioeconomic, housing, and demographic variables to demonstrate just how <u>ordinary</u> New Bedford actually is.
2. Much of Eastern Massachusetts is classified by the US Census as the Boston-Cambridge-Quincy, MA-NH Metropolitan Statistical Area.
3. See Putnam (2000).
4. New Bedford has maintained an active working waterfront despite external efforts to convert the waterfront to a museum, tourist attraction, or residential enclave. Today, the city generates much of its employment and tax revenues from active commercial operations at the waterfront.

Bibliography

Barkin, Solomon. 1981. Management and Ownership in the New England Cotton Textile Industry. *Journal of Economic Issues*. Social Science Premium Collection [ProQuest]. Web 23 January 2017.

Beauregard, Robert A. 2009. Urban Population Loss in Historical Perspective: United States, 1820–200. *Environment & Planning A* 41 (3): 514–528.

California Department of Finance. 2015. E-1 Population Estimates for Cities, Counties, and the State. Accessed January 11, 2016. http://www.dof.ca.gov/Forecasting/Demographics/Estimates/E-1/.

Gittell, Ross Jacobs. 1989. A Critical Analysis of Local Initiatives in Economic Revitalization. Order No. 9013286 Harvard University. Ann Arbor: ProQuest. Web 26 February 2017.

Hartford, William F. 1996. *Where Is Our Responsibility?: Unions and Economic Change in the New England Textile Industry, 1870–1960*. Amherst: University of Massachusetts.

Hobbs, Frank, and Nicole Stoops. 2002. *Demographic Trends in the 20th Century*. Washington, DC: U.S. Census Bureau.

Lucy, William H., and David L. Phillips. 2000. *Confronting Suburban Decline: Strategic Planning for Metropolitan Renewal*. Washington, DC: Island Press.

McCabe, Marsha, and Joseph D. Thomas. 1995. *Not Just Anywhere: The Story of WHALE and the Rescue of New Bedford's Waterfront Historic District*. New Bedford, MA: Spinner Publications.

Melville, Herman. 1988/1851. *Moby-Dick or, The Whale*. New York, NY: Penguin Books.

Nugent, Rory. 2009. *Down at the Docks*. New York, NY: Pantheon.

Putnam, Robert D. 2000. *Bowling Alone: The Collapse and Revival of American Community*. New York, NY: Simon & Schuster.

U.S. Census. 2014. Census Website. Accessed July 1, 2015.

Schneider, Paul. 2006. 36 Hours in New Bedford, Mass. *New York Times*, May 26.

Voyer, Richard A., Carol Pesch, Jonathan Garber, Jane Copeland, and Randy Comeleo. 2000. New Bedford, Massachusetts: A Story of Urbanization and Ecological Connections. *Environmental History*. ProQuest SciTech Collection. Web 11 July 2017.

Wolfbein, Seymour L. 1944. *The Decline of a Cotton Textile City: A Study of New Bedford*. New York, NY: Columbia University Press.

CHAPTER 2

Planning for Growth and Decline in America: A Concise History

Although cities have not always been planned, the North American experience tells us that most were quite well thought out from their very beginnings (Reps 1992; Southworth and Ben-Joseph 2013). Early planning was grounded in traditional sensibilities, using the design and layout of the city to emphasize military or economic might, celebrate religious symbols or buildings, or codify other traditional practices or rituals (Chudacoff 1981; Reps 1992; Alanen and Eden 2014).

New Bedford's urban morphology can be traced back to the influence of these early, premodern planners. Orientation of the street network around the city's harbor speaks to the role of commerce in shaping the port city, as does the erection of thousands of triple-decker homes within walking distance of the city's major mill complexes. The influence of immigrants from the Azores is evident by the thousands of grapevines grown throughout the city, which are homages to traditional practices as well as a source of raw materials for making wine.

But a seismic shift in planning practice arrived with the advent of modernism and the growing commitment to universal ideas of progress, efficiency, and rationality (LeCorbusier 2000; Scott 1998; Porter and Shaw 2013). The planning of cities became a chance to perfect society, and utopian ideas flourished (see Howard 1902, Fishman 1982, Ryan 2012). The race to "better" the city resulted in some of the worst tragedies in modern American history, such as the clearing of the West End of Boston

© The Author(s) 2018
J.B. Hollander, *An Ordinary City*,
DOI 10.1007/978-3-319-60705-4_2

and the construction of slum public housing across the country. However, modernist pioneers, like Robert Moses, who was vilified in the acclaimed *Power Broker* (Caro 1974), have been celebrated of late (Ballon and Jackson 2008).

The legacy of modernism reveals itself, too, in the streets of New Bedford. A wide highway cuts north-south through the city, and acres of public housing replaced "slum" housing in the middle of the twentieth century. Blank street walls line portions of downtown, where modernist ideas about simplicity collide with the chaotic urban scenery.

But the rise of a postmodern-planning approach in recent decades (see Healey 1996; Sandercock 1998; MacCallum 2016, and Innes and Booher 2010) has opened ground for a new type of planning that is grounded in the life experience of residents, rather than the minds of planners. This new kind of planning has been a work in progress, but its central tenets revolve around new definitions of successful planning and successful cities. By downplaying the potency of quantitative measures of success like population, employment, educational level, or poverty, postmodern planning begins with the people who live in a place and seek to address their own construction of their corresponding identities.

Rather than telling local residents that they live in a poor neighborhood that needs to be "fixed," postmodern planning instead taps their ideas and values around what they like and do not like about their community, what they would like to see change, and how. The interference of the modernist planner in this kind of process imposes the discourse of economic development and growth; but devoid of such a distraction, his post modern planning can be effective in generating consensus around the issues that affect a place and how to address those issues. The planner's role then becomes that of facilitator, guide, and coach, helping those with the most intimate local knowledge of a place to talk about it. Then, the planner shapes those citizen voices into a coherent vision or plan for the future, drawing on other data sources like maps, statistics, or photographs.

The influence of postmodernism in New Bedford is less obvious. Due to its development in planning practice over just the last couple of decades, there are few examples where New Bedford appears to have embraced this approach. But for a city that faces depopulation and growth, sometimes simultaneously, I argue that postmodernism offers new and creative approaches to planning. In the next section, I offer some perspective on the fast growth urbanization so familiar to the urban planning world. Then, the remainder of the chapter provides an introduction to the very idea of shrinkage, offering some key definitions, laying out the mechanisms at work when a place depopulates, and describing the policy responses available to respond to depopulation. These are all themes and ideas that will serve as the basis for the empirical investigation of what New Bedford does do in subsequent chapters, thereby answering the question of how traditional, modern, or postmodern the city really is.

This chapter ends on a personal note, where I describe how work experiences I have had shaped a key organizing principle for much of this book and my other research: that protecting and maintaining vacant and abandoned property is the most important thing that cities can do to manage depopulation.

Fast Growth Urbanization and Smart Growth

The population boom globally has led to the rise of megacities (over 10 million in population) and a rising interest in the problems of growth. The urban planning literature is full of research documenting the perils of fast growth, both through the lens of suburbanization (Jackson 1985; Southworth and Ben-Joseph 2013; Mcdonald 2015) and the lens of global cities (Sassen 2001). Those global cities act as magnets, attracting increasing numbers of new jobs, educational opportunities, and greater and greater population levels.

Local governments can really struggle to manage this cycle of growth and expansion, coordinate new development projects, inhibit gentrification (Freeman 2006), and create just, sustainable settlements (Agyeman 2013). The environmental and social costs of growth have been documented well since 1981 with the Council of Environmental Quality's Costs of Sprawl report. Cities like Phoenix, Las Vegas, and Atlanta experienced double-digit growth in the 1990s and early 2000s, garnering extraordinary attention and interest (Bruegmann 2006; Squires 2002; Gonzalez 2009), only to see their population growth crash along with the housing market during the Great Recession (Hollander 2011; Johnson et al. 2014; Immergluck 2012; Hackworth 2014).

But these things repeat themselves cyclically, and places like San Francisco and New York City are growing rapidly, facing rapidly escalating rents and property values and shaping themselves into increasingly homogenous, wealthy enclaves (Hutson 2015; Angotti 2008).

Such are not the problems of ordinary cities like New Bedford. Instead, New Bedford faces the more mundane and prosaic growth pressures of small-scale new development, downtown renaissance, and gentrification of historically low-income neighborhoods. Faced with this kind of growth pressure, cities today largely embrace the policy response of smart growth. Originally conceived of in the 1990s, smart growth offers a suite of policy and planning tools to maintain affordable housing, protect environmental quality, reduce low density sprawl-style development, and reinvest in centralized, transit-oriented village or urban centers (Chapple 2015). For fast growth cities, the scale and power of the population pressure and associated real estate boom provides little room for effective smart growth (Angotti 2008). But in ordinary cities, smart growth represents a realistic approach to managing change and shaping new development.

Shrinking Cities Movement, Smart Shrinkage

A number of cities have shrunk in recent decades, with some experiencing tremendous population declines since just 2006, when the world economy began to slow. Shrinkage has affected cities internationally, with estimates showing that even before the 2006 downturn, 25% of all cities with more than 100,000 were in decline (Oswalt & Rieniets 2006). Researchers have shown heavy population declines in the cities of former East Germany, in the United Kingdom, and France (Sousa and Pinho 2015; Pallagst et al. 2014; Mace et al. 2004; Cunningham-Sabot and Fol 2007; Oswalt & Rieniets 2006; Wiechmann 2008).

In the US, the litany of shrinking cities is a veritable alphabet soup, as cities like Akron, Buffalo, Cleveland, and Detroit have all succumbed to massive depopulation in recent years. According to the U.S. Census, the City of Detroit lost 25% of its population from 2000 to 2010. But this trend is no longer confined to postindustrial Rust Belt cities as some of the most prominent population losses in this recent period can be found in Sun Belt locales that exploded in population in the 1990s and early 2000s, including cities like Las Vegas, Atlanta, Modesto, and Phoenix. The numbers are striking: I examined Postal Service data to show and found that 20% of Sun Belt cities with more than 100,000 persons ($n = 138$) experienced a net loss in housing units from 2006 to 2009 (Hollander et al. 2010). More than 80% of those cities contained at least one zip code that lost housing units during the same period. Among the most striking examples are Scottsdale, Arizona, which lost 1575 housing units; St. Petersburg, Florida, which lost 3122 units; and San Bernardino, California, with 876 units lost.[1] Since 2009, many of those cities have reversed course and are now growing again.

The groundswell of popular media coverage of the shrinking city phenomenon began several years ago with a short article in *Time* magazine, "Detroit Tries to Get on a Road to Renewal" (Altman 2009). Many commentators writing on this issue provide a relatively balanced view of decline, while others tend to couch it as a major problem that must be overcome at all costs, especially in localities accustomed to recent growth. Nearly every major U.S. daily has covered this issue, including *The New York Times* ("An Effort to Save Flint, Mich., by Shrinking It," Streitfeld 2009) and the *Los Angeles Times* ("Empty Florida Homes May Return to Nature," Fausset 2009). But no headline caused more furor and debate than the *Daily Telegraph*'s (UK) article "US Cities May Have to Be Bulldozed in Order to Survive," (Leonard 2009). The provocative piece prompted significant debate and commentary in the U.S. press—even meriting a spirited Morning Edition discussion on National Public Radio in July 2009—although it was speculative and no major bulldozing program had begun (see Glaeser 2009).

At the same time, a number of broad-based coalitions and research centers such as the Shrinking Cities International Research Network, the National Vacant Properties Campaign, and the $3 million German government-sponsored Shrinking Cities research project have tried to temper the rhetoric by providing more empirically backed research and, sometimes, solutions to these perceived ills. Recently, the popular planning and development blog Planetizen asked its readers—many of them professional planners—for suggestions on how cities might "shrink gracefully." Several dozen solutions were offered, debated, and even voted on during the several days the feedback forum was posted.

In addition, popular articles with titles like "Demolition a Wrong Answer for Imperiled Neighborhoods" (Gratz 2009) and "Bulldozing Our Cities May Wreck Our Future," (Rodriguez 2009) acknowledge the need for less drastic, longer-term proposals.

The Landscape of Shrinking Cities[2]

Economists have developed models showing that municipalities offering different baskets of goods in the form of government services attract residents who make rational migratory decisions that satisfy their desired balance between services and costs (Tiebout 1956; Zodrow and Mieszkowski 1986). An extension of these assumptions suggests that, when employment falls in a territory, people are expected to act rationally, leaving that territory and relocating to a place where new employment exists. There are several problems that arise when this expectation is met, however. Crucial among these problems is that when people leave a neighborhood, the physical form of the city does not naturally shrink. Glaeser and Gyourko (2005) studied the durability of housing in their time-series sample of 321 U.S. cities and towns with at least 30,000 residents in 1970, showing how housing prices declined at a faster rate in depopulating cities than prices grew in growing cities. Their research suggests that the durability of housing poses a long-term threat to neighborhood stability because houses do not disappear when people leave, but instead remain and largely sit unoccupied for years. Another key facet of understanding neighborhood quality is how increased abandonment and vacancy lead to higher levels of criminal activity. If housing does not disappear as quickly as people do, then those abandoned structures will serve as havens for criminal activity (Wallace 1989; Kelling and Wilson 1982).

Furthermore, widespread past and present discrimination in hiring and in the housing market have systematically limited relocation options for African-Americans and Latinos (McDonald 2015; Jargowsky 1997; Massey and Denton 1993; Sugrue 1995). During times of population declines, urban residents with means can relocate, leaving behind the poorest and most destitute residents. With fewer middle- and upper-income residents in a neighborhood, there is a greater and largely unmet need for role models available to youth, while prospects for upward mobility remain dim (Sugrue 1996; Wilson 1987; McDonald 2015). As a neighborhood loses jobs, African-Americans and Latinos continue to have fewer choices for places to move to, which causes further racial concentration and economic segregation in ghettos. A portion of the racial differences in employment can be attributed to a geographic mismatch between where a person lives and where potential jobs are located (Stoll 2005), which is particularly concerning for minorities and lower-income workers with fewer transportation options and less economic stability.

In depopulating residential neighborhoods, housing units change from being new high rent (with affluent residents) to lower rent (with less affluent residents) as demand declines. In a process described as filtering, poorer economic conditions result in lower demand for housing and a filtering through of economic classes of owners or renters ensues (Hoyt 1933; Temkin and Rohe 1996; Dewar et al. 2015). Specifically, "as most structures age, wear, and become obsolete, they filter down to lower-income occupants" (Bier 2001, p. 6; Bear and Williamson 1988). This is notably an uneven process whereby poor neighborhoods tend to depopulate more rapidly than wealthier neighborhoods (Guerrieri et al. 2012).

Access to housing, in terms of both tenure and neighborhood characteristics, has long been racialized, dating back to the earlier portions of the twentieth century and the advent of an American society of homeowners (Lloyd 2014; Crossney and Bartelt 2005, 2006; Metzger 2000). Ultimately, when demand sinks to a certain threshold level, owners tend to abandon their structures (Henderson 2015; Keenan et al. 1999). In time, many abandoned structures become derelict and may be subject to arson. Thus, in a depopulating neighborhood, occupied housing units are replaced by unoccupied housing units, derelict structures, and vacant lots where fire consumed the unit(s). This process suggests the pressing need for analyzing physical change through the lens of occupied housing unit density.

Rust's (1975) study of population and employment decline in 30 U.S. metropolitan areas from the 1800s to the 1970s revealed much about both *why* and *how* places decline. He found that these shrinking places experienced dramatic population loss and then "a long period of profound resistance to demographic or economic change which continues until the people, artifacts, and institutions which were assembled in the truncated growth era gradually erode away" (p. 169). The very physical fabric of neighborhoods—these artifacts—is expected to "erode away" in a period of decline.

This erosion process has been widely characterized as negative (Beauregard 2003), but population loss does not have to be a bad thing for a community. In my last book, *Sunburnt Cities*, I explored how less people can mean less congestion and leading to more open space and recreational opportunities. Less people in a city can mean lower student to teacher ratios in the classroom and faster response times from the police and fire departments. A smaller population has a smaller environmental footprint, helping a city to reduce its impacts on global climate change. Fewer jobs mean fewer cars on the roads and improved air quality. Fewer factories mean less pollution and better water quality. While population and employment declines are never the aim of public policy and planning (and are usually associated with negative outcomes), such declines, if managed properly, can be potentially beneficial to residents and workers left behind.[3]

Cities know very little about what it takes to manage decline. More often, the loss in population is either caused by or contributes to a wide range of social, economic, and fiscal challenges. So, in a knee-jerk fashion, local governments simply work to reverse the process of depopulation—a skill that only a handful have mastered.

But household size is shrinking nationally, as well (Ryan 2012). Some might argue that a city with a smaller population, but smaller household size, would need fewer housing units. That hypothesis was tested using a simulation model and researchers found just the opposite (Lauf et al. 2012). The study of the Leipzig region of Germany found that as the region contracted in population, modeling predictions showed that housing demand fell. The results showed that household size may not be shrinking enough to compensate for overall depopulation in some locales.

Rust's study also found that for many cases he studied, the effects after decline begins are "expected to be felt most strongly a generation after the cessation of growth and to persist for up to 50 years" (p. 187). For this reason, it is important to look at both contemporary and historical planning approaches when studying a city like New Bedford.

Conventional Responses to Shrinkage

Local officials effectively face three choices when presented with population decline: public redevelopment, smart shrinkage, or no action. With public redevelopment, planning agencies are essentially fighting population loss by attempting to manipulate both endogenous and exogenous factors to encourage private investment to create new jobs and generate new demand for real estate. Smart shrinkage (the antonym of smart growth) is a way to accommodate population loss in a way that does not require a manipulation of exogenous factors, but rather a focus on quality of life improvements in a neighborhood. Lastly, communities may simply do nothing (this is the most popular choice).

For local government policymakers and planners, there is very little they can do about changing their population and employment levels.[4] After completing an exhaustive study of 30 metropolitan areas in the USA over 200 years of boom and bust, Rust (1975) concluded that "national forces often overshadow local efforts to direct growth and change" (p. 169). Dewar's (1998) close examination of the effectiveness of economic development policies in Minnesota reached the same conclusion. Bradbury et al. (1981) ran a series of rigorous mathematical models to study how public redevelopment policies might impact on the continuing depopulation and economic decline of Cleveland. They also found little to no effect of such policies on the broader trends of economic decline, housing abandonment, and population loss.

Despite these challenges of trying to combat decline, politics make doing so a popular choice. On its own or through a redevelopment agency, a local government may choose to fight decline through publicly financed redevelopment, streetscape improvements, grants or loans to encourage new private investment, or other economic development strategies. An example of public redevelopment is when local Detroit government funded Community Development Corporations (CDCs) develop affordable housing in shrinking neighborhoods in the city (Thomas 2013). Another example is when local governments in Tennessee encouraged people, using financial incentives, to move to cities in an urban homesteading program (Accordino and Johnson 2000). The dearth of public monies available for the redevelopment of vacant and abandoned property makes partnerships with nonprofits and private companies an appealing avenue for many local governments.

In a study of six large U.S. cities that attempted to intervene and shift the underlying forces shaping economic and population forces, Perloff (1980) found that none considered the possibility of failure. In devising long-term plans to address urban problems, none of these cities confronted the possibility that their efforts to shape exogenous forces might not work. Perloff calls on planners to draw on decision theory in approaching possible futures. Decision theory suggests that since the dangers and risks of certain outcomes are higher than others, the risk that decline could occur (with all its potential dangers) ought to be part of community planning efforts.

Perloff goes on to conclude his study of planning-in-action:

> Growth is commonly regarded as an aid to reducing unemployment and raising levels of living within a city, but a review of the statistics suggests that the connections are often tenuous. Population growth in some cases attracts many unemployed persons and many poor families so that the problems remain or are exacerbated. (Perloff 1980, p. 201)

A recent study of the effectiveness of the Low Income Housing Tax Credit Program[5] in Detroit found that after publicly subsidizing the rehabilitation of over 6000 housing units from 1990 to 2007, any clear neighborhood benefit remains elusive (Deng 2013).

Where fighting decline may be effective in some places, the urban studies and planning literature suggest that a real opening exists for an alternative policy response that is not economic growth-oriented.

Free market advocates argue that no local government response is needed to address decline. Clark (1989) devoted much scholarship to this perspective, proposing that governments "facilitate, even ... encourage, the run-down of cities and ... use such resources as may be released to promote the growth of new urban forms in the locations most suited to the needs of modern industry" (p. 129). But more often, cities do nothing because they are not able to acknowledge population decline, either for political reasons or simply out of embarrassment. Indiana County, in southwest Pennsylvania, has been consistently losing population every decade since 1980, yet all its planning is focused on growth—officials seem to be ignoring the demographic trends and projections that point to further decline. In fact, there is only one city-government master plan produced in the USA that has ever truly come to terms with population decline (Youngstown, Ohio, in 2004), and the other scores of plans produced every year in shrinking cities simply tend to ignore population decline.

Critics of the do-nothing policy approach point to research that demonstrates a contagion effect with population decline—if you do nothing, the extent and level of the population loss can increase. Wilson and Margulis (1994) showed that neighborhoods that were economically and socially vital in the 1980s experienced severe decline in the 1990s, largely due to the spread of abandonment and crime from proximate declining neighborhoods. By doing nothing, whether by ignoring or taking a stance away from public action, communities may be exacerbating their problems.

A New Approach to Address Shrinkage

Popper and Popper (2002) define smart shrinkage as "planning for less—fewer people, fewer buildings, fewer land uses" (p. 23). Beauregard (2013) explained the approach well in a contribution to Dewar and Thomas' (2013) edited volume *The City after Abandonment*:

... the privileging of quality-of-life concerns and neighborhood-based efforts over economic development ... The overriding goal is to make the city livable rather than to expand the economic base for the sake of growth. The model embraces the notion that the city might be better off smaller and that urban neighborhoods can become less dense and remain viable, thereby becoming more desirable. (pp. 242–243)

The clearest practical example of smart shrinkage is Popper and Popper's proposal to establish a Buffalo Commons in severely shrinking parts of the Great Plains (Matthews 2002 [1992]). The Poppers' research (1987) found that the preservation of a large portion of the Great Plains as "somewhere between traditional agriculture and pure wilderness" offered "ecologically and economically restorative possibilities" (Popper and Popper 2004, 4). Vergara (1999) proposes an American Acropolis in downtown Detroit to preserve the scores of abandoned skyscrapers, seeing cultural benefit in establishing a park at the site to attract visitors to walk the crumbling streets.

Other areas of Detroit have become naturalized as greenery has taken over land where abandoned structures were razed (Millington 2013), with results described by Ryan (2012) as "a beautiful, successional landscape of wildflowers" (p. 74). Clark (1989) called for an active promotion of this beauty, arguing that these vacated areas should be greened for "parkland and recreational spaces" (p. 143)—a suggestion echoed by Schilling and Logan (2008). Others have looked into the potential for urban forestry in those abandoned spaces of shrinking cities (Haase 2013; Kowarik and Korner 2005; Rink 2009), while still others, including myself, have considered the potential use of urban agriculture for emptied out land (Rosenman and Walker 2015; Rugare and Schwarz 2008; Hollander 2011).

Armborst et al. (2005) introduced the idea of widespread side-yard acquisitions of vacant lots as a means of reducing housing density, a process they described as blotting. They found that the urban fabric of Detroit was changing on a daily basis not by city plan or regulation but by the actions of individual landowners expanding their lots to more closely mirror density patterns seen in suburbia.

Ryan's (2012) research into historic patterns of housing density in shrinking cities found quite a few examples of active redesigning of urban neighborhoods for lower densities. The 1980s-era Charlotte Gardens complex of detached single-family homes resulted in 6.8 housing units per acre, whereas the prior landscape had been dominated by five-story tenement buildings with a density of 290 housing units per acre.

Likewise, the Jefferson Square 180-unit two-story apartment complex in Detroit in 1980 was built on a 3.5 block area that had previously been comprised of 302 units of housing (Ryan 2012). This approach to managing depopulation was quite common in Detroit, Ryan (2012) found that from 1990 to 2001, a total of fifteen single-family detached housing developments were built all over the city, effectively de-densifying Detroit.

With less land available for housing, the question becomes: what happens to the land that used to be devoted to residential use? In Ryan's (2012) research in Detroit, he found that the additional land in the Jefferson Square project was largely devoted to "collective open spaces" (p. 97). But, certainly expanded parking areas were also a major land use.

What all of the above smart shrinkage responses have in common is a commitment to non-residential future uses for land and buildings that had previously been residential in nature. For the remainder of this book, I will use this as the core definition of smart shrinkage: *local government policies that contribute to the conversion of land and buildings from residential to non-residential use.* That is a deceivingly simple definition, but it does capture a qualitatively unpopular and relatively uncommon practice in cities. Certainly, there are examples of homes being acquired for the expansion of industry (as was famously proposed by the City of New London in the Supreme Court case validating the use of eminent domain for economic development purposes, see *Kelo v. New London*). But in a city with stable population levels, rarely does the government kick people out of their homes to generate new, non-residential uses.[6] From what I have seen, that only happens when there is a concerted effort to deal with shrinkage, vacancy, and abandonment.

In my own research, I have used the non-residential framework to organize land use planning in shrinking places. For several years, I have been working with Professor Michael P. Johnson at the University of Massachusetts Boston on using operations research to help cities make these land-use decisions. In one of our studies, we explicitly created two categories of future use in a given neighborhood—residential investments and non-residential investments (Johnson et al. 2014). With this approach, a vacant lot can either be redeveloped for housing, consistent with an economic development strategy, or reused for a non-residential use, consistent with smart shrinkage.

If a city is seeking to get smaller, what better way to deal with it than to redraw municipal boundaries to fit around a geographically smaller area? In the early twentieth century, major northeastern and midwestern cities grew through annexation, including New York, Chicago, Detroit, and Boston. Annexation continues to be an avenue to accommodate new growth in the Sun Belt. But what about de-annexation? Can a city shed zones or neighborhoods that are no longer beneficial to the overall city?

If de-annexation was possible, it would leave the de-annexed areas outside of municipal government control, and oversight and county rule would apply. In a place like Fresno, California, this is easy to visualize because the city has dozens of county islands within the city limits. These unincorporated areas are diverse across income levels and with regard to overall neighborhood conditions. In an interview I conducted with a county planner in Fresno County, she expressed exasperation at the difficulties in providing services across these isolated county islands. However difficult, the de-annexation approach offers one strategy for cities to apply the same logic which drove them to annex land in the past: the action will positively affect the overall city.

Slightly more extreme than de-annexation is the notion of dissolution or disincorporation. Anderson's (2012) *Yale Law Review* treatise called Dissolving Cities reports on this growing trend of entire local governments dissolving into their respective counties or townships, ultimately abandoning local services in order to presumably meet a precipitous drop in population. In her research, Anderson found that 130 cities have dissolved since 2000. She found that the majority of all the dissolutions ever to have occurred in the USA happened within the last fifteen years (Anderson 2012, p. 1364).

Anderson argues that dissolution "offers a backdoor way of achieving regionalism and defragmentation…" (p. 1431). A different breed of regionalism, to be sure. Conventional regional solutions call for new regional government agencies—Metro in Portland is a celebrated type. Anderson's version of shrinking governance touts that "dissolution offers the hope that removal of suburban and rural local governments can strengthen counties as rational, responsive governments capable of strategic land-use control across larger areas of suburban and rural land" (p. 1432). At the very least, Anderson is right about dissolution meaning reduced local fragmentation—a desirable goal when the typical metropolitan area in the USA has over 100 local governments (Lucy 2010).

The Genesis and Maturity of the Shrinkage Idea

In the last few decades, mass migration from the former East Germany to West Germany following the fall of the Berlin Wall has left cities and towns emptied. The German Federal Cultural Council responded in 2004 by funding an arts-grounded Shrinking Cities Project (Oswalt 2006). The project included an international ideas competition that generated scores of ideas on how to make smart shrinkage happen—in the process defining the scope of the problem and outlining the boundaries of policy and planning responses—and initiated a sketch of what smart shrinkage looks like.

The Shrinking Cities Project then spawned a traveling exhibit showcasing these novel ideas in dozens of cities throughout the world. The interest created by the project resulted in a conference on the topic sponsored by Kent State University in 2005 and another in 2006 convened by a newly formed group—Shrinking Cities in a Global Perspective—at the University of California, Berkeley (Pallagst 2008).

While academics and artists were singing the praises of shrinkage, the popular media was slow to catch on. In fact, for some years after the German event, the media was still using the same old language of decline as death. *Forbes* magazine, which loves to rank the best and worst of everything—the richest CEOs, the best place to vacation, the worst places to work, et cetera—may have hit a new low by profiling the Fastest Dying Cities in its August 2008 issue (Zumbrun 2008). The issue took specific aim at Buffalo, New York; Canton, Ohio; Charleston, West Virginia; Cleveland, Ohio; Dayton, Ohio; Detroit, Michigan; Flint, Michigan; Scranton Pennsylvania; Springfield, Massachusetts; and Youngstown, Ohio.

Activists in Dayton, Ohio—hurt and inspired by such a label—decided to fight back. Co-opting the term "dying," they organized local officials and activists for a Forbes 10 Fastest Dying Cities Symposium and Art Exhibition held in August 2009. Over 200 people from 8 of the 10 cities attended, celebrating certain dimensions deemed well and alive about their cities like spirit and passion, that are not so easily calculated in *Forbes*' statistical analysis. Dayton's city planner argued for a shrinking cities approach to city planning, saying, "The future in front of us is different from what we knew in the past. We won't recreate the Dayton of the 1950s and 1960s."

The Brookings Institution tried a few years before the "Dying Cities" raucous to rebrand declining cities as "Weak Market Cities." Their effort garnered some attention and helped somewhat to reframe the discussion around depopulation (Burnett 2003). More recently, Brookings issued two reports on what the federal government should do about shrinkage (Mallach 2010) as well as a policy guide directed specifically at Ohio local and state governments (Mallach and Brachman 2010).

The federal report calls for a rethinking of the concept of affordable housing in shrinking cities, questioning what is gained by providing government-subsidized affordable housing (through the low-income tax credit program) in places where market-rate housing is already quite affordable. The result, the author of the report argues, is the proliferation of new, federally subsidized affordable housing in areas desperately in need of a reduction in housing units to meet a smaller population. Silverman et al.'s (2016) book on affordable housing in shrinking cities examines the same conundrum.

Mallach (2010) also criticizes U.S. Department of Housing and Urban Development (HUD) policies that require an annual consolidated plan without any meaningful consideration of future demographic change. Mallach (2010) calls for new HUD language that requires communities to design "targeted strategies for reconfiguration of land uses and economic activity around the reality of population loss" (p. 27). The Ohio report echoes some of the same themes as the federal report, adding the need for state and local policies to promote urban agriculture and land banking.

The Federal Reserve Bank (FRB) has also been toying around with the benefits of shrinkage. The FRB of Cleveland produced a report in 2008 which held the Youngstown planning example up as a good practice and called for demolishing vacant homes. The recommendations are intended to fix a broken housing cycle that occurs in a period of economic malaise. The FRB of Cleveland is on record for arguing that demolition of vacant housing is an effective way to break this cycle of crisis and help stabilize neighborhoods. It is a radical policy recommendation to call for destroying sound structures that could help meet society's housing needs. But at the very core of the shrinking cities idea is that the needs of neighborhoods to maintain some kind of equilibrium in their housing market trumps policies that purport to increase the stock of affordable housing. If the physical changes that occur in shrinking cities cannot be stabilized through management (demolition, reconfiguration, or reuse), the FRB of Cleveland and the Brookings Institution argue that the overall quality of life in these places will fall so low that these new affordable housing units will be quite undesirable.

In 2004, I traveled through the Brightmoor neighborhood in northwest Detroit, which was physically ravaged by the effects of decades of depopulation. My guide was a community development professional, and as we drove the streets he kept pointing out the new housing built through low-income tax credits or by Habitat for Humanity. The vast majority of these affordable housing units, although not all, were either damaged by arson or partially abandoned.

Brightmoor was not able to reach an equilibrium between the supply of housing and the demand for housing. Instead of pursuing an active demolition program, the city government was working closely with affordable housing developers to build more housing, further straining the housing market and leading to more and more abandoned buildings, derelict structures, and poorly maintained public spaces and infrastructure.

Critics will worry about the unintended consequences of major demolition efforts, concerned about outcomes for urban aesthetics and the broken teeth look of a crumbling streetscape (Bertron and Rypkema 2012; Ryan 2012). Recent research offers some tantalizing evidence to the contrary. Haase et al. (2010) developed an agent-based model to measure the expected benefits of actively programming nonhousing uses for abandoned buildings. They found that a selective demolition program could effectively balance the supply-demand disequilibrium described in the earlier section. In the city of Leipzig, Germany, Haase et al. tested the introduction of aggressive demolitions and found that it would theoretically work to reduce vacancy rates, from a peak of 17% in 2002 to 9% in 2020.

Mallach (2011) writes about the importance of maintaining active demolition programs in shrinking cities, but doing so in a way that reframes historic preservation, from protecting buildings to neighborhoods. He draws on the work of noted historic preservationist Ned Kaufman by calling for moving "away from 'historic' preservation to what might better be called 'community' preservation" (Mallach 2011, p. 391). By attending to the culturally and aesthetically important elements in a community, a smart-shrinkage approach *can* thoughtfully include demolition.

PROTECTION AND MAINTENANCE IS THE KEY

The aforementioned books, articles, and reports are all piling up high on my desk and filling up my laptop's hard drive. This accumulated knowledge about how cities shrink and the emergence of the smart-shrinkage approach serves as a useful foundation for this intensive study of one such shrinking city. But there is something else that orients this inquiry: my own experience as a community planner with the nation's public real estate agency.

From 2000 to 2006, I worked as an urban planner for the Public Building Service of the U.S. General Services Administration (GSA). My assignment was with the Property Disposal Division, an office charged with the disposition of federally owned real estate. I sat in a cubicle on the seventh floor of the Tip O'Neill Federal Office Building in Boston, helping to plan for the reuse of shuttered military bases, decommissioned light houses, and closed Army supply depots, among other more exotic properties. Together with a team of about a dozen other civil servants, we managed the end-of-life for government land and buildings throughout the northeastern USA.

Through scores of site visits and my own review of hundreds of case files, I learned a great deal about the corporeal experience of decline. In one coastal New Jersey lighthouse, I will never forget the decaying staircase, the rusting beer cans on the ground, and the obscene graffiti on the wall. I recall being overwhelmed by the sense that the place was regularly visited by intruders, but at the same time, the Coast Guard functions seems to have had been frozen in time: a calendar displaying 1992 was still on a desk, a dated emergency operations guide remained plastered on the wall, and a rusting Coast Guard sign still guarded the front.

For the neighbors of this former lighthouse, there was much anxiety around the lighthouse and its future. But the one thing that mattered most, and particularly struck me during my countless tours of vacated federal facilities, was that these buildings and land had to be protected and maintained. They sometimes were, which made a difference for the surrounding neighborhoods. Through relatively modest efforts of regular maintenance of fences, grass, building exteriors, and entrances, as well as regular surveillance and patrols of an area, dramatic results in maintaining order and peace in the surrounding areas could be yielded. When the government failed to do those things—for instance allowing squatters to live in or party in old lighthouses, or neglecting to mow the lawn or repaint the signs—a powerful message of stability—or lack of—was sent to the surrounding community.

Urban studies research cited earlier in the chapter supports this notion, but it was through the experience I had at GSA that I saw it with my own eyes. Protection and maintenance of vacant and abandoned properties is what really makes a difference between depopulation being an absolutely bad thing for a place, and depopulation being something that a place *can* manage and adapt to.

Notes

1. While there are differences between a city losing population and housing units over three years and the kind of prolonged population and economic loss experienced by cities such as Detroit, Manchester, and Leipzig over decades, the basic physical processes and policy responses have much in common.
2. Adapted from Chap. 2 in *Sunburnt Cities* (2011).
3. If not beneficial, well-managed shrinkage can potentially eradicate the worst impacts of employment and population decline.
4. Despite the small set of tools available to cities, some have had success in changing their basic economic structure to effectively increase employment and population levels through expensive firm recruitment strategies (Wilmington, Delaware), arts and cultural investments (San Francisco), and an asset-based approach that builds on existing strengths (Boston). The problem is that most cities have not been able to do so and no evidence exists to suggest that current strategies that have worked *can* be transferred to other locales.
5. The Low Income Housing Tax Credit Program was enacted as part of the Tax Reform Act of 1986 and nationally provides nearly $8 billion annually in tax credits, representing one of the most significant contemporary federal policy initiatives to address urban disinvestment (Leng 2013).
6. Robert Moses was famous for doing it, in the interest of creating large-scale parks and infrastructure projects (Caro 1974).

Bibliography

Accordino, John, and Gary T. Johnson. 2000. Addressing the Vacant and Abandoned Property Problem. *Journal of Urban Affairs* 22 (3): 301–315.

Agyeman, Julian. 2013. *Introducing Just Sustainabilities: Policy, Planning, and Practice*. London: Zed Books.

Alanen, A.R., and J.A. Eden. 2014. *Main Street Ready-Made: The New Deal Community of Greendale*. Wisconsin: Wisconsin Historical Society.

Altman, Alex. 2009. Detroit Tries to Get on a Road to Renewal. *Time Magazine*, March 26.

Anderson, Michelle. 2012. Dissolving Cities. *Yale Law Journal* 121: 1364–1447.

Angotti, Tom. 2008. *New York for Sale: Community Planning Confronts Global Real Estate*. Cambridge, MA: MIT Press.

Armborst, Tobias, Daniel D'Oca, and Georgeen Theodore. 2006. However Unspectacular. In *Shrinking Cities. Volume 2: Interventions*, ed. Philipp Oswalt, 324–329. Ostfildern, Germany: Hatje Cantz.

Ballon, Hilary, and Kenneth T. Jackson. 2008. *Robert Moses and the Modern City: The Transformation of New York*. New York, NY: W.W. Norton.

Bear, William C., and Christopher B. Williamson. 1988. The Filtering of Households and Housing Units. *Journal of Planning Literature* 3 (2): 127–152.

Beauregard, Robert A. 2003. *Voices of Decline: The Postwar Fate of U.S. Cities.* 2nd ed. New York, NY: Routledge.

———. 2013. Chapter 10. Strategic Thinking for Distressed Neighborhoods. *The City After Abandonment.* doi:10.9783/9780812207309.227.

Bertron, Cara, and Donovan Rypkema. 2012. Historic Preservation and Rightsizing. Accessed March 23, 2017. http://www.achp.gov/achp-rightsizing-report.pdf.

Bier, Thomas. 2001. *Moving Up, Filtering Down: Metropolitan Housing Dynamics and Public Policy.* Washington, DC: Brookings Institution, Center on Urban and Metropolitan Policy.

Bradbury, Katharine L., Anthony Downs, and Kenneth A. Small. 1981. Forty Theories Of Urban Decline. *Journal of Urban Affairs* 3 (2): 13–20. doi:10.1111/j.1467-9906.1981.tb00007.x.

Bruegmann, Robert. 2006. *Sprawl: A Compact History.* Chicago, IL: University of Chicago press.

Burnett, Kim. 2003. Strengthening Weak Market Cities: A 10-Step Program for CDCs. *Shelterforce* 131 (September/October). Accessed May 29, 2013. http://www.shelterforce.com/online/issues/131/weakmarkets.html.

Caro, Robert A. 1974. *The Power Broker: Robert Moses and the Fall of New York.* New York, NY: Knopf.

Chapple, Karen. 2015. *Planning Sustainable Cities and Regions: Towards More Equitable Development.* New York, NY: Routledge.

Chudacoff, Howard P. 1981. *The Evolution of American Urban Society.* Upper Saddle River, NJ: Prentice Hall.

Clark, David. 1989. *Urban Decline: The British Experience.* London: Routledge.

Crossney, Kristen B., and David W. Bartelt. 2005. Residential Security, Risk, and Race: The Home Owners' Loan Corporation and Mortgage Access in Two Cities. *Urban Geography* 26 (8): 707–736.

———. 2006. The Missing Link: An Assessment of the Legacy of the Home Owners' Loan Corporation. *Housing Policy Debate* 16 (3/4): 547–574.

Cunningham-Sabot, E., and S. Fol. 2007. Schrumpfende Städte in Westeuropa: Fallstudien aus Frankreich und Grossbritannien. *Berliner Debatte Initial* 1: 22–35.

Deng, Lan. 2013. Building Affordable Housing in Cities After Abandonment: The Case of Low-Income Housing Tax Credit Developments in Detroit. In *The City After Abandonment*, ed. Margaret Dewar and June Manning Thomas, 41–63. Philadelphia: The University of Pennsylvania Press.

Dewar, Margaret. 1998. Why State and Local Economic Development Programs Causes so Little Economic Development. *Economic Development Quarterly* 12 (1): 68–87.

Dewar, Margaret, and June Manning Thomas. 2013. *The City After Abandonment.* Philadephia: University of Pennsylvania Press.

Dewar, Margaret, Matthew Weber, Eric Seymour, Meagan Elliot, and Patrick Cooper-McCann. 2015. Learning from Detroit: How Research on a Declining City Enriches Urban Studies. In *Reinventing Detroit: The Politics of Possibility*. New Brunswick, NJ: Transaction.
Fausset, Richard. 2009. Empty Florida Homes May Return to Nature. *Los Angeles Times*, April 16.
Fishman, Robert. 1982. *Urban Utopias in the Twentieth Century: Ebenezer Howard, Frank Lloyd Wright and Le Corbusier*. Cambridge, MA: MIT Press.
Freeman, L. 2006. *There Goes the Hood*. Philadelphia: Temple University Press.
Glaeser, Edward. 2009. Bulldozing America's Shrinking Cities. *New York Times*, Economix blog. June 16. Accessed February 10, 2012. http://economix.blogs.nytimes.com/2009/06/16/bulldozing-americas-shrinking-cities/.
Glaeser, Edward, and Joseph Gyourko. 2005. Urban Decline and Durable Housing. *Journal of Political Economy* 113 (2): 345–375.
Gonzalez, George A. 2009. *Urban sprawl, Global Warming, and the Empire of Capital*. Albany, NY: SUNY Press.
Gratz, Roberta Brandes. 2009. Demolition a Wrong Answer for Imperiled Neighborhoods. *Citiwire.net*, June 18. http://citiwire.net/columns/demolition-a-wrong-answer-for-imperiled-neighborhoods/.
Guerrieri, Veronica, Daniel Hartley, and Erik Hurst. 2012. Very Local House Price Dynamics. *American Economic Review: Papers & Proceedings* 103 (3): 120–126.
Haase, Dagmar. 2013. Shrinking Cities, Biodiversity and Ecosystem Services. In *Urbanization, Biodiversity and Ecosystem Services: Challenges and Opportunities*. Netherlands: Springer.
Haase, Dagmar, Sven Lautenbach, and Ralf Seppelt. 2010. Modeling and Simulating Residential Mobility in a Shrinking City Using an Agent-Based Approach. *Environmental Modelling & Software* 25 (10): 1225–1240.
Hackworth, J. 2014. The Limits to Market-Based Strategies for Addressing Land Abandonment in Shrinking American Cities. *Progress in Planning* 90: 1–37.
Healey, P. 1996. The Communicative Work of Development Plans. In *Explorations in Planning Theory*, ed. Seymour Mandelbaum, Luigi Mazza, and Robert Burchell, 263–288. New Brunswick, NJ: Center for Urban Policy Research.
Henderson, Steven R. 2015. State Intervention in Vacant Residential Properties: An Evaluation of Empty Dwelling Management Orders in England. *Environment and Planning C: Government and Policy* 33 (1): 61–82.
Hollander, Justin B. 2011. *Sunburnt Cities: The Great Recession, Depopulation and Urban Planning in the American Sunbelt*. London: Routledge.
Hollander, Justin B., Colin Polsky, Dan Zinder, and Dan Runfulo. 2010. The New American Ghost Town: Foreclosure, Abandonment and the Prospects for City Planning. *Land Lines* 23 (2): 2–7.
Howard, Ebenezer. 1902. *Garden Cities of To-morrow, etc*. London: Swan Sonnenschein & Co.

Hoyt, Homer. 1933. *One Hundred Years of Land Values In Chicago; The Relationship of the Growth Of Chicago to The Rise in Its Land Values, 1830–1933*. Chicago, IL: University of Chicago Press.

Hutson, Malo André. 2015. *The Urban Struggle for Economic, Environmental and Social Justice: Deepening Their Roots*. London: Routledge.

Immergluck, D. 2012. Distressed and Dumped Market Dynamics of Low-Value, Foreclosed Properties during the Advent of the Federal Neighborhood Stabilization Program. *Journal of Planning Education and Research* 32: 48–61.

Innes, Judith Eleanor, and David E. Booher. 2010. *Planning with Complexity: An Introduction to Collaborative Rationality for Public Policy*. Milton Park, Abingdon, Oxon and New York, NY: Routledge.

Jackson, Kenneth T. 1985. *Crabgrass Frontier: The Suburbanization of the United States*. New York, NY: Oxford University Press.

Jargowsky, Paul A. 1997. *Poverty and Place: Ghettos, Barrios, and the American City*. New York, NY: Russell Sage Foundation.

Johnson, M.P., J. Hollander, and A. Hallulli. 2014. Maintain, Demolish, Re-purpose: Policy Design for Vacant Land Management Using Decision Models. *Cities* 40 (Part B): 151–162.

Keenan, Paula, Stewart Lowe, and Sheila Spencer. 1999. Housing Abandonment in Inner Cities-The Politics of Low Demand for Housing. *Housing Studies* 14 (5): 703–716.

Kelling, George L., and James Q. Wilson. 1982. Broken Windows – The Police and Neighborhood Safety. *The Atlantic*, March 1.

Kowarik, Ingo, and Stefan Körner. 2005. *Wild Urban Woodlands New Perspectives for Urban Forestry*. Berlin: Springer.

Lauf, Steffen, Dagmar Haase, Ralf Seppelt, and Nina Schwarz. 2012. Simulating Demography and Housing Demand in an Urban Region under Scenarios of Growth and Shrinkage. *Environment and Planning B: Planning and Design* 39 (2): 229–246. doi:10.1068/b36046t.

Le Corbusier. 2000. A Contemporary City. In *The City Reader*, ed. Richard T. LeGates and Frederic Stout, 2nd ed., 336–343. London: Routledge.

Leonard, Tom. 2009. US Cities May Have to Be Bulldozed in Order to Survive. *The Telegraph*, June 12. http://www.telegraph.co.uk/finance/financialcrisis/5516536/US-cities-may-have-to-be-bulldozed-in-order-to-survive.html.

Lloyd, Christopher D., Ian G. Shuttleworth, and David W. Wong, eds. 2014. *Social-Spatial Segregation: Concepts, Processes and Outcomes*. Bristol, UK: Policy Press.

Lucy, William. 2010. *Foreclosing the Dream: How America's Housing Crisis is Reshaping our Cities and Suburbs*. Washington, DC: APA Planners Press.

MacCallum, D. 2016. *Discourse Dynamics in Participatory Planning: Opening the Bureaucracy to Strangers*. Routledge.

Mace, Alan, Nick Gallent, Peter Hall, Lucas Porsch, Reiner Braun, and Ulrich Pfeiffer. 2004. *Shrinking to Grow: The Urban Regeneration Challenge in Leipzig and Manchester*. London: Institute of Community Studies.

Mallach, Alan. 2010. *Facing the Urban Challenge: Reimagining Land Use in America's Distressed Older Cities--The Federal Policy Role*. Washington, DC: Brookings Institution.
———. 2011. Comment on Hollander's 'The Bounds of Smart Decline: A Foundational Theory for Planning Shrinking Cities'. *Housing Policy Debate* 21 (3): 369–375.
Mallach, Alan, and Lavea Brachman. 2010. *Ohio Cities at a Turning Point: Finding the Way Forward*. Washington, DC: Brookings Institution Press.
Massey, Douglas S., and Nancy A. Denton. 1993. *American Apartheid: Segregation and the Making of the Underclass*. Cambridge, MA: Harvard University Press.
Matthews, Anne. 1992. *Where the Buffalo Roam: Restoring America's Great Plains*. Chicago, IL: The University of Chicago Press.
McDonald, John F. 2015. *Urban America: Growth, Crisis, and Rebirth*. Routledge.
Metzger, John T. 2000. Planned Abandonment: The Neighborhood Life-Cycle Theory and National Urban Policy. *Housing Policy Debate* 11 (1): 7–40.
Millington, Nate. 2013. Post-industrial Imaginaries: Nature, Representation and Ruin in Detroit, Michigan. *International Journal of Urban and Regional Research* 37 (1): 279–296.
Oswalt, Philipp. 2006. *Shrinking Cities. Interventions*. Hatje Cantz Verlag.
Oswalt, Philipp, and Tim Rieniets. 2006. *Atlas of Shrinking Cities = Atlas der schrumpfenden Städte*. Ostfidern, Germany: Hatje Cantz.
Pallagst, Karina M. 2008. Shrinking Cities: Planning Challenges from an International Perspective. Cities Growing Smaller. Accessed March 23, 2017. http://cudcserver2.cudc.kent.edu/publications/urban_infill/cities_growing_smaller/cities_growing_smaller_chapter_01_screen.pdf.
Pallagst, Karina, Thorsten Wiechmann, and Cristina Martinez-Fernandez. 2014. *Shrinking Cities: International Perspectives and Policy Implications*. Vol. 8. New York, NY: Routledge, Taylor & Francis Group.
Perloff, Harvey S. 1980. *Planning the Post-Industrial City*. Washington, DC: Planners Press.
Popper, Deborah E., and Frank J. Popper. 2002. Small Can Be Beautiful: Coming to Terms with Decline. *Planning* 68 (7): 20–23.
———. 2004. The Great Plains and the Buffalo Commons. *WorldMinds: Geographical Perspectives on 100 Problems*: 345–349. doi:10.1007/978-1-4020-2352-1_56.
Porter, L., and K. Shaw. 2013. *Whose Urban Renaissance?: An International Comparison of Urban Regeneration Strategies*. Routledge.
Reps, John W. 1992. *The Making of Urban America: A History of City Planning in the United States*. Princeton, NJ: Princeton University Press.
Rink, Dieter. 2009. Wilderness: The Nature of Urban Shrinkage? The Debate on Urban Restructuring and Restoration in Eastern Germany. *Nature & Culture* 4 (3): 275–292.

Rodgriguez, Gregory. 2009. Bulldozing Our Cities May Wreck Our Future. *Los Angeles Times*, June 22.
Rosenman, Emily, and Samuel Walker. 2015. Tearing Down the City to Save It? 'Back-Door Regionalism' and the Demolition Coalition in Cleveland, Ohio. *Environment and Planning A* 48 (2), 273–291.
Rugare, Steve, and Terry Schwarz. 2008. *Cities growing smaller*. Cleveland, OH: The Cleveland Urban Design Collaborative, College of Architecture and Environmental Design, Kent State University.
Rust, Edgar. 1975. *No Growth: Impacts on Metropolitan Areas*. Lexington, MA: Lexington Books.
Ryan, Brent D. 2012. *Design After Decline: How America Rebuilds Shrinking Cities*. 1st ed. Philadelphia: University of Pennsylvania Press.
Sandercock, Leonie. 1998. *Towards Cosmopolis: Planning for Multicultural Cities*. New York, NY: John Wiley and Sons.
Sassen, Saskia. 2001. *The Global City: New York, London, Tokyo*. Princeton, NJ: Princeton University Press.
Schilling, Joseph, and Jonathan Logan. 2008. Greening the Rust Belt: A Green Infrastructure Model for Right Sizing America's Shrinking Cities. *Journal of the American Planning Association* 74 (4): 451–466.
Scott, James C. 1998. *Seeing Like a State: How Certain Schemes to Improve the Human Condition Have Failed*. New Haven, CT: Yale University Press.
Silverman, Robert Mark, Kelly L. Patterson, Li Yin, Molly Ranahan, and Wu. Laiyun. 2016. *Affordable Housing in US Shrinking Cities: From Neighborhoods of Despair to Neighborhoods of Opportunity?* Bristol, UK: Policy Press.
Sousa, Sílvia, and Paulo Pinho. 2015. Planning for Shrinkage: Paradox or Paradigm. *European Planning Studies* 23 (1): 12–32.
Southworth, M., and E. Ben-Joseph. 2013. *Streets and the Shaping of Towns and Cities*. Island Press.
Squires, Gregory D. 2002. *Urban Sprawl: Causes, Consequences and Policy Responses*. Washington: The Urban Institute Press.
Stoll, Michael A. 2005. Geographical Skills Mismatch, Job Search and Race. *Urban Studies* 42 (4): 695–717.
Streitfeld, David. 2009. An Effort to Save Flint, Mich. by Shrinking It. *New York Times*, April 21.
Sugrue, Thomas J. 1995. Crabgrass-Roots Politics: Race, Rights, and the Reaction Against Liberalism in the Urban North, 1940–1964. *Journal of American History* 82 (2): 551–578.
———. 1996. *The Origins of the Urban Crisis: Race and Inequality in Postwar Detroit*. Princeton, NJ: Princeton University Press.
Temkin, Kenneth, and William Rohe. 1996. Neighborhood Change and Urban Policy. *Journal of Planning Education and Research* 15 (3): 159–170.
Thomas, June Manning. 2013. *Redevelopment and Race: Planning a Finer City in Postwar Detroit*. Detroit: Wayne State University Press.

Tiebout, Charles M. 1956. A Pure Theory of Local Expenditures. *Journal of Political Economy* 64 (5).

Vergara, Camilo J. 1999. *American Ruins*. New York, NY: Monacelli Press.

Wallace, R. 1989. 'Homelessness', Contagious Destruction of Housing, and Municipal Service Cuts in New York City: 1. Demographics of a Housing Deficit. *Environment and Planning A* 21 (12): 1585–1602.

Wiechmann, Thorsten. 2008. Errors Expected—Aligning Urban Strategy with Demographic Uncertainty in Shrinking Cities. *International Planning Studies* 13 (4): 431–446.

Wilson, William J. 1987. *The Truly Disadvantaged: The Inner City, the Underclass, and Public Policy*. Chicago, IL: The University of Chicago Press.

Wilson, D., and H. Margulis. 1994. Spatial Aspects of Housing Abandonment in the 1990s: The Cleveland Experience. *Housing Studies* 9 (4): 493–511.

Zodrow, George R., and Peter Mieszkowski. 1986. Pigou, Tiebout, Property Taxation, and the Underprovision of Local Public Goods. *Journal of Urban Economics* 19 (3).

Zumbrun, Joshua. 2008. America's Fastest-Dying Cities. *Forbes Magazine*, August 5.

CHAPTER 3

Theories of Smart Shrinkage and Smart Growth

The very practical matter of protecting and maintaining properties is central to what I see as the goal of local governments facing depopulation. The overview offered in the previous chapter helps to situate the problems that New Bedford faces, the problems briefly introduced in Chap. 1. New Bedford is hardly alone in addressing decades of stagnation, decline, and some growth. Chapter 2 showed how prevalent these demographic and economic patterns are, how very ordinary New Bedford is.

Before diving into the empirical results of my research into New Bedford, which comprise the remainder of the book, this chapter offers a gift: a chance to step back from the practical realities of things, like mowing lawns and boarding up windows. Here, I offer a chance to connect the processes of decline and growth to broader and deeper normative questions about the kind of communities we want to live in. How should decisions about managing change happen? What does it mean for a city to be successful? For city planners, are some values around equity and justice more important than other values like efficiency and order?

Many urban studies and planning scholars tend to focus on outcome over process—an important aim, but one that draws away attention from issues of representation, inclusion, and deliberation in planning and policy development. Research I conducted with my colleague Jeremy Nemeth resulted in a foundational theory[1] of "smart shrinkage" that holds at its core *process* notions of equity and social justice (Hollander and Nemeth 2011).[2] The principles we outline are relevant to both cities experiencing growth and decline and offer an intellectual roadmap for ordinary cities like New Bedford.

In our work, we attempted to advance a foundational theory that takes as its starting point discussions of ethics, equity, and social justice in the planning and political theory literature but is well grounded in observations of successful smart growth and shrinkage practice. Present day proposals for addressing change are debated in public meetings, town-hall discussions, and council hearings. By providing a means to judge and evaluate the merits of potential solutions to both growth and decline, this theory aims to guide the burgeoning cadre of professional planners, policymakers, urbanists, students, and academics attempting to manage change in a more thoughtful and broad-based manner.

It is important to note, however, that this theory provides very little guidance—if any at all—as to the proper physical, outcome-based solutions to a locality's decline. Economic, historical, cultural, and political circumstances differ from context to context, and any theory claiming to provide specific proposals will inevitably fall short. Accordingly, the theory offers a set of broad criteria for judging the functioning of the planning *process* itself, while also touching on issues of scale, power, and agency. As such, it is rooted in more expansive notions of procedural justice, political representation, and participatory planning, all central concerns in much of the recent literature on cities and social justice.

PLANNING THEORY AND DEPOPULATION

There is no single explanation as to why a place depopulates. Depopulation has been blamed on forces including natural disasters (Vale and Campanella 2005), deindustrialization (Bluestone and Harrison 1982; McDonald 2008), suburbanization (Jackson 1985; Clark 1989), globalization (Sassen 1991; Hall 1997), and of course the natural economic cycle of boom and bust (Rust 1975). Beauregard's (2009) analysis of shrinking US cities from 1820 to 2000 argued against such wholesale claims, concluding instead that causes of population decline vary from one historical period to another. A conference report from the Urban Affairs Association annual meeting—where a global group of scholars discouraged a "one-size-fits-all" explanation for why places lose population (Grossmann et al. 2012)—affirmed that view.

Understanding the theoretical and conceptual explanations for decline is important but not the focus of this analysis. Instead, we explored the theoretical frames available in *evaluating* smart-shrinkage practice. To understand those frames, it is crucial to first explicate two distinct bodies of thought on why neighborhoods depopulate: neighborhood life-cycle theory and alternative neighborhood change theory.

By viewing neighborhood change in terms of a life cycle, the first theory posits that places grow and die in a way analogous to the human body: "the constant cycle of birth, life, and death is inevitable in both" (U.S. Federal Home Loan Bank Board 1940, p. 3). Hoover and Vernon (1962) described five stages in a neighborhood's life cycle: new development, transition, downgrading, thinning-out, and renewal. The Real Estate Research Corporation (1975) outlined five similar steps along a continuum: healthy, incipient decline, clearly declining, accelerating decline, and abandoned.

Neighborhood life-cycle theory was developed in order to better understand and rationalize the declining city. Many, who wrote on the topic, set out to identify planning and policy interventions that might either arrest or reverse this "natural" process (Bradbury et al. 1982). The stated goal of policymakers was to help revitalize devastated places, while preventing future deterioration of existing stable neighborhoods. Neighborhood life-cycle theory has been tremendously influential in US urban policy and planning but has been subject to insightful critique (see Metzger 2000).

Believing that such policies can arrest the slow death of neighborhoods, Blakely (1994) and others in the economic development tradition draw on neighborhood life-cycle theory in advocating public intervention through monetary investments in vacant land. Described as redevelopment or revitalization, this approach is often top-down in nature and uses forced relocation via eminent domain to achieve its objectives. The City of New London's Supreme Court victory allowed it to move forward with the condemnation of 64 privately owned homes in order to allow the expansion of a large corporation (Langdon 2005; Salzman and Mansnerus 2005). The *Kelo v. City of New London*, 125 S. Ct. 2655 (2005) case generated a groundswell of popular sentiment against eminent domain for the purposes of economic development and provoked a rash of new state laws and public protests against government taking of private property for economic development (Egan 2005).

The dominant interpretation of neighborhood life-cycle theory is that public investment is needed to stop an out-of-control process. This view of neighborhood change fails to account for a scenario where a city loses population but does so without suffering the expected accompanying blight. Rather than look for ways to manage population loss so that blight does not occur, the theory only allows for the neighborhood to be seen as growing or declining, alive or dead (Hollander et al. 2009).

According to Metzger (2000), the future of a city depends not on its stage in a "natural" life cycle "but on whether residents had access to financial resources within an environment of community control" (p. 7). Metzger draws on a body of critical theory which rejects the modernist notions of advance and retreat, growth and decline. Beauregard (2003) also explores this dialectic in examining the discourse of urban decline. He finds that urban decline was incorporated into a socially constructed story of the rise of suburbia and fall of the city—a fictional account reified into the public consciousness through oral and written communication.

Critics such as Dear and Flusty (1998) advance a postmodern notion of neighborhood change that escapes this grand narrative and allows the details of each city, neighborhood, and block to speak for itself. Mitchell (2002) also contributes to this alternative theory in his account of planning in Egypt. He shows how the "informal, clandestine, and unreported" activities of society determined planning outcomes, not the "fabricated" script developed by Western colonizers. An understanding of urban decline as a disaggregated, finely complex phenomenon is possible under this alternative theoretical framework. This alternative theory of neighborhood change allows planners to be cognizant of urban problems and to avoid the inevitability embedded in the discourse of urban decline. Such an unshackling from the structures of urban decline opens up the possibility for the planner to work toward proactively managing depopulation.

A planner or policy analyst drawing on this alternative theoretical framework may attempt creative intervention as described above, or avoid action altogether. Hoch (1996) suggests that a consequence to postmodern planning practice is that a sense of hopelessness may infect the planner as all interventions are somehow intertwined with the forces of power. The planner who embraces alternative neighborhood change theories may be reluctant in labeling his or her city as "in decline," or might be timid about his or her own ability to manipulate power relations in an affected neighborhood.

Indeed, we can attribute much of the success of community development professionals in general, and community development corporations (CDCs) in particular, to their grounding in this alternative neighborhood change theory. For decades, CDCs and grassroots organizations have fought for a higher quality of life for residents of some of the poorest neighborhoods in America. For the most part, CDCs reject conventional views of neighborhood death and dying and instead promote new building and growth, often through the construction of new affordable housing. New movements are underfoot, however, that recognize a certain inevitability of decline but plan for these demographic and socioeconomic shifts in proactive ways.

TOP-DOWN SMART SHRINKAGE

Smart shrinkage is hardly a new idea. For at least 80 years, cities have implemented various policies with mixed success throughout the world. Next, we present several examples of smart-shrinkage processes. What they all have in common is that they were devised and implemented in a top-down[3] manner, with little regard for the advances in bottom-up planning and policy approaches that are so widely accepted today.

In the UK before the outbreak of World War II, federal officials devised a strategy for shutting down mining towns in the countryside where mines had closed (Pattison 2004). Following the basic premise of smart shrinkage, the UK government saw widespread unemployment and declining population levels in a geographically concentrated area, and reduced the number of homes, streets, and other infrastructure to meet that lower employment supply. Their top-down approach led to major pushback from activists and residents, halting the program after only just a single village was dismantled.

A similar program was developed by officials in New York City in the 1960s under the banner of triage planning and planned shrinkage. Facing fiscal disaster due to declining tax revenues associated with population loss, New York City Housing Commission Roger Starr led an effort to remove housing for the poorest residents and invest in the city's most economically viable areas (Sites 2003). Starr was ultimately removed from his position due to the political uproar his policies generated, but his ideas persisted: when New York City faced its worst fiscal crisis ever in the 1970s, planned shrinkage once again gained favor among the policy elite. Wallace and Wallace (1998) document in fastidious detail how the city, working with the RAND Corporation, orchestrated the closing of dozens of fire stations in parts of the city experiencing the highest depopulation levels. Their research demonstrates a strong causal link between the closures and the rampant arson and public health emergency that followed. The closure of fire stations in impoverished neighborhoods is indicative of the weakness of applying smart shrinkage from the top down.

This triage planning practice was not isolated to New York City. Schmidt's (2011) history of its use in Milwaukee in the 1970s demonstrates the dangers of investing primarily in "savable" neighborhoods and largely writing off "unsavable" ones. One of the leading proponents of triage planning, Anthony Downs (1975), divided neighborhoods into those that were healthy, those beginning to transition to a state of decline, and those that were unhealthy. Downs recommended that the unhealthy neighborhoods "be targeted with job training, social services, and demolition of deteriorated housing" (Schmidt 2011, p. 572). For those zones of Milwaukee that were unhealthy, the city committed to maintaining vacant land and associated public improvements, and "eliminating pockets of deterioration"—a euphemism for demolition. In addition, the city built physical barriers (two-foot tall timber and concrete pylons) along the street frontage of vacant lots to discourage illegal dumping.

The contemporary application of smart shrinkage in US cities suggests the potential for a repetition of past top-down planning. While Youngstown's innovative Master Plan employed a bottom-up planning process, the implementation of the plan so far suggests otherwise (Schatz 2010). In fact, my own (2009) research on the Youngstown experiment shows that neighborhood district boundaries were drawn for the express purpose of limiting citizen participation in smart-shrinkage strategies. Some districts, known to have few residents, were created so that city officials could fully control land-use decisions. While current public outreach efforts are stepping back from such a top-down posture, Youngstown Mayor Jay Williams set the tone early by boasting publicly about plans to pay residents to leave depopulating neighborhoods—even hinting at the potential use of the city's eminent domain powers (Schatz 2010).

Assumption of Blank Slate

The German Federal Cultural Foundation (2006) published a book titled *Interventions*, which broke smart-shrinkage practice into four categories: deconstruction, reevaluating, reorganizing, and imagining. Throughout the book, these terms are used to presume a blank slate at each location, or a place that ostensibly can be deconstructed, reevaluated, reorganized, or imagined without reverence for history, culture, or ecology. Most postmodern planning theory—including feminist and collaborative approaches—presents alternatives in response to this blank slate assumption. Much of this literature critiques Habermasian theories of communicative rationality that assume an "ideal speech situation," instead arguing that planning processes must recognize the inherent imbalance of power between community members and the powers that control decision-making avenues.

Quieted Public

Related to the top-down planning heading above, many smart-shrinkage processes to date require a docile or disengaged public, happy for any crumbs city leaders or outside experts might throw to a desperate community. The Youngstown 2010 planning process began with the idea that city residents were waiting for something to happen, eager to be told what would become of their shrinking city (Schatz 2010; Hollander 2009). Due to such passivity, outside planning consultants, along with the city's director of community development Jay Williams,[4] were able to develop a comprehensive vision for what a smaller Youngstown could look like. The lack of community activism or resistance is well documented in Safford's (2009) book *Why the Garden Club Couldn't Save Youngstown: The Transformation of the Rust Belt* and serves as a principle explanation for why smart shrinkage is happening in the city.

Still, the purpose of this analysis is not to provide an assessment of recent attempts at smart-shrinkage planning. This would require extensive knowledge of each locality's history, understanding of its political and economic engines, awareness of existing power structures, and extensive familiarity with the norms, values, and cultures of its community members. So we are less concerned with outcomes than we are with process, or *how* a city, town, or municipality decides what solution is appropriate for itself. Still, though, we find a lack of theoretically grounded guidance when it comes to assessing the merits of the planning process, especially as it relates to the fast-moving subfield of smart shrinkage. This is a serious flaw in this recent discourse, as much of the discussion surrounding the shrinking cities phenomenon is eerily reminiscent of Urban Renewal-era policies of "creative destruction" (Schumpeter 1975 [1942]).

Social Justice and Smart Shrinkage

Responding to the various criticisms posited above, I developed with Professor Nemeth a theory of smart shrinkage rooted in a social justice framework. It is important to put forth a theoretical framework that is both unifying and universal but also adaptable to various contexts and circumstances. For this, our starting point is the work of both David Harvey (1973, 1996) and Iris Marion Young (1990, 2000), the latter a geographer and political scientist whose normative work on social, spatial, and procedural justice is explicitly intent on developing a framework for defining and interpreting the 'justness' of planning actions. Some—most postmodernists included—might argue that no unified discourse is possible, that no higher-order arguments are worth pursuing, and that there is no way to universalize criteria for judging the success of a venture. These same critics might also contend that universal claims to rationality—to "one right answer"—were deconstructed decades ago in the humanizing civil rights movements of the 1960s and 1970s. There is significant merit to these arguments, but they are also deeply disconcerting to those in search of transformative practice (see Sandercock 1998). As David Harvey (2003 [1992]) offers: "If we accept that fragmented discourses are the only authentic discourses and that no unified discourse is possible, then there is no way to challenge the overall qualities of a social system" (p. 107).

But what discourse—what frame—could possibly liberate the argument from the traps of formless relativism and deconstructionism indicative of postmodern social theory? Here, Harvey (2003 [1992]) turns to Marx and Engels for his position:

> The stick used to measure what is right and what is not is the most abstract expression of right itself, namely justice ... nothing more than a striving to bring human conditions, so far as they are expressed in legal terms, ever closer to the ideal of justice, eternal justice. (1951, p. 562)

We maintain that justice is at the core of planning ethics discussion, as it is "the first virtue of social institutions" (Rawls 1971, p. 586). We also argue, however, that any such overarching theory depends on the availability of a coherent and concise set of principles that can guide practice. Our discussion provides some basic principles that should be met in any just process.

Still, a number of definitions of social justice exist, ranging from the utilitarian, relativist, egalitarian, or social contract views of justice, each differing from place to place and society to society. Therefore, we use as our starting point David Harvey's (1973) simple assertion that social justice describes a "just distribution, justly arrived at" (p. 97). In this statement, Harvey is critical of John Rawls (1971) and his focus on simple *distributive* justice; instead, he posits a model that also accounts for justice of process, or *procedural* justice.

Responding to, or simply assessing, the level of justice distributed to a population is extremely difficult due to aforementioned concerns about knowing a locality's history and understanding its economic realities. In addition, as McConnell (1995) argues, the assumption that a just distribution can be arrived at via bottom-up process is flawed. When trying to assess how principles of distributive justice might be met, questions would likely include how need should be specified and what types of mechanisms would justly allocate shared resources. The answers to these questions traditionally depend on the political views and values of the decision makers charged with determining whether (and how) proposals are implemented (McConnell 1995, p. 44). Put another way, while distributive justice proponents argue for "the greatest benefit for the least advantaged" (Rawls 1985, p. 224)—a goal we find laudable and necessary—the decision of who gets what and who qualifies as the "least advantaged" is left to the powers that be.

The distributive paradigm also makes some problematic assumptions as it focuses solely on possession and does not consider what people actually *do*, what rules govern their actions, and how people are positioned in society. As such, distributive justice theories concern themselves more with allocation and less with essential issues of domination, oppression, power, language, inclusion, and representation. Young (1990) argues that such assertions are situated outside of specific social contexts and assume a homogeneous, undifferentiated public that shares the same desires and needs. She further claims that any conception of social justice must attend to *both* the just distribution of resources *and* a framework that allows full, effective participation in decision making (1990, p. 35; see Mitchell 2003, p. 31). Young, Harvey, and Mitchell (2003) all argue for decentralized, bottom-up control over the *means* of distribution. Individuals or groups must be able to determine their own actions and the conditions for these actions in order to combat structures of oppression and domination. Indeed, Mitchell argues, this is a fundamental right that must be protected—the right of "groups and individuals to make their desires and needs known, to represent themselves to others and to the state ... as legitimate claimants to public consideration" (pp. 32–33). This right of representation and inclusion in the public forum provides the core of our model of bottom-up planning for smart shrinkage.

We next sketched out the five fundamental propositions of our foundational theory, each rooted in a conception of procedural justice and each addressing the weaknesses of smart shrinkage (and growth) practice today. Below each proposition we also provide some actions that planners can take to make those a reality. It is important to note that these propositions are neither novel nor innovative on their own, but their packaging and application to planning serves to remind us of the potential these tenets have for guiding future practice. The planning theory and smart-shrinkage literature help us understand that just processes in ordinary cities experiencing both shrinking and growth demand a uniquely tailored set of propositions.

Smart Shrinkage and Growth Planning Processes Must Include and Explicitly Recognize Multiple Voices
As stated above, a central goal of a just planning process must be the inclusion of multiple parties and multiple voices, removing the barriers that effectively quiet the public. It is especially important to initiate and nurture processes that are broad-based and inclusive because each community and each individual can impart certain meanings and values on what should occur in a locality. Every account of what is good or appropriate is a personalized account, since "justice is relative to social meanings" (Walzer 1983, p. 312). In this regard, social justice necessarily involves producing "the institutional conditions for promoting self-development and self-determination of a society's members" (Young 2000, p. 33).

Harper and Stein (1996) argue that it is important to not only search for some consensus in just planning processes but also recognize different voices and claims for presence (p. 425). They offer a number of reasons why processes must be broadly inclusive, namely that any attempt at progress *requires* a rich critique of past actions, that all persons have a right to be heard, and that active participation increases the chance for disparate individuals to find that a "common good" does indeed exist (Ibid., p. 425). In this reading, it is the planner's job to raise consciousness of competing views among groups maintaining divergent opinions on what actions should be taken (or not). At the same time, the planner must be utterly realistic about expectations for consensus of compromise lest they mislead and frustrate stakeholders (Healey 1996, p. 266).

Recognizing that divergent viewpoints often hold at their core similar truths or aims, some theorists argue that radical or insurgent planners should help like-minded groups form coalitions around higher-order, and often progressive, causes (Friedmann 1987; Sandercock 1998). Harvey (2003 [1992]) finds fault with this coalition-building exercise, instead arguing that "to hold the divergent politics of need and desire together with some coherent frame may be a laudable aim, but in practice far too many of the interests are mutually exclusive to allow their mutual accommodation" (p. 104). We agree that coalitions of progressive causes can be important in struggling against the status quo but maintain that voices from all sides need to be heard, and that disagreement and deliberation must occur before any consensus or coherence is formed. Fernandez Agueda (2009) lends further credibility to this proposition by providing evidence that shrinking cities are more likely to "rebound"—not necessarily grow—if they diversify industries, economies, and actions. Multiple voices allow for multiple policies and proposals to be struggled over and acted upon.

How exactly to engage such a multitude of voices and make meaning of their contributions has been a question at the heart of planning practice for a generation (Arnstein 1969). My own work through the Open Neighborhood Project in harnessing the power of technology to improve public outreach processes has yielded some powerful results, lending greater credence to the notion that a hybrid digital/analog process can enhance collaborative rationality (Hollander 2011).

I developed the Open Neighborhood Project in a partnership between local officials, Ann Sussman (a Massachusetts-based architect), and my students at Tufts University. The goal was to begin to address the core weaknesses of collaborative rationality that have caused planning theorists to view it as only an ideal, not a reality. While conventional planning practices may allow citizens to attend a public hearing or go for a site visit to inspect a property, today's immersive planning practices (Gordon et al. 2011) provide potentially better instruments to realize collaborative rationality. These new instruments do not fundamentally alter the uneven power relations present in society or change the way we understand deliberation, but they do allow us to better approach the ideal vision of what it means to run a collaboratively rational planning process.

For the Open Neighborhood approach, we began by inviting a broad spectrum of a community to join an electronic conversation on a website and virtual neighborhood using Second Life. Extensive web-based and paper-based marketing is used to get the word out about the web-based process underway. Then, a full real-world outreach to stakeholders not accustomed to using the Internet (seniors, non-English speakers) ended up enlisting a diversity of actors.

Next, we introduced a suite of web-based applications that allow stakeholders to see their own issues and values in contrast to others' on screen. A virtual mapping of values in wiki format allows for stakeholders to edit and add to a common document that confirms the interdependence of the participants.

We ended up providing greater access to speech and dialog among community members than through conventional methods, either through the anonymity provided by an avatar or by name. While a skilled facilitator may be able to approach these conditions in an in-person collaborative process, the Open Neighborhood virtual dialog can go further in managing and monitoring such conversations with the combined powers of a web-based human moderator and highly sophisticated computer software. Comprehensibility, logic, sincerity, and legitimacy can, technically, be monitored and controlled both through embedded software coding and through control of access and conversation by the web-based moderator. Tools for participation are not limited only to dialog in the Open Neighborhood process, but instead include web-based games, activities, and even quizzes which allow stakeholders to express themselves, learn from others, and reach consensus around wicked problems. These alternate activities allow for values and meaning to be shared without the express work of a facilitator in a traditional in-person event.

In a test of this approach in suburban Acton, Massachusetts, 35 miles west of Boston, we involved over 500 residents in the Open Neighborhood process. With planners playing a very limited facilitation role, the residents' voices spoke over all else. They collectively expressed a range of values and beliefs about the future of Kelley's Corner, and through the discussion spaces of the Google Map, the gallery walls, the Post-It boards, and the public meetings, a vision of the neighborhood came to be articulated—a neighborhood that would be pedestrian-oriented, with a focus at the intersection, and improved bicycle access and greenery. The common vision was then reprocessed by my team and reported back at a public meeting several months after the planning process. The response was astounding: Acton residents were in consensus about the future vision of Kelley's Corner after being presented back with their collective ideas. In an interview with a local newspaper, Acton assistant planner Kristen Alexander said, "It seems that everyone kind of agrees on these things, and they're achievable" (Harrington-Davis 2010). The Open Neighborhood Process, employing a collaborative rationality model of planning, successfully brought people of diverse backgrounds to experience a place together and coalesce around a common vision. While planning is still ongoing, the community now has a blueprint to move forward with that has the consensus of the community.

Smart Shrinkage and Growth Planning Processes Should Be Political and Deliberative in Nature
Here we follow theoretical assertions by Mouffe (1996), who claims that the struggle over personal rights and limited resources is constantly redefined through deliberation over value-laden claims of diverse groups. This

model, which Benhabib (1996) calls the "agonistic model of democratic politics," is necessarily oppositional, as it involves the "the incessant contestation over ethical and cultural questions" (p. 9). But some, including Wolin (1996), contend that this is precisely what we mean by a "deeply democratic" politics, or a politics that celebrates "the legitimized and public contestation, primarily by organized and unequal social powers, over access to resources available to the public authorities of the collectivity" (p. 31).

The smart shrinkage and growth practices of today are often top-down, but we call for a bottom-up, deliberative style of planning. Young (2000) argues that while we recognize that participants are differently positioned in society, a just process is one in which "differentiated social groups must attend to their particular situation *of others* and be willing to work out just solutions to their conflicts and collective problems from across their situated positions" (Young 2000, p. 7, *emphasis added*). Broad-based inclusion is vital, and planners must facilitate discussion and debate about what the state "ought to do": ethics, values, and passions are thus brought to the fore (Young 2000, p. 177). Still, there can be no presupposition of effective communication within and among groups; instead, planners must help varying groups empathize with the plight and conceptual frameworks of others. The ultimate barometer of a socially just process is the simple recognition and appreciation of other people's claims, or an acknowledgement of difference. Therefore, planners must recognize the important fact that groups can dwell together in cities without forming a normative public, or a "community" of like-minded individuals (Young 1990, p. 227; see Staeheli and Mitchell 2008).

Again, my own research using an Open Neighborhood approach has found that a hybrid digital-analog process can help participants check their power at the door and be more open to shaping a deliberative space together.

Smart Shrinkage and Growth Planners Should Be Cognizant of Differential Communication Techniques and Should Provide Information That Enables Citizens to Recognize and Challenge Power Imbalances and Structures of Domination

The ability for groups—especially traditionally marginalized groups—to express political power, engage in self-expression, and simply "be heard" are fundamental rights often overlooked in traditional planning processes (see Harvey 2003 [1992]). Planners should aim to create processes in which participants recognize each other as vital participants in deciding future action (Young 2000, p. 61). But as these individuals and groups are differently positioned within society, planners must explicitly recognize structures of domination and oppression as well as any extant imbalances of power. In this sense, planners can no longer be value-neutral, but rather committed to the "possibility of a non-oppressive society" (Friedmann 1987, p. 306). Planning and development activities are shaped by both relations and distributions of power, and these relations must be explicitly revealed (Healey 1996, p. 266). But while planners should strive to expose uneven power relations, they must be careful not to speak *on behalf* of any particular individual or group, lest they disempower them by robbing them of their voice. Still, "the temptation always stands, for even the most politicized of us, to speak for others without listening to them" (Harvey 2003 [1992], p. 112).

Planners must ensure that stakeholders are aware of power differences and should attend to the dynamics of rhetoric that can influence the manner in which face-to-face communication takes place, reducing the quieting effect present in smart-shrinkage practice today. Specifically, planners should aim to expose the ways in which rhetorical devices are employed to foster or deter inclusion in the planning process (Young 2000, p. 70). At its core, planning is an exercise that asks what life can be. It raises the hopes of a better life for many. Therefore, as Forester (1996) argues, planners must attend not only to process and products but also to a good amount of passion (p. 256).

Fundamental to any comprehensive planning is the recognition of the political and economic factors and forces shaping growth, shrinkage, and the potential for just processes. In particular, the planner must provide relevant information that allows citizens to better understand, recognize, and potentially challenge structures of domination. Among other things, this information should describe the fiscal rationale for redevelopment, especially as the federal government, banks, and redevelopment agencies are often the primary drivers for housing clearance and renovation; the mandates of the infrastructure sector, including agencies dedicated to utilities, energy, and service delivery; and the exigencies of the housing market, along with an understanding of its principal actors and historical trends.

Smart Shrinkage and Growth Planning Processes Must Be Transparent and Value Different Types and Sources of Information
Good science must be freely available to all participants, and different types of information must be considered equally relevant. Data sourced from

experts and professionals—including demographic models, decline node predictions, land-use patterns, or zoning overlays—should not be automatically prioritized over data derived from community members' experiences, perceptions, and observations made on the ground (Sandercock 1998). Put another way, planners should value equally multiple styles of communication, including both official data projections and impassioned narratives from engaged community members (Young 2000, p. 71). In this sense, they must be active mediators between the "clashing rhetorics" of participants in the planning process (Howe 1995, p. 138).

A number of participatory visualization and mapping devices exist in the planner's toolbox to ensure more bottom-up community participation. These tools can uncover less official or measurable sets of information, and as these observations are inherently differentiated from individual to individual, they can produce alternative, and often competing, sets of knowledge about the same space, place, or project. Such methods utilize all community members as sources of relevant information, recognizing alternative, subjective, perceptual, and indigenous knowledge and visions as acceptable data forms (Dunn 2007). These participatory methods can also encourage communities to question the assumptions inherent in any official model presented by decision makers and acknowledge instead that any such "reality" is still socially constructed (Lejano 2008). This commitment further challenges the viability of planning processes aimed at forging consensus at the expense of active, discursive, and deliberative processes. Instead, more bottom-up methods serve to legitimize knowledge from the community or other non-expert participants (Dunn 2007).

Smart Shrinkage and Growth Planning Processes Should Be Regional in Scope, but Local in Control and Implementation
The question then arises as to where to draw the geographical bounds of the smart-shrinkage process. While we acknowledge that the scope of justice must be global, we argue that the broader planning process should be regional in scope and local in implementation, in order to best block the kind of "blank slate" thinking that currently dominates smart shrinkage and smart growth (see Frug 1999). We follow Young's definition of a region as a place where 50% or more of residents live in the population center, where residents experience similar climatic/topographical conditions throughout the area, and where nearly all of those in the labor market both live and work in the region (Young 2000, p. 232).

Our rationale for taking the region as bounds for the process is that regional plans have the ability to focus on major smart-shrinkage (and growth) issues about which disparate groups can debate, deliberate, agree and disagree, such as transportation plans, infrastructure development, environmental protection, heritage and historical preservation, and proposed regional economic drivers (see Fernandez Agueda 2009). These interventions can serve to connect populations and activity centers, bringing people together around fundamental improvements. Regional planning processes can serve to expose political-economic conditions operating outside of a locality's borders, while coordinating future actions taken in the region as a whole. However, the regional plan must not dictate what is to be done in each locality comprising the region, and it must leave localities in control of the built environment and the construction (or destruction) of actual places, spaces, and structures. This is an especially critical point in smart-shrinkage planning in the USA, because there the region often has neither legislative authority nor decision-making capacity. Rather, the city, town, or municipality most often holds these powers (Fernandez Agueda 2009). Since regional planning is so weak in the USA, this proposition is important to remind federal and state actors to be particularly attentive to the broader metropolitan area perspective, while maintaining the systems in place to allow for strong local power and voice.

This briefly sketched model of governance "requires that local governments take the interests of others in the region into account, especially where they are affected by the actions and policies of that locale" (Young 2000, p. 233). The regional plan can set a framework and protocol for inter-local negotiation and conflict resolution that then "trickles down" to local-planning activities. Indeed, since communities of difference cluster locally, local governments must remain autonomous in the sense that "their citizens, through their political institutions, have the right to decide the form and policies of social services" (Young 2000, p. 233).

Justice in Practice?

Whereas a number of groups are dedicated to revitalization in shrinking cities, few recognize explicitly the importance of just planning processes. Our general criteria can be used to determine levels of procedural justice in any planning intervention, although we stop short of enumerating specific policies conducive to social justice in a particular place and time. We leave our criteria general and context-dependent since measuring justice of *process* is, perhaps, more elusive than an assessment of just *outcomes*. A burgeoning urban literature, most strongly represented by work from Purcell (2008), Soja (2010), and Fainstein (2010), revisits and reinterprets foundational philosophies of justice to present more concrete rubrics for understanding justice as manifested in urban space. In particular, Fainstein identifies a list of specific criteria that must be embraced by any planner or elected official dedicated to attaining just outcomes. Although none of these focuses specifically on the context of shrinking cities—indeed, nearly all focus on world-class global cities like Amsterdam, London, Los Angeles, and New York City—all are useful attempts in understanding how justice plays out "on the ground" and in the trenches, that is, the messy everyday world of planning and politics.

So can we point to a planning or development process wherein a commitment to just, bottom-up process influenced strategic decision making? London's Coin Street development immediately comes to mind: although the centrally located project occurred in a (now) high-profile location on the edge of London, the lessons learned with regard to process are relevant in shrinking contexts, especially since the successful redevelopment occurred on land that had sat vacant for decades.[5]

In this case, two mixed-use development proposals were presented for this site in 1980, one by a major developer and the other a community-based scheme to be developed by the non-profit Coin Street Community Builders (CSCB). An effective local grassroots campaign resulted in the selection of the latter scheme, and once CSCB was selected as developer it immediately bequeathed the land to the Society for Co-operative Dwellings, which eventually served as housing developer for the project. This move ensured that all units slated to be "affordable" would remain so. In addition, the CSCB redeveloped a nearby landmark for use as local craft workshops and a restaurant, and stipulated that all proceeds would be reinvested in future CSCB endeavors (Fainstein 2010). CSCB also redeveloped the wharf area adjacent to the Coin Street housing; this area now hosts independent local merchants, frequent community festivals, a neighborhood-serving community center, and similar community-driven amenities.

Most attribute the success of Coin Street to the commitment of CSCB to a bottom-up and inclusive participatory process as well as the cycling of benefits back to the neighborhood associations involved since the outset. Fainstein (2010) agrees, but with a caveat: while the planning process *initially* resulted in "the reinforcement of democracy, diversity and equity," the resulting popularity of the area 25 years later has served to increase gentrification pressures and attendant commitments to design and consumption over social equity and redistributional priorities (p. 128). This example reflects both the trade-offs inherent in development strategy and the importance of recognizing the spatiotemporal contexts in which these strategies are deployed.

A New Theory of Smart Shrinkage and Growth

By setting out the bounds of a theory of smart shrinkage and growth, we argue that new opportunities and challenges arise for both the theoretician and the practitioner.

As Beauregard (2009) pointed out, decline is just one stage in a cycle of boom and bust that characterizes US cities for at least 200 years, and it represents an opportunity to reflect on community change patterns. While a time of growth is busy with new development and the associated fights that accompany it, citizen groups and non-profits can use the period of decline to focus on long-term goals for improving quality of life in their communities.

But depopulation has traditionally been a great challenge for planners attempting to achieve any degree of social justice. During times of growth and vitality, the poor and politically marginalized need to fight for their seat at the table and attempt to pick up the crumbs of capital that fall to them. During times of decline and disinvestment, there is often no table at all and certainly few crumbs. When jobs are scarce and city services meager, the poorest segment of a community often need to struggle to meet their very basic needs and are less likely to be able to focus on urban planning processes.

The propositions presented here provide a foundation for making a real difference on the ground in ordinary places like New Bedford. Through socially just processes, grounded in principles of fairness and equity, planning may result in just outcomes. Neighborhoods can have more green spaces, streets can be less congested, more food can be locally produced, and inner-city wilderness can provide habitat for endangered species and enhance regional biodiversity. To avoid the mistakes of 1970s experiments in triage planning, there is an important opportunity to build on the weaknesses of those approaches, both in terms of process and outcomes. The Milwaukee examples introduced above demonstrate that explicit attention to reprogramming future uses of vacant lots and abandoned buildings toward non-residential uses can be an important innovation over the triage-planning approaches of the past.

The remainder of this book explores the empirical causes, consequences, and responses to demographic change in the ordinary city of New Bedford. The theory of smart shrinkage and growth provides bounds by which to judge and evaluate the actions undertaken historically and in recent years. What follows is the result of a multi-year investigation of the people and places of New Bedford. I will return in the final chapter to the question of how *just* and *fair* the city has acted in how it has managed its change and will return again to these propositions to guide future recommendations for action.

Notes

1. I am using the term "theory" here in the way that Allmendinger's (2009) categories of theories includes "prescriptive" theories which are "concerned with best means of achieving a desired condition" (p. 11). What is presented later in the chapter is not an "explanatory theory," helping us to understand why cities decline, but rather sets the agenda for how a city might go about implementing a smart-shrinkage approach. I will use this agenda to organize much of the analysis in the book and use it to reflect in the conclusion on how well New Bedford managed its decline.
2. This chapter is adapted, with permission, from Hollander and Nemeth (2011).
3. Here I define "top-down" as any policies or plans that originate and are implemented from political and administrative leadership within a city government. This approach is in contrast to "bottom-up" policies that come from grassroots organizations or neighborhood groups with implementation duties shared across governmental and non-governmental organizations.
4. Mr. Williams later became mayor of Youngstown.
5. Details of this case are widely available but are drawn principally from Fainstein (2010) and Brindley, Rydin, and Stoker (1996).

Bibliography

Allmendinger, Philip. 2009. *Planning Theory*. 2nd ed. Basingstoke: Palgrave Macmillan.

Arnstein, Sherry R. 1969. A Ladder of Citizen Participation. *Journal of the American Institute of Planners* 35 (9): 216–224.

Beauregard, Robert A. 2003. *Voices of Decline: The Postwar Fate of U.S. Cities*. 2nd ed. New York, NY: Routledge.

———. 2009. Urban Population Loss in Historical Perspective: United States, 1820–200. *Environment & Planning A* 41 (3): 514–528.
Benhabib, Seyla. 1996. *Democracy and Difference: Contesting the Boundaries of the Political.* Princeton, NJ: Princeton University Press.
Bluestone, Barry, and Bennett Harrison. 1982. *The Deindustrialization of America: Plant Closing, Community Abandonment and the Dismantling of Basic Industry.* New York, NY: Basic Books, Inc.
Bradbury, Katharine L., Anthony Downs, and Kenneth A. Small. 1982. *Urban Decline and the Future of American Cities.* Washington, DC: Brookings Institution.
Brindley, Tim, Yvonne Rydin, and Gerry Stoker. 1996. *Remaking Planning.* 2nd ed. New York, NY: Routledge.
Clark, David. 1989. *Urban Decline: The British Experience.* London: Routledge.
Dear, Michael, and Steven Flusty. 1998. Postmodern Urbanism. *Annals of the Association of American Geographers* 88 (1): 50–72.
Downs, Anthony. 1975. Using the Lessons of Experience to Allocate Resources in the Community Development Program. In *Recommendations for Community Development Planning: Proceedings of the HUD/RERC Workshops on Local Urban Renewal and Neighborhood Preservation.* Chicago: Real Estate Research Corporation.
Dunn, Christine E. 2007. Participatory GIS—A People's GIS? *Progress in Human Geography* 31 (5): 616–637.
Egan, Timothy. 2005. Ruling Sets Off Tug of War Over Private Property. *The New York Times*, July 30.
Fainstein, Susan S. 2010. *The Just City.* Ithaca: Cornell University Press.
Fernandez Agueda, B. 2009. Urban Planning in Industrial Cities: The Reversibility of Decay. Presentation at City Futures Conference, Madrid, June 4–6.
Forester, John. 1996. Argument, Power and Passion in Planning Practice. In *Explorations in Planning Theory*, ed. Seymour Mandelbaum, Luigi Mazza, and Robert Burchell, 241–262. New Brunswick, NJ: Center for Urban Policy Research.
Friedmann, John. 1987. *Planning in the Public Domain: From Knowledge to Action.* Princeton, NJ: Princeton University Press.
Frug, Gerald E. 1999. *City Making: Building Communities without Building Walls.* Princeton, NJ: Princeton University Press.
German Federal Cultural Foundation. 2006. In *Shrinking Cities, Volume 2: Interventions*, ed. Philipp Oswalt. Ostfildern, Germany: Hatje Cantz Verlag.
Gordon, Eric, Steven Schirra, and Justin Hollander. 2011. Immersive Planning: A Conceptual Model for Designing Public Participation with New Technologies. *Environment and Planning B: Planning and Design* 38 (3): 505–519. doi:10.1068/b37013.
Grossmann, Katrin, Caterina Cortese, Annegret Haase, and Iva Ticha. 2012. How Urban Shrinkage Impacts on Patterns of Socio-Spatial Segregation: The Cases

of Leipzig/Germany, Ostrava/Czech Republic and Genova/Italy. Presentation at Urban Affairs Association 42nd Annual Conference, Pittsburgh, PA, April 18–21.

Hall, Peter. 1997. Modeling the Post-Industrial City. *Futures* 29 (4–5): 311–322.

Harper, Thomas L., and Stanley M. Stein. 1996. Postmodernist Planning Theory: The Incommensurability Premise. In *Explorations in Planning Theory*, ed. Seymour Mandelbaum, Luigi Mazza, and Robert Burchell, 414–429. New Brunswick, NJ: Center for Urban Policy Research.

Harrington-Davis, B. 2010. Residents Have Their Say on Vision for Acton's Kelley's Corner, Acton Beacon, July 2.

Harvey, David. 1973. *Social Justice and the City*. Baltimore, MD: John Hopkins University Press.

———. 1996. *Justice, Nature and the Geography of Difference*. London: Blackwell.

———. 2003. Social Justice, Postmodernism and the City. In *Designing Cities: Critical Readings in Urban Design*, ed. Alexander R. Cuthbert, 101–115. Malden, MA: Blackwell Publishing.

Healey, P. 1996. The Communicative Work of Development Plans. In *Explorations in Planning Theory*, ed. Seymour Mandelbaum, Luigi Mazza, and Robert Burchell, 263–288. New Brunswick, NJ: Center for Urban Policy Research.

Hoch, Charles. 1996. A Pragmatic Inquiry about Planning and Power. In *Explorations in Planning Theory*, ed. Seymour Mandelbaum, Luigi Mazza, and Robert Burchell, 30–44. New Brunswick, NJ: Center for Urban Policy Research.

Hollander, Justin B. 2009. *Polluted and Dangerous: America's Worst Abandoned Properties and What Can Be Done About Them*. Burlington, VT: University of Vermont Press.

———. 2011. *Sunburnt Cities: The Great Recession, Depopulation and Urban Planning in the American Sunbelt*. London: Routledge.

Hollander, Justin B., and Jeremy Nemeth. 2011. The Bounds of Smart Decline: A Foundational Theory for Planning Shrinking Cities. *Housing Policy Debate* 21 (3): 349–367.

Hollander, Justin B., Karina Pallagst, Terry Schwarz, and Frank J. Popper. 2009. Planning Shrinking Cities. *Progress in Planning* 72 (4): 223–232.

Hoover, Edgar M., and Raymond Vernon. 1962. *Anatomy of a Metropolis: The Changing Distribution of People and Jobs within the New York Metropolitan Region*. Cambridge, MA: Harvard University Press.

Howe, Elizabeth. 1995. Introduction: Part II—Ethical Theory and Planning Practice. In *Planning Ethics: A Reader in Planning Theory, Practice and Education*, ed. Sue Hendler, 123–140. New Brunswick, NJ: Center for Urban Policy Research.

Jackson, Kenneth T. 1985. *Crabgrass Frontier: The Suburbanization of the United States*. New York, NY: Oxford University Press.

Kelo, Susette, et al. 2005. *v. City of New London, Connecticut, et al.*, 125 S. Ct. 2655.

Langdon, Philip. 2005. NOTE FOR SALE. *Planning* 71 (4): 12–15.
Lejano, Raul P. 2008. Technology and Institutions: A Critical Appraisal of GIS in the Planning Domain. *Science, Technology and Human Values* 33 (5): 653–678.
Marx, Karl, and Friedrich Engels. 1951. *Selected Works.* New York, NY: International Publishers.
McConnell, Shean. 1995. Rawlsian Planning Theory. In *Planning Ethics: A Reader in Planning Theory, Practice and Education*, ed. Sue Hendler, 30–48. New Brunswick, NJ: Center for Urban Policy Research.
McDonald, John F. 2008. *Urban America: Growth, Crisis, and Rebirth.* Armonk, NY: M.E. Sharpe.
Metzger, John T. 2000. Planned Abandonment: The Neighborhood Life-Cycle Theory and National Urban Policy. *Housing Policy Debate* 11 (1): 7–40.
Mitchell, Timothy. 2002. *Rule of Experts: Egypt, Techno-Politics, Modernity.* Berkeley, CA: University of California Press.
Mitchell, Don. 2003. *The Right to the City: Social Justice and the Fight for Public Space.* New York, NY: Guilford Press.
Mouffe, Chantal. 1996. Democracy, Power and the Political. In *Democracy and Difference: Contesting the Boundaries of the Political*, ed. Seyla Benhabib, 245–256. Princeton, NJ: Princeton University Press.
Pattison, Gary. 2004. Planning for Decline: The "D"-Village Policy of County Durham, UK. *Planning Perspectives* 19 (3): 311–332.
Purcell, Mark. 2008. *Recapturing Democracy: Neoliberalization and the Struggle for Alternative Urban Futures.* New York, NY: Routledge Chapman & Hall.
Rawls, John. 1971. *A Theory of Justice.* Cambridge, MA: Harvard University Press.
———. 1985. Justice as Fairness: Political not Metaphysical. *Philosophy & Public Affairs* 14 (3): 223–251.
Real Estate Research Corporation. 1975. *The Dynamics of Neighborhood Change.* Washington, DC: U.S. Department of Housing and Urban Development, Office of Policy Development and Research.
Rust, Edgar. 1975. *No Growth: Impacts on Metropolitan Areas.* Lexington, MA: Lexington Books.
Safford, Sean. 2009. *Why the Garden Club Couldn't Save Youngstown: The Transformation of the Rust Belt.* Cambridge, MA: Harvard University Press.
Salzman, Avi, and Lauren Mansnerus. 2005. For Homeowners, Frustration and Anger at Court Ruling. *The New York Times.* The New York Times Company. Web.
Sandercock, Leonie. 1998. *Towards Cosmopolis: Planning for Multicultural Cities.* New York, NY: John Wiley and Sons.
Sassen, Saskia. 1991. *The Global City: New York, London, Tokyo.* Princeton, NJ: Princeton University Press.
Schatz, Laura. 2010. What Helps or Hinders the Adoption of "Good Planning" Principles in Shrinking Cities? A Comparison of Recent Planning Exercises in

Sudbury, Ontario and Youngstown, Ohio. Doctoral dissertation, University of Waterloo.
Schmidt, Deanna H. 2011. Urban Triage: Saving the Savable Neighbourhoods in Milwaukee. *Planning Perspectives* 26 (4): 569–589. doi:10.1080/02665433.2011.601609.
Schumpeter, Joseph. 1942. *Capitalism, Socialism and Democracy*. New York, NY: Harper.
Sites, William. 2003. *Remaking New York: Primitive Globalization and the Politics of Urban Community*. Minneapolis, MN: University of Minnesota Press.
Soja, Edward W. 2010. *Seeking Spatial Justice*. Minneapolis, MN: University of Minnesota Press.
Staeheli, Lynn, and Don Mitchell. 2008. *The People's Property? Power Politics and the Public*. New York, NY: Routledge.
United States Federal Home Loan Bank Board. 1940. *Waverly: A study in Neighborhood Conservation*. United States Federal Home Loan Bank Board.
Vale, Lawrence J., and Thomas J. Campanella. 2005. *The Resilient City: How Modern Cities Recover from Disaster*. New York, NY: Oxford University Press.
Wallace, Deborah, and Rodrick Wallace. 1998. *A Plague on Your Houses: How New York was Burned Down and National Public Health Crumbled*. New York, NY: Verso.
Walzer, Michael. 1983. *Spheres of Justice: A Defense of Pluralism and Equality*. New York, NY: Basic Books.
Wolin, Sheldon. 1996. Fugitive Democracy. In *Democracy and Difference: Contesting the Boundaries of the Political*, ed. Seyla Benhabib, 31–45. Princeton, NJ: Princeton University Press.
Young, Iris M. 1990. *Justice and the Politics of Difference*. Princeton, NJ: Princeton University Press.
———. 2000. *Inclusion and Democracy*. Oxford, England: Oxford University Press.

CHAPTER 4

How Much Change Is Too Much: A Look at the Numbers

Following the gentle voice of my GPS navigator, I turn off the highway onto the narrow, winding streets to the edge of New Bedford's historic downtown. Retrieving a camera and clipboard from my car, I feed the meter and set off to explore Herman Melville's old stomping grounds.

The imagery of a former whaling town is completed as the narrow storefronts and cobblestone roads depicted in *Moby Dick* come to life. Well, not exactly. The streets are largely dead. The historic buildings are true to archeological records, but merchants no longer hawk their wares on the streets, and the bustle is gone.

As I continue on my path toward City Hall, though, the energy increases: college students rush to and fro, lawyers escort their clients to court, and the people on the street share a laugh with one another. New Bedford is the legal, political, and cultural capital of three-quarters of a million people who live in the Southeastern Massachusetts region and here, in downtown, you can see it (South Coast Rail 2009; see Fig. 4.1).

The downtown is hardly teeming with the electricity of the late nineteenth century, but things are happening. The University of Massachusetts established a campus in nearby suburban Dartmouth in 1964 and, in 2001, opened a satellite campus for their arts school right in downtown New Bedford. The results have been astounding.

A new burrito café, art galleries, coffee shops—the very face of downtown is drastically different than it was for most of the 1970s, 1980s, and 1990s. The downtown has a new vibrancy that comes through in discus-

© The Author(s) 2018
J.B. Hollander, *An Ordinary City*,
DOI 10.1007/978-3-319-60705-4_4

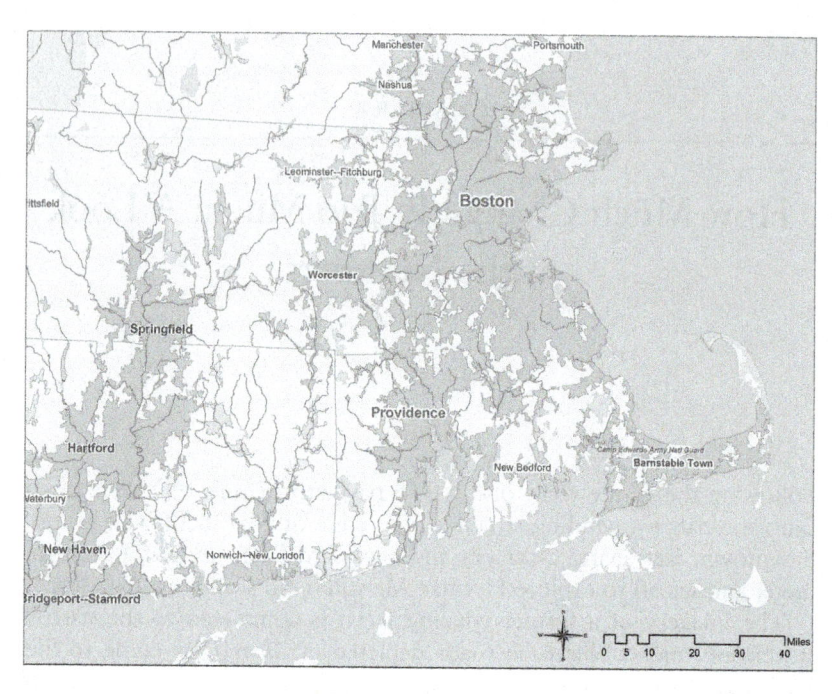

Fig. 4.1 Locus map of New Bedford

sions with residents, business owners, activists, and government officials. But for all the excitement, the "For Rent" signs remain in abundance. City parking lots are rarely full.

Decades of economic decline wreaked havoc on New Bedford's downtown, and there were simply not enough businesses to fill the office and retail space at the core of a city that was built at its peak for 150,000 people. The siting of the UMass satellite campus had a primary impact by filling up empty buildings but also had the secondary impact of attracting new businesses catering to students as well as a burgeoning arts scene.

Frieden and Sagalyn's (1991) *Downtown, Inc.* pronounced the death nail in the coffin of downtowns and offered up public–private partnerships as an effective rebirth strategy. Urban theory suggests that a strong and vital downtown will be a source for economic growth throughout a city. While certainly a point of pride, people I interviewed in New Bedford, however, were not convinced that the downtown boom would translate to growth in the neighborhoods.

I employed a nested research design in this book, focusing both on the city of New Bedford and on three case study neighborhoods. The three neighborhoods were selected based on a full review of all New Bedford neighborhoods. I began a search for several neighborhoods to focus on by considering some key criteria for inclusion in the research: (1) an active neighborhood association so that I would have access to residents for interviews, (2) modest to high levels of housing abandonment or foreclosure issues, and (3) some degree of geographic diversity present in the city that is represented in the neighborhood. After consulting with city officials and conducting interviews with community leaders, I arrived at my three study neighborhoods: South Central, Bullard Street, and Cove Street (see Fig. 4.2). Each of the neighborhoods has been affected differently by eight decades of depopulation. Each has enjoyed a slightly unique development path, but what they share is a growth and decline pattern: early settlement in the nineteenth century, full built-out by the twentieth century, and steady decline in number of structures since.

South Central is located due south of New Bedford's downtown area and is one of the city's oldest neighborhoods. It grew with the construction of several large mill complexes in the South End of New Bedford, including the renowned Howland Mill (the site of an historic district now listed on the National Register of Historic Places). And when many of these mills closed, demand weakened for housing within walking distance of empty factories and scores of working families left the area.

In recent decades, South Central has experienced high levels of foreclosure and abandonment. Historically, South Central was affected by government intervention in the 1930s–1960s via the construction of public housing along Acushnet Avenue and the demolition of residential neighborhoods connected to the South Terminal urban renewal project. In recent years, community activists from South Central have been heavily involved in public policy and planning, making the neighborhood a useful case study throughout this book.

The Bullard Street neighborhood was settled later in New Bedford's history, with most of the homes constructed in the early twentieth century. Also driven by close walking distance to numerous textile mills, Bullard Street's growth was driven largely by mill expansion—particularly the Wamsutta Mills just a few blocks away. Wamsutta is considered the first of the city's great textile mills, having fueled much of the city's explosion in population in the early decades of the twentieth century. A local New Bedford historian explained Wamsutta's unusual influence:

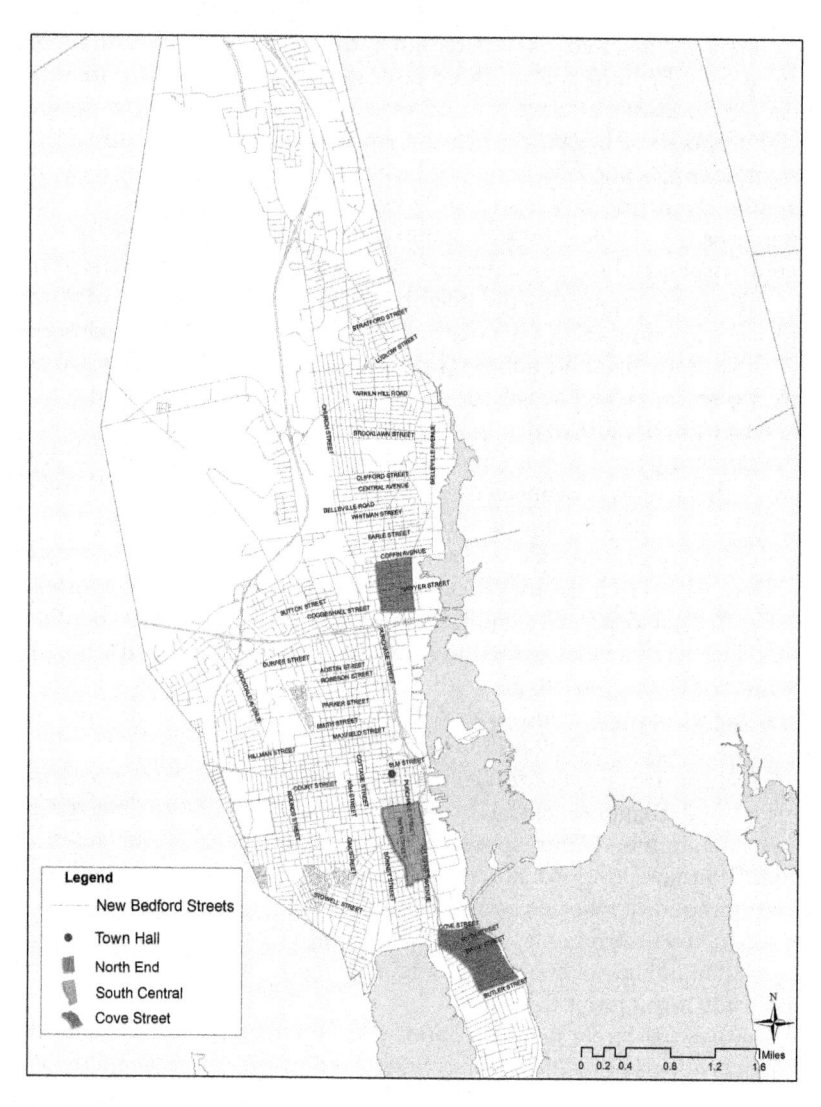

Fig. 4.2 Map of New Bedford

the Mills got into developing mill housing. Wamsutta Mills did it and a matter of fact there are still a couple of blocks in the Wamsutta Mills that are still in existence. And those are not tenements they were more like small two story Greek revival town houses. And Wamsutta Mill is so interesting because it had such an impact on the city. It grew very fast. Did very well. And began drawing down French Canadians from the Quebec area who came to work in the New Bedford Mills.

In recent years, the neighborhood has had the worst foreclosure rate in the city. Nevertheless, it remains a bustling place full of economic activity. Located north of Downtown, Bullard Street is proximate to the North Terminal urban renewal project but was outside the project boundaries and did not experience any of the demolition that impacted South Central.

Cove Street Neighborhood began to be built around the time of the Bullard Street neighborhood, but only came to its current boundaries by the 1920s. Built up around a cluster of industrial mill buildings wedged between Cleveland Street and the Acushnet River, Cove Street was a highly desirable neighborhood for much of the twentieth century. Its proximity to the Hathaway Mill fed much of the new housing built in the 1920s and 1930s and when that and other nearby mills began to close, demand for the neighborhood's historic housing waned and vacancy set in. A long-time Cove Street neighborhood leader took me on a tour and pointed out the Hathaway Mill and all its numerous pieces and outbuildings. It is where her father, grandfather, and uncles all worked. It was her family's sustenance. Esteemed Omaha, Nebraska, investor Warren Buffet bought the Hathaway Mill in the 1960s and witnessed huge financial losses. According to local residents, Mr. Buffet visited the mill often and he was known to say that it was the worst investment decision he ever made. He subsequently named his investment firm Berkshire Hathaway to remind himself and others of the miscalculation.

Despite mill closings and disinvestment, Cove Street was largely untouched by the urban renewal wrecking ball. While present day statistics show that the neighborhood has elevated foreclosure rates, Cove Street offers an interesting glimpse at how a relatively stable neighborhood has managed population loss.

Together, these three neighborhoods offer a lens to view both past and current change in one ordinary city. And together, they offer clues to how this kind of change can be managed.

Socioeconomic and Demographic Change

A close review of the demographic and housing characteristics of the city as a whole, and the three study neighborhoods, confirms a larger discourse of depopulation and housing abandonment. Tables 4.1 and 4.2 demonstrate a clear and steady trend toward fewer residents, smaller households, and less occupied housing units from 1970 to 2000, followed by a modest uptick in population in 2010.[1] During the 40-year period depicted in the tables, the city's population density dropped from 5089 persons per square mile to 4754, a reduction in 7%.

This drop in population was accompanied, generally, by higher poverty levels and an influx of African-Americans and non-white Hispanics (see Table 4.2). Similar patterns were evident in the three study neighborhoods (see Tables 4.3, 4.4, 4.5, 4.6, 4.7, and 4.8), where population and housing occupancy has dropped fairly consistently since 1970.

Spatially, Figs. 4.3 and 4.4 show how that population has, historically, been distributed throughout the city. The central portions of New Bedford had the most population in 1970 (shaded dark gray and black in Fig. 4.3) and that population experienced severe decline in the following decades (except 1980–1990, when the central portions of the city grew). Looking at population change across the entire period (1970–2015), the

Table 4.1 City-wide demographic data, New Bedford, 1970–2010

	1970	1980	1990	2000	2010	% ch 1970–2010
Total population	101,777	98,478	99,922	93,768	95,072	−7%
% female	52.5%	53.7%	53.1%	52.9%	52.0%	−1%
% male	45.3%	46.3%	46.9%	47.1%	48.0%	6%
% white[a]	93.8%	89.4%	87.6%	78.9%	74.5%	−21%
% African-American[a]	3.1%	2.7%	4.1%	4.4%	6.4%	106%
% Hispanic or Latino of any race[b]	1.4%	4.6%	6.7%	10.2%	16.7%	1055%
% foreign born	17.7%	23.8%	20.9%	19.6%	20.6%	16%
% <age 18	30.0%	26.2%	25.0%	20.8%	23.2%	−23%
% >age 64	13.8%	16.2%	17.4%	16.7%	14.6%	6%

Source: US Census Bureau State & County QuickFacts, 2010 and 2000

US Census Bureau, Census 2010 Summary File 1, 2000 Summary Files 1 and 3

1970 and 1980 data from NHGIS at http://www.nhgis.org or U.S. Census files

[a]Includes persons reporting only one race

[b]Hispanics may be of any race, so also are included in applicable race categories

Table 4.2 City-wide demographic and housing data, New Bedford, 1970–2010

	1970	1980	1990	2000	2010	% ch 1970–2010
Total population	101,777	98,478	99,922	93,768	95,072	−7%
% female	52.5%	53.7%	53.1%	52.9%	52.0%	−1%
% male	45.3%	46.3%	46.9%	47.1%	48.0%	6%
% white[a]	93.8%	89.4%	87.6%	78.9%	74.5%	−21%
% African-American[a]	3.1%	2.7%	4.1%	4.4%	6.4%	106%
% Hispanic or Latino of any race[b]	1.4%	4.6%	6.7%	10.2%	16.7%	1055%
% foreign born	17.7%	23.8%	20.9%	19.6%	20.6%	16%
% <age 18	30.0%	26.2%	25.0%	20.8%	23.2%	−23%
% >age 64	13.8%	16.2%	17.4%	16.7%	14.6%	6%

Source: US Census Bureau State & County QuickFacts, 2010 and 2000

US Census Bureau, Census 2010 Summary File 1, 2000 Summary Files 1 and 3

1970 and 1980 data from NHGIS at http://www.nhgis.org or U.S. Census files

[a]Includes persons reporting only one race

[b]Hispanics may be of any race, so also are included in applicable race categories

Table 4.3 North End (Bullard Street) demographic data

Census tract 6507

North End (Bullard St)

Demographic data, 1970–2010

	1970	1980	1990	2000	2010	% ch 1970–2010
Total population	3273	2534	2461	2256	2583	−21%
% female	54%	53%	53%	51%	45%	−18%
% male	46%	47%	47%	49%	55%	21%
% white[a]	99%	98%	91%	77%	49%	−51%
% African-American[a]	1%	0%	2%	7%	8%	1331%
% Hispanic or Latino of any race[b]	0%	7%	7%	23%	46%	–
% foreign born[c]	23%	29%	29%	24%	31%	31%
% <age 18	32%	29%	26%	29%	27%	−14%
% >age 64	14%	15%	12%	7%	8%	−42%

Source: US Census Bureau Neighborhood Change Database (1970–2000)

US Census Bureau American FactFinder, Census 2010 Summary File 1 (2010)

[a]Includes persons reporting only one race

[b]Hispanics may be of any race, so also are included in applicable race categories

[c]% foreign born for 2010 from American Community Survey five-year estimates (2010)

Table 4.4 North End (Bullard Street) demographic and housing data

Census tract 6507

North End (Bullard St)

Demographic and housing data, 1970–2010

	1970	1980	1990	2000	2010	% ch 1970–2010
Total population	3273	2534	2461	2256	2583	−21%
Total households	1212	1019	1019	944	887	−27%
Total housing units	1262	1157	1145	1045	1052	−17%
% occupied housing units	96%	90%	87%	87%	84%	−12%
Tenure (% rent) of OHU	90%	89%	85%	80%	86%	−4%
Tenure (% owned) of OHU	10%	11%	15%	20%	14%	37%
% vacant housing units of Total	4%	10%	13%	13%	16%	296%
% vacant housing units (other)1 of total	2%	3%	2%	3%	4%	152%
Median household income[a]	N/A	N/A	15,650	16,929	26,274	–
% people of all ages in poverty[a]	20%	23%	25%	35%	29%	45%
% unemployed of 16+ labor force	7%	11%	13%	17%	7%	4%
Land area in square miles	14%	14%	14%	14%	14%	0%
Persons per square mile	23,378.57	18,100	17,578.57	16,114.29	18,450	−21%

Source: US Census Bureau Neighborhood Change Database (1970–2000)

US Census Bureau American FactFinder, Census 2010 Summary File 1 (2010)

[a]For 2010, 2005–2009 American Communities Survey (five-year estimates, 2010); out of measured population

Table 4.5 Cove Street demographic data

Census tract 6527

Cove Street

Demographic data, 1970–2010

	1970	1980	1990	2000	2010	% ch 1970–2010
Total population	4110	4121	4074	3616	3762	−8%
% female	55%	56%	54%	51%	51%	−7%
% male	45%	44%	46%	49%	49%	8%
% white[a]	100%	97%	93%	84%	72%	−28%
% African-American[a]	0%	2%	1%	6%	6%	3667%
% Hispanic or Latino of any race[b]	1%	8%	8%	13%	29%	3226%
% foreign born[c]	23%	35%	24%	28%	23%	0%
% <age 18	30%	28%	27%	28%	27%	−10%
% >age 64	15%	17%	16%	15%	14%	−4%

Source: US Census Bureau Neighborhood Change Database (1970–2000)
US Census Bureau American FactFinder, Census 2010 Summary File 1 (2010)
[a]Includes persons reporting only one race
[b]Hispanics may be of any race, so also are included in applicable race categories
[c]For 2010, Data from American Community Survey (five-year estimates, 2010)

maps show a stark pattern of population declines of 5–27% in all census tracts of the city where data was available, except for the downtown tract, which experienced growth. While 1970–1980 and 1990–2000 were ones where much of the core of the city experienced population decline, the city's western and northern tracts grew during both periods. In other decades, numerous tracts even in the core of the city witnessed modest population growth. Altogether, a portrait of an ordinary city: one that experiences growth, decline, and stagnation.

With such variation and complexity, these trends can be viewed through the lens of the Reverse Transect Model. While conducting research on the impact of the Great Recession on American Sun Belt cities, I saw a need to create a conceptual model to rethink the outcomes of population change, particularly decline (Hollander 2011). The model builds off of the work of New Urbanists, a national movement of architects and planners committed to form-based solutions to manage growth and development. In their transect, each ecozone cuts across different segments of the land-

Table 4.6 Cove Street demographic and housing data

	1970	1980	1990	2000	2010	% ch 1970–2010
Total population	4110	4121	4074	3616	3762	−8%
Total households	1526	1714	1706	1539	1578	3%
Total housing units	1574	1805	1900	1786	1808	15%
% occupied housing units	97%	94%	89%	86%	87%	−10%
Tenure (% rent) of OHU	76%	77%	76%	76%	80%	4%
Tenure (% owned) of OHU	24%	23%	24%	24%	20%	−14%
% vacant housing units of Total	3%	6%	11%	14%	13%	317%
% vacant housing units (other)1 of total	0%	1%	2%	5%	3%	635%
Median household income[a]	N/A	N/A	15,063	18,942	21,803	–
% people of all ages in poverty[a]	19%	22%	22%	33%	31%	65%
% unemployed of 16+ labor force[a]	6%	10%	21%	15%	4%	−37%
Land area in square miles	0.28	0.28	0.28	0.28	0.26	−7%
Persons per square mile	14,678.57	14,717.86	14,550	12,914.29	14,469.23	−1%

Source: US Census Bureau Neighborhood Change Database (1970–2000)
US Census Bureau American FactFinder, Census 2010 Summary File 1 (2010)
[a]For 2010, American Communities Survey (five-year estimates, 2010); out of measured population

Table 4.7 South End demographic data

Census tract 6519, 6520

South End

Demographic and housing data, 1970–2010

	1970	Mean	1980	Mean	1990	Mean	2000	Mean	2010	Mean	% ch 1970–2010
Total population 6519	2267	**2929.5**	1885	**2441.5**	2036	**2530**	1865	**2353.5**	1942	**2309**	−21%
Total population 6520	3592		2998		3024		2842		2676		
% female 6519	0.5373	**0.54565**	0.57741	**0.548715**	0.56222	**0.548305**	0.52225	**0.53839**	0.528	**0.5295**	−3%
% female 6520	0.554		0.52002		0.53439		0.55453		0.531		
% male 6519	0.46269	**0.45434**	0.42258	**0.451275**	0.43777	**0.451685**	0.47774	**0.4616**	0.472	**0.4705**	4%
% male 6520	0.44599		0.47997		0.4656		0.44546		0.469		
% white[a] 6519	0.71327	**0.8203**	0.44137	**0.600435**	0.43418	**0.63607**	0.38874	**0.587225**	0.384	**0.536**	−35%
% white[a] 6520	0.92733		0.7595		0.83796		0.78571		0.688		

(*continued*)

Table 4.7 (continued)

Census tract 6519, 6520

South End

Demographic and housing data, 1970–2010

	1970	Mean	1980	Mean	1990	Mean	2000	Mean	2010	Mean	% ch 1970–2010
% African-American[a] 6519	0.27393	0.169675	0.06949	0.05609	0.08447	0.06009	0.19892	0.140275	0.135	0.106	−38%
% African-American[a] 6520	0.06542		0.04269		0.03571		0.08163		0.077		
% Hispanic or Latino of any race (b) 6519	0.01488	0.00855	0.08912	0.082585	0.16159	0.088895	0.23646	0.145145	0.326	0.2245	2526%
% Hispanic or Latino of any race[b] 6520	0.00222		0.07605		0.0162		0.05383		0.123		
% foreign born 6519[c]	0.23467	0.182895	0.3395	0.3507	0.24508	0.29466	0.18069	0.230735	0.257	0.3075	68%
% foreign born 6520[c]	0.13112		0.3619		0.34424		0.28078		0.358		
% <age 18 6519	0.32465	0.302775	0.2732	0.252175	0.28634	0.256925	0.2815	0.249475	0.281668	0.247523	−18%

(*continued*)

Table 4.7 (continued)

Census tract 6519, 6520

South End

Demographic and housing data, 1970–2010

	1970	Mean 1980	Mean 1990	Mean 2000	Mean 2010	Mean	% ch 1970–2010
% <age 18 6520	0.2809	0.23115	0.22751	0.21745	0.213378		
% >age 64 6519	0.17556	0.20053	0.16453	0.17694	0.179		
	0.1674	**0.177645**	**0.175845**	**0.18488**		**0.1855**	11%
% >age 64 6520	0.15924	0.15476	0.18716	0.19282	0.192		

Source: US Census Bureau Neighborhood Change Database (1970–2000)
US Census Bureau American FactFinder, Census 2010 Summary File 1 (2010)

[a] Includes persons reporting only one race

[b] Hispanics may be of any race, so also are included in applicable race categories

[c] For 2010, American Communities Survey (five-year estimate, 2010); out of measured population

Table 4.8 South End demographic and housing data

Census Tract 6519, 6520

South End

Demographic and housing data, 1970–2010

	1970	Mean	1980	Mean	1990	Mean	2000	Mean	2010	% ch 1970–2010
Total population 6519	2267	**2929.5**	1885	**2441.5**	2036	**2530**	1865	**2353.5**	1942	−21%
Total population 6520	3592		2998		3024		2842		2676	
Total households 6519	817	**1039**	843	**980**	832	**960.5**	771	**957**	825	−7%
Total households 6520	1261		1117		1089		1143		1098	
Total housing units 6519	831	**1079.5**	882	**1045**	929	**1060.5**	849	**1037**	932	0%
Total housing units 6520	1328		1208		1192		1225		1224	
% occupied housing units 6519	0.98315	**0.966345**	0.89569	**0.90852**	0.92142	**0.92925**	0.90341	**0.915375**	0.885	**0.891**	−8%

(*continued*)

Table 4.8 (continued)

Census Tract 6519, 6520

South End

Demographic and housing data, 1970–2010

	1970	Mean	1980	Mean	1990	Mean	2000	Mean	2010	Mean	% ch 1970–2010
% occupied housing units 6520	0.94954		0.92135		0.93708		0.92734		0.897		
Tenure (% rent) of OHU 6519	0.78824	**0.7141**	0.82278	**0.706535**	0.77102	**0.66393**	0.76401	**0.678655**	0.806	**0.7105**	−1%
Tenure (% rent) of OHU 6520	0.63996		0.59029		0.55684		0.5933		0.615		
Tenure (% owned) of OHU 6519	0.21419	**0.28711**	0.17848	**0.29409**	0.22897	**0.33606**	0.23598	**0.321335**	0.194	**0.2895**	1%
Tenure (% owned) of OHU 6520	0.36003		0.4097		0.44315		0.40669		0.385		
% vacant housing units of total 6519	0.01564	**0.033045**	0.10317	**0.09132**	0.07857	**0.07074**	0.09658	**0.084615**	0.115	**0.109**	230%

(*continued*)

Table 4.8 (continued)

Census Tract 6519, 6520

South End

Demographic and housing data, 1970–2010

	1970	Mean	1980	Mean	1990	Mean	2000	Mean	2010	Mean	% ch 1970–2010
% vacant housing units of total 6520	0.05045		0.07947		0.06291		0.07265		0.103		
% vacant housing units (other)1 of total 6519	0.00601	0.00451	0.0068	0.014985	0.00107	0.00976	0.06124	0.044085	0.031	0.03	565%
% vacant housing units (other)1 of total 6520	0.00301		0.02317		0.01845		0.02693		0.029		
Median household income 6519[a]	N/A	N/A	N/A	N/A	11,071	17,862.5	16,426	23,222	20,085	26,673	–
Median household income 6520[a]	N/A		N/A		24,654		30,018		33,261		

(continued)

Table 4.8 (continued)

Census Tract 6519, 6520

South End

Demographic and housing data, 1970–2010

	1970	Mean	1980	Mean	1990	Mean	2000	Mean	2010	Mean	% ch 1970–2010
% People of all ages in poverty 6519[a]	0.26422	**0.198785**	0.23948	**0.21375**	0.3136	**0.222365**	0.3216	**0.224835**	0.433	**0.334**	68%
% People of all ages in poverty 6520[a]	0.13335		0.18802		0.13113		0.12807		0.235		
% Unemployed of 16+ labor force 6519[a]	0.0898	**0.066695**	0.11621	**0.11657**	0.21592	**0.15523**	0.18379	**0.13455**	0.042	**0.058**	−13%
% Unemployed of 16+ labor force 6520[a]	0.04359		0.11693		0.09454		0.08531		0.074		
Land area in square miles 6519	0.38	**0.275**	0.38	**0.275**	0.38	**0.275**	0.38	**0.275**	0.38	**0.275**	–

(*continued*)

Table 4.8 (continued)

Census Tract 6519, 6520

South End

Demographic and housing data, 1970–2010

	1970 Mean	1980 Mean	1990 Mean	2000 Mean	2010 Mean	% ch 1970–2010
Land area in square miles 6520	0.17	0.17	0.17	0.17	0.17	
Persons per square mile 6519	5965.789	13,547.6	11,573.07	10,812.77	10,425.85	−23%
		4960.526	5357.895	4907.895	5110.526	
		11,297.91				
Persons per square mile 6520	21,129.41	17,635.29	17,788.24	16,717.65	15,741.18	

Source: US Census Bureau Neighborhood Change Database (1970–2000)

US Census Bureau American FactFinder, Census 2010 Summary File 1 (2010)

[a]For 2010, American Communities Survey (five-year estimate, 2010); out of measured population

Fig. 4.3 Population by the decade, 1970–2015

scape, beginning out in the remote rural zones with T1 (Rural Preserve) through T2 (Rural Reserve), T3 (Sub-urban), T4 (General Urban), T5 (Urban Center), and culminating in the heart of a metro area, T6 (Urban Core) (Duany and Talen 2002).

Associated with each ecozone of the transect are maximum density levels and associated urban design and landscape elements. T2 has homes on large lots with narrow winding roads and scenic vistas, while T3 allows for limited multi-family housing, woodlands, and arterial roads. T4 and T5 allow for increasing levels of housing density and higher capacity roadways, along with mixes of uses (particularly retail and office uses). The key, Duany and Talen (2002) argue, is to preserve and protect the cohesiveness of each distinct ecozone.

The transect model teaches us that when growth happens, it does not have to be a bad thing for communities and neighborhoods if it is planned for and managed such that each ecozone is preserved. In the Reverse Transect, the same argument is made for decline: it does not need to be a

82 4 HOW MUCH CHANGE IS TOO MUCH

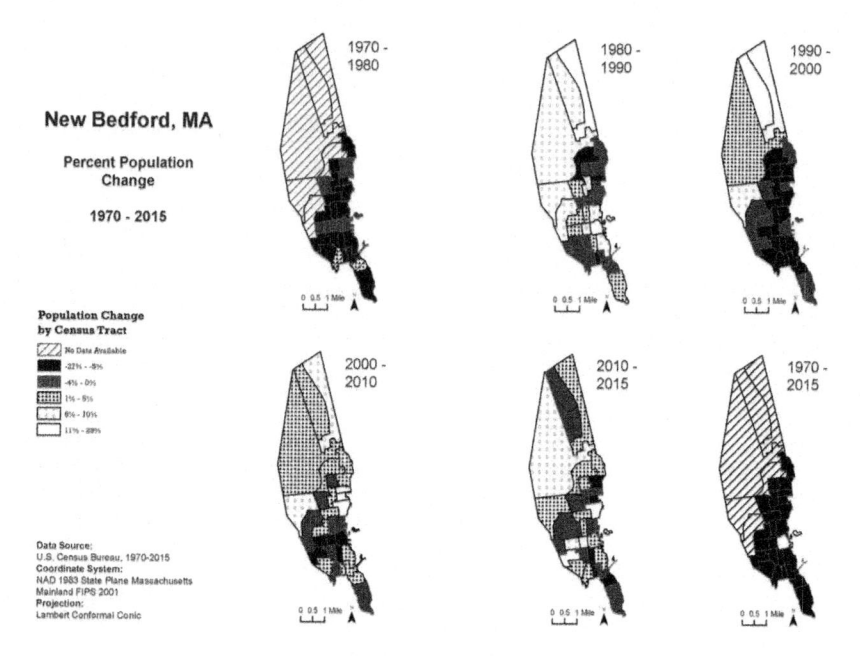

Fig. 4.4 Percentage population change, 1970–2015

bad thing for communities and neighborhoods if it is well planned for and ecozones are properly preserved.

In the Reverse Transect, we assume that an example neighborhood begins at T5 with 15 housing units per acre (see Fig. 4.5). If the neighborhood loses 20% of its housing units due to depopulation, it will have just 12 units per acre and will appear now in the T4 ecozone. Normally, such a loss would be viewed as tragic, but the transect concept teaches us that neighborhood change does not have to be a bad thing. From the New Urbanists, we learn that T4 is no better or worse than T5, simply different. We also learn from them that a variety of urban design and landscape architecture techniques can be useful to retrofit a neighborhood to install or redesign elements within the ecozone to protect and preserve its integrity.

Returning to New Bedford, a close examination of housing density changes shows a movement along the Reverse Transect for each case study neighborhood (see Table 4.9). By dividing the number of occupied hous-

THE REVERSE TRANSECT

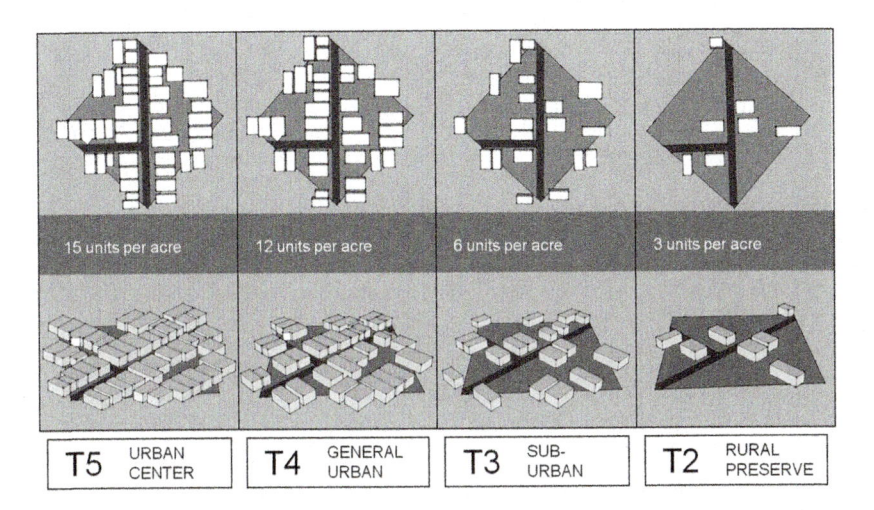

Fig. 4.5 Reverse tract model

ing units by the area of the census tract(s) of the neighborhood, I can estimate rough housing density.[2]

The patterns that emerged in the North End fit nicely with the Reverse Transect Model and illustrate the broader trend of increased vacancy in the neighborhoods since 1970 (see Table 4.10). The neighborhood went from 14 occupied housing units per acre in 1970 down to 12 in 1980, then 11 in 1990, and finally 10 in both 2000 and 2010. This pattern fits nicely with the trend depicted in Fig. 4.3: the North End began as a T5 Urban Center ecozone and then became a T4 General Urban ecozone and is beginning to approach the density levels of T3 Sub-urban.

Interestingly, neither the South End nor Cove Street experienced such a steady, consistent downward pattern. In fact, Cove Street experienced a modest uptick in number of occupied housing units from 1970 to 2010 and only registered a slight overall loss in population, with its overall housing stock having both risen and fallen during the 1970–2010 period. The South End, likewise, experienced flat housing unit growth during a period of large-scale population decline.

Table 4.9 Occupied housing density in city of New Bedford, 1970–2000

City-wide (land area = 20 sq miles = 12,800 acres)	1970	1980	1990	2000	2010
Total housing units	36,597	39,482	41,760	41,511	42,933
% occupied housing units	97%	95%	93%	92%	90%
Occupied housing units	35,389	37,389	38,795	38,190	38,768
Occupied housing units per acre	2.8	2.9	3.0	3.0	3.0

Table 4.10 Occupied housing density for three study neighborhoods, 1970–2010

South End[a] (land area = 0.17 sq miles = 108.8 acres)	1970	1980	1990	2000	2010
Total housing units	2159	2090	2121	2074	2156
% occupied housing units	96%	90%	93%	92%	89%
Occupied housing units	2073	1882	1971	1898	1919
Occupied housing units per acre	19	17	18	17	18

North End (land area = 0.14 sq miles = 89.6 acres)	1970	1980	1990	2000	2010
Total housing units	1262	1157	1145	1045	1052
% occupied housing units	96%	90%	87%	87%	84%
Occupied housing units	1212	1042	993	909	887
Occupied housing units per acre	14	12	11	10	10

Cove Street (land area = 0.28 sq miles = 179.2 acres)	1970	1980	1990	2000	2010
Total housing units	1574	1805	1900	1786	1808
% occupied housing units	97%	94%	89%	86%	87%
Occupied housing units	1526	1703	1692	1540	1578
Occupied housing units per acre	17	19	19	17	18

[a]Used sum of the two census tracts that compromise the neighborhood, 6519 and 6520

For the South End and Cove Street, each experienced movement along the Reverse Transect, just not in a predictable, steady way. Both neighborhoods maintained a relatively stable footing around 17–19 occupied housing units per acre from 1970 to 2010, staying comfortably settled in the T5 Urban Center ecozone. The North End is unique among the case neighborhoods in that it continued to experience high levels of further depopulation in tandem with decreasing levels of occupied housing. Chapter 6 includes a detailed examination of the pre-1970s era, offering further insights into how each neighborhood fared.

Notes

1. The focus of this detailed tabular demographic and housing review is the period from 1970 to 2010. I delimited the scope of data collection to this period because of the high levels of validity and reliability of U.S. Census data at the census tract level during this period. In fact, I drew data from the Neighborhood Change Database for the 1970–2000 periods, whereby census tract boundaries have been normalized across all periods. Prior to 1970, it becomes increasingly difficult to make fair comparisons for many indicators for the same geographic areas over time. Additional spatial population-only data was available to construct 2015 maps.
2. This is a technique I have employed elsewhere, see Hollander (2010, 2011).

Bibliography

Duany, Andres, and Emily Talen. 2002. Transect Planning. *Journal of the American Planning Association* 68 (3): 245–266.

Frieden, Bernard J., and Lynne B. Sagalyn. 1991. *Downtown, Inc.: How America Rebuilds Cities*. Cambridge, MA: MIT Press.

Hollander, Justin B. 2010. Moving Towards a Shrinking Cities Metric: Analyzing Land Use Changes Associated with Depopulation in Flint, Michigan. *Cityscape: A Journal of Policy Development and Research* 12 (1): 133–151.

———. 2011. *Sunburnt Cities: The Great Recession, Depopulation and Urban Planning in the American Sunbelt*. London: Routledge.

Massachusetts Executive Office of Transportation and Massachusetts Executive Office of Housing and Economic Development. 2009. *South Coast Rail Economic Development and Land Use Corridor Plan*. Boston, MA: Commonwealth of Massachusetts.

CHAPTER 5

The Legacy of Change: Depopulation and Growth's Impact on New Bedford Today

Change can be difficult for anyone. The psychological and social dimensions of community decline have been viewed among scholars as some of the most heart-wrenching and stressful types of change people face. Research in Youngstown, Ohio, showed how residents of a declining steel town grieved over the loss of jobs, residents, and overall prosperity (Linkon and Russo 2003). This concept of community depression builds on Robert Bellah's (1985) communitarianism notion, where places are viewed as having memories, constituted inter-subjectively by residents, past and present. New Bedford residents continue to experience these emotional difficulties as they regularly witness the continued emptying out of neighborhoods. A famous study of former mining towns in Western Pennsylvania found that it took a generation before city leaders could fully accept that their mines were closed for good and take steps to plan for the future (Mayer and Greenberg 2001).

The malaise often associated with employment and population decline is palpable among many of today's residents of New Bedford. Over the course of two years, I conducted over a dozen individual interviews and three focus groups with neighborhood residents, government officials, and community leaders (each compromising of between 8 and 15 participants).[1] I conducted the interviews and focus groups anonymously with the assistance of several Tufts graduate students.

In both interviews and focus groups, I sought to understand three dimensions of community change:

1. What do residents see as their neighborhoods' biggest challenges?
2. What are the major physical changes they have witnessed in their neighborhood?
3. For vacant lots and abandoned buildings in their neighborhood, what new uses do they see as possible?

What Residents See as Their Neighborhoods' Biggest Challenges

During the focus groups and interviews, three major categories of challenges emerged: blaming the "other," absentee landlords, and real estate market stagnation. While all interconnected, each deserves some attention independently.

Blaming the "Other"

Over and over in my research, I heard the complaints of long-term residents that their neighborhoods were changing because poor people were moving in and ruining the status quo. One resident explained it like this: "There have been a lot of changes in New Bedford—you used to know all your neighbors, could walk on your street. Boston fixed up its neighborhoods and sent them all down here."

The anger reached a fever pitch during two of the focus groups, where much of the vitriol was downright anti-poor: "I'd say the majority of the people who pass through the street—everybody's on some form of SSI or disability, so there are people who can't, and don't, work." These "people" are also viewed as the source of a broader moral decay in the city:

> One conversation I overheard: three nine-year-olds found some pills, wondered what they were, and one said "Let's ask my dad, he's a drug dealer." … total moral decay of society.
>
> When the mills closed down, it forced a lot of people to go [to] other places and it was hard for landlords to rent out these tenements, so a lot of these low income people came in. With them came drugs and disrespect. Guns, for instance. I lived on Brock Avenue growing up and we had a group that was mischievous. We would climb Roosevelt to the roof and the police would come, but there were no guns. We were always the South End versus the West End, but we were nothing like this. They don't think about taking a life.

This discourse of Boston sending its poor people to New Bedford was a powerful one, repeated a number of times to me in both the interviews and focus groups. Even more surprising, I found it again in Rory Nugent's (2009) book about the fishing industry in New Bedford, *Down by the Docks* (introduced in Chap. 1). This tale of Boston shipping its poor to New Bedford really resonated with those I spoke to, so enchanted by the notion that the source of their problems lay in the state's capital city. I had to investigate.

Weeks later, I had independently verified that the compelling yarn is, in fact, a fictitious one. There is no government or non-governmental office in Boston that sends poor people anywhere. Throughout the state, a system of housing referral non-profit organizations provide counseling for those people who qualify for Section 8 federally subsidized housing vouchers. During the boom years of 2000–2007 in Boston, it became increasingly difficult for people holding such vouchers to find suitable housing in and around Boston as rents skyrocketed and a shrinking list of landlords were willing to rent out to Section 8 voucher holders.

The Section 8 program is entirely voluntary, so landlord willingness to rent does restrict the spatial reach of where poor people can live (you won't find many Section 8 apartments in the ritzy Back Bay or Beacon Hill neighborhoods of Boston, for instance). So, as rents and housing prices went up, Section 8 voucher holders did leave Boston for other places where their vouchers would be accepted: Brockton, Providence, Hartford, and beyond. Did Boston send their poor people to New Bedford? No. I interviewed several key administrative officers at the non-profit counseling agency that serves the city of Boston's Section 8 voucher recipients, the Metropolitan Boston Housing Partnership. They do not encourage voucher holders to relocate to any specific location—all they do is provide apartment listings. A quick perusal of those listings actually indicates that New Bedford apartments are not even included. To find New Bedford apartments, a voucher holder would need to reach out to another agency, far outside Boston, to be able to even access New Bedford listings.

Absentee Landlords

In many ways, the influx of poor residents and the change that has meant for neighborhoods is conflated with a different "bad guy": the absentee landlord. As employers and people left the city, the real estate market also softened and increasing numbers of out-of-town investors bought up the low value homes for sale. With the foreclosure crisis of 2008–2009, the problem became even more acute. Homes that had been selling for around $100,000 were on the auction block for $10,000.

Investors with little personal connection to the New Bedford community bought these homes and rented them largely to poor residents, in many cases Section 8 holders. But the problem seen by those I interviewed had much to do with those investors who were viewed as absentee; that is, they do not reside in their new homes (much of New Bedford's housing stock consists of multi-family houses) or in the immediate area. One longtime resident explained the problem:

> If a landlord lives there in the house it's OK. If you have absentee landlords, it's a different story. They get people in there that just don't care. A lot of garbage in the backyard. Rats going in and out when there are open containers. When you see owners who live there, people are more careful.

It is not just that the owners are buying buildings cheap, that they are charging low rents, or that they are renting to Section 8 voucher holders. The biggest problem is that they "just don't care" and are not present in the neighborhood and community.

Some residents organized in early 2010 and fought back against the scourge of absentee landlords. A group chartered a bus and drove to the affluent suburbs around New Bedford to picket in front of the homes of these absentee landlords. "We want to embarrass them in front of their neighbors with pictures of their properties." One particular absentee landlord has amassed a small empire of multi-family rental units, estimated to be nearly 300 through the city.

> He's been a horrible landlord and you can't stop him from buying property. Someone's going to get hurt. Services are not like it used to be, and they know. We want to kinda shake him a little. The homes like he has here, nobody should be living that way. It's not right. There should be a suit of community against absentee landlords to not have to live this way.

The city government also responded by creating a task force to look more closely at absentee landlords. Their work has resulted in better code enforcement and more attention to garbage collection. But the overall impression from New Bedford residents is that these absentee landlords are part of the problem and should be stopped. While the city government could be more proactive, these absentee landlords are acting in their self-interest and will be appropriately motivated to only make the most modest of investments in their houses as long as the real estate market continues to be weak in the city.

Real Estate Market Stagnation

The same forces that create the economic advantages of absentee landlord practices and that attract Section 8 voucher holders also generate a third problem for New Bedford residents: real estate market stagnation. The shrinking job base has meant falling population levels, which has translated into falling home prices and rents. For home owners in New Bedford, that makes leaving the city quite difficult. The feeling of being trapped, and that the city is mired in crime and poverty, is tied in the minds of many residents to the health of the real estate market.

One resident was clear about his inability to relocate out of New Bedford at the present:

> My mother owns the house, she's in her 80s, and when the day comes she passes away I'm definitely leaving. I want to go out to a quiet neighborhood. I want to go to the suburbs. I'm tired, it's the drugs, the shootings, I'm tired.

Others expressed a more conflicted relationship to the city:

> I can't afford to live somewhere else. I'm not stuck here, I choose to live here. I'm happy where I am, I've lived here 10 years. But it's the kind of thing you deal with. You're either part of the problem or part of the solution. And I've never been part of the problem, I'm part of the solution.

This resident was expressing her concern with not being able to afford to live anywhere else but refused to draw on the discourse of "being stuck." Instead, she argues that her refusal to leave the city is part of a noble tradition of being "part of the solution." But her lack of financial resources to relocate (due perhaps to owning a home that is worth less than she purchased it for or due to the high costs of moving) is framing her own understanding of why she remains in the city.

Another community leader I interviewed expressed the same conflicted relationship to the city. In one interview, she recounted her complicated commitment to New Bedford:

> Why should I have to leave? Why can't I make ends meet in the city I live in? This is supposed to be the land of opportunity, but I can't find a job in my own country—that's pitiful. ... My friends, we're all on Facebook, we grew up with—all my friends who left home, they would love to come home. They can't afford to. They can't make the salaries they make [there], they went to Florida, Texas, Chicago. ... I take care of my step-dad, so I can't leave him.

After lamenting the poor job prospects in the city and how those limit her friends' ability to migrate back to New Bedford, this community leader ends by saying she really cannot leave because she has to take care of her step-dad. This theme was repeated by others I interviewed again and again. They want to help make New Bedford better, they care deeply about the city, they want more job opportunities, but until that happens, they still would leave if they could.

So, then, what are the *real* problems in New Bedford?

There is a familiar refrain of the anonymous subject pronoun of "they" or the generic "Boston" in the tall tale of how Boston sent its poor to New Bedford and ruined the city. This tale is viewed by many in the city as the source of the city's problem and general moral decline, absentee landlords, and the real estate market stagnation that has made many residents stuck in the city. By using an anonymous pronoun, people are suggesting a larger strategic intention and purpose in the way that a steady stream of poor residents migrated into New Bedford's previously middle-class neighborhoods. I have found no evidence of such a grand plan to "ruin" New Bedford, rather a reversal of fortunes: as Boston's neighborhoods got wealthier, fewer housing options were available for the poor. As jobs left New Bedford, its formerly middle-income and stable neighborhoods began to see lower rents, opening the door for larger and larger numbers of landlords willing to accept Section 8 vouchers. Why and how this economic restructuring occurred is largely lost to New Bedfordians I spoke to, but the result is clear to many of them: "I've lived in my same house all my life; I've seen a lot of changes in the neighborhood, and it's just deteriorated."

This anger at new, largely poor neighbors, was striking to me. The long-time residents were adamant that there is something morally and ethically inferior about these people, the "other." Interviewees spoke about the work ethic of new residents ("They don't get off their rear end and get out"), their attitude toward crime and violence ("They run wild"), and basic norms about raising children and treating others ("These kids have no guidance. They're out on the street. Guess it's the TV, too. No respect"). New residents certainly had different, if similarly negative, attitudes toward the long-time residents, seeing them as vestiges of the past.

We know cities are melting pots, and Sandercock (1998) and others teach us that neighborhoods in transition are on the front lines in embracing (or rejecting) that difference. Research on gentrification has shown this clash during periods of growth, but we have only the "white flight" literature to understand decline. With the development of the Interstate Highway System and growth of suburbs in the 1950s through the 1980s, middle and upper income (largely white) residents fled urban neighborhoods, moving to homogeneous suburbs outside the city (Jackson 1985). How do we conceptualize difference and diversity in the face of vitriol and hidden racism spewing from long-time residents?

Change can be hard for city governments to manage. Shrinkage means more than just a change in how many people live in a neighborhood or how many houses are vacant. In New Bedford and other places, shrinkage has also meant a change in the type of people who live in a place. Lucy and Phillips (2000) remind us that any place is continuously changing, people are always moving in, moving out, dying, and being born. To create stable neighborhoods, which maintain roughly steady income levels, rental rates, and housing values, the neighborhood must continuously remain attractive to new residents (Lucy and Phillips 2000).

Called neighborhood succession, the general idea promoted in the Neighborhood Life Cycle literature is that neighborhoods decrease in various quality measures as new lower-income residents succeed the last residents to depart. New Bedford neighborhoods are in a regular state of change but a better model exists in what I have called the Alternative Neighborhood Change theory (Hollander 2009) (see Chap. 2).

Rather than neighborhoods getting worse and more morally corrupt, the Alternative Neighborhood Change theory allows for a value-neutral change. Nobody wants lower incomes, but it is reasonable to believe that every city will have some poor people. Some great minds have argued that a certain balance between rich, middle income, and poor—normatively speaking—creates the ideal city (Jacobs 1961; Gans 1962). Others have argued that some level of poorness is fine, but a steady decline in income over time is troubling (Lucy and Philips 2000). Both of these are sound arguments and ought to inform policymaking in a shrinking city.

However, the Alternative Neighborhood Change theory stands to both arguments. Concerning the former, a construction of a perfect balance of rich, middle income, and poor will most certainly have costs, and the calibration of benefits are so entirely value based that a city could potentially achieve such a balance but also end up creating a new caste system. Without a clear moral compass, the building of a city population around income levels ends up being discriminatory, likely resulting in a system of quotas. As an extreme case, I can imagine that in order to attract wealthy residents, housing is given to them at a nominal cost, where poor residents have to pay a premium for rent.

A community with declining income will mean that individuals and families will have to live on fewer and fewer dollars. In theory, this is a problem, but not if expenses continue to fall. In many shrinking cities, property values tend to fall as employment drops. This can result in declining rents and declining cost of living. Again, the Alternative Neighborhood Change theory stands up to this critique, offering a fairer and more balanced way to view changes in neighborhoods. The theory provides a less critical view of declining incomes in a shrinking neighborhood as those falling incomes may reflect lower costs for households or indicate employment in more enjoyable (but less lucrative) careers.

More Abandoned Buildings, More Vacant Lots

When I asked residents what they saw as the biggest problems in their neighborhood, few responded first with abandoned buildings and vacant lots. Most New Bedfordians (as well as most scholars) believe that abandoned buildings and vacant lots are a symptom of more deep-seeded problems like the ones discussed in the previous section: new influx of poor people, absentee landlords, and real estate market stagnation. The physical fabric of the neighborhood was not seen as the cause of problems, but the result. Adopting a smart-shrinkage perspective, I argue the opposite. In fact, it is the very problem of too many homes (too much supply to meet shrinking demand) that causes declining real estate values, which leads to the city as an attractive location for absentee landlords actively bringing in increasingly lower and lower socioeconomic classes into previously middle-income neighborhoods.

This argument begins with the notion that an abandoned building is the first domino to fall in what can be a spiral of falling rents and disinvestment that can destroy stable neighborhoods. If buildings can be adapted for other uses and if vacant lots can be reused quickly, the larger real estate market can be stabilized, thus preserving home values and rent prices. If we think of the abandonment of a building as the beginning of the process, policy intervention is possible, and neighborhood stabilization can happen. If we begin with the buildings and lots, we can theoretically prevent the kinds of problems identified in the above section.

Abandoned Buildings

In the three study neighborhoods, abandoned buildings are viewed as a problem by some. "I have to say the sad thing to this is, we didn't have as many abandoned homes as we do now" remarked one long-time resident. For many, abandoned buildings are not an abstract problem for other parts of the city, but a reality right next door. One community leader said:

> There is [a] house 2 blocks away from my house and another ... that is empty and has been on the market for a couple of years. The house was set on fire. The house next to that one was vacant, but now it has tenants and it makes a huge difference.

Tenants are central to maintaining stability in neighborhoods. According to this community leader, they make a "huge difference." Despite all of the concerns about who those tenants are and what kinds of problem they generate for a community, the very presence of tenants counts.

Vacant Lots

While conceptually related to abandoned buildings, vacant lots pose a unique challenge to neighborhood well-being. If the lots are being cared for, protected, and maintained, then they are hardly a problem at all. If they are not, they are considered a major threat to community stability (Kelling and Wilson 1982; Hollander 2009). This distinction is sometimes hard to measure and most local governments tend to not have the means to do so. In Chaps. 6 and 8, I introduce an approach for collecting data on, and classifying vacant lots into, these two categories for the purposes of effective planning. In those chapters, I also present the results of a detailed review of the conditions and status of vacant lots in the three study neighborhoods. Here, I present summary statistics on that investigation and the impressions of residents, community leaders, and government officials regarding the vacant lot problem in the city.

When resident activists see a vacant lot, they tend to report it to the city ("We don't like to see empty lots because it becomes a trash issue and we have to call it in"). Dumping is very common on lots that are not being protected and maintained—in New Bedford and in general.

Groups of activist citizens have gone around their neighborhoods cleaning up lots with trash. This can help build civic pride and community cohesion but can also be a source of frustration when more dumping occurs later.

Policy Options for Reusing Empty Buildings and Lands

This is not just a book about what New Bedfordians believe and how they make meaning of their shrinking city. This is also a book about action, about the ways that the city has changed, and how it ought to change in the future. What do residents, community leaders, and government officials see today as the ways to manage shrinkage? What are their attitudes around the reuse of vacant lots and abandoned buildings? My research has revealed two primary means by which future uses are viewed, in terms of (1) green space and (2) decline in density.

Green Space

One focus group participant called on the city government to take a lead: "They should do what they do in Brockton—as a house gets dilapidated, they should level it and build more green space." Brockton is a medium-sized city about one-hour north of New Bedford. To many New Bedfordians, the notion of demolishing housing to make room for more green space is appealing. Here, green space is meant to be any property which is predominantly grass or other vegetation—without respect to the exact use of the land.

A community leader echoed the need for more green space in the city:

> If there was a block that was blighted then it would be a good idea to take down the housing and create some open space. A neighborhood park would be nice, but it would take money to maintain. A dog park would be ideal.

Others saw gardens as a valuable way to use green space, saying that the city should have "community gardens similar to what was done during the Depression and WWII. You get fresh food and gardening is good therapy." A new resident, enthusiastic about the contemporary grow local movement, added: "I have raised beds in the backyard and all the neighbors are like 'Wow, that's great'."

Decline in Density

A critical dimension of reusing or repurposing vacant land and abandoned buildings is *how*. For most of the residents, community leaders, and officials I spoke to, there was an understanding about the limitations of the real estate market in New Bedford to foster growth. Put another way, the conventional urban planning approach to decline described in Chap. 2 was largely ignored by those I interviewed in favor of a more pragmatic approach to reusing land and buildings. The conventional approach suggests that through government subsidy and incentives, vacant lots and abandoned buildings could be redeveloped for new housing, retail, or office uses (primarily).

As articulated in Chap. 2, there are major challenges to that approach for cities that are shrinking. For a place like New Bedford, there is little enthusiasm among public agencies for subsidizing reuse scenarios that are not grounded in the realities of the real estate market. Instead, the green space ideas mentioned above and others focused largely on uses that could be economically viable in New Bedford.

One government official explained that "some homes have been turned commercial: hair salons, real estate offices." Certainly, a conventional planning for growth strategy would support new uses where demand exists (hair salons and real estate offices), but there exists little interest in new housing with the exception of converting former mills into luxury housing. The vast majority of the current housing stock in New Bedford is of low to moderate quality, so city officials have supported luxury housing as a viable reuse for former industrial buildings.

In the downtown of the city, there is support from at least one government official to turn an eyesore of a vacant lot into parking, by intervening and taking over the situation from an absentee owner:

> People want to take them [vacant lots] over. There is one building downtown where the owner has not done anything with it while waiting for the economy to turn around. We've been putting on the peer pressure and they are talking about making it into a parking lot, to charge for parking spaces until the economy gets better. But we've got to put on the peer pressure to change it.

What about policy solutions to housing vacancy and abandonment? For those issues, I asked about converting some multi-family units into single-family housing. One resident recounted how that conversion did occur in his neighborhood, when a three-story, three-unit building had a fire. "The top floor burns down and they don't rebuild it, so then it's a two-family. Unless they burn down nothing happens." This resident felt that little is being done to proactively reduce the number of housing units or the density of residential neighborhoods—it takes a fire to do it.

Not all I spoke to were so pessimistic. Some saw the opportunities for turning some homes into half-way houses: "There's one for AIDS-infected people somewhere nearby. If they're a state run program they don't pay taxes, so that doesn't help the city." But a half-way house can make sense for a new use for an otherwise abandoned building.

For some owners, their homes are not fully occupied by design. One long-time resident explained:

> You actually have a lot of one-floor vacancy because if an elderly person, owner-occupied, has paid off their mortgage, they worry about what tenants might do to the property. So if they don't need the money they leave it vacant.

Respondents at one of the focus groups agreed that "as much as 20% of owner occupied homes have vacant units." This thinning-out of occupied housing units is less about finding creative new uses for old buildings or vacant lots and more about a decline in density. While certainly not all, many of the people I spoke to saw value in making their neighborhood less congested, with more green space and access to gardens, and with fewer occupied housing units. The results here presage what I found looking historically, that is, for the past few decades the very physical fabric of the city has effectively reprogrammed itself to meet a smaller population. The following chapter takes a step back and looks at the history of depopulation in New Bedford, its impact on the physical landscape, and how the city responded to this new threat.

NOTE

1. We took detailed notes, including verbatim quotes, during both the interviews and focus groups. In addition, the focus groups and some group interviews were recorded, which allowed us to check the accuracy of our notes. I conducted an open reading of these notes and then thematically analyzed them to pull out key topics and themes (see Kvale 2007).

BIBLIOGRAPHY

Bellah, Robert N. 1985. *Habits of the Heart: Individualism and Commitment in American Life*. Berkeley, CA: University of California Press.
Gans, Herbert J. 1962. *The Urban Villagers: Group and Class in the Life of Italian-Americans*. New York, NY: The Free Press of Glencoe.
Hollander, Justin B. 2009. *Polluted and Dangerous: America's Worst Abandoned Properties and What Can Be Done About Them*. Burlington, VT: University of Vermont Press.
Jackson, Kenneth T. 1985. *Crabgrass Frontier: The Suburbanization of the United States*. New York, NY: Oxford University Press.
Jacobs, Jane. 1961. *The Death and Life of Great American Cities*. New York, NY: Random House.
Kelling, George L., and James Q. Wilson. 1982. Broken Windows – The Police and Neighborhood Safety. *The Atlantic*, March 1.
Kvale, Steinar. 2007. *Doing Interviews*. London: Sage.
Linkon, Sherry L., and John Russo. 2003. *Steeltown U.S.A.: Work and Memory in Youngstown*. Lawrence, KA: University Press of Kansas.
Lucy, William H., and David L. Phillips. 2000. *Confronting Suburban Decline: Strategic Planning for Metropolitan Renewal*. Washington, DC: Island Press.
Mayer, Henry J., and Michael R. Greenberg. 2001. Coming Back from Economic Despair: Case Studies of Small and Medium-size American Places. *Economic Development Quarterly* 15 (3): 205–216.
Nugent, Rory. 2009. *Down at the Docks*. New York, NY: Pantheon.
Sandercock, Leonie. 1998. *Towards Cosmopolis: Planning for Multicultural Cities*. New York, NY: John Wiley and Sons.

CHAPTER 6

After the Hurricane: Government Responses to Employment and Population Decline, 1929–1975

From its humble beginnings to the self-appointed title of "Whaling Capital of the World," the politics and culture of New Bedford have always been shaped by an image of self-grandeur. But "grand" would hardly describe New Bedford today. Something very important happened to this port city, and it is something that has been lamented among long-time residents and leaders: the overall decline of New Bedford's population starting around 1929.

While I offered a sketch of the history of the city in Chap. 1, here I continue unpeeling the onion to help explain how the city first began to respond to a shrinking of the physical plant of the city. It is easy to say that once more people began to leave New Bedford than arrive, a problem was at hand. But cities are much too complex for such a platitude. Problems abound in both growing and shrinking cities. What really matters is how change is managed. And with that in mind, what did New Bedford do about its decline?

By the time of the Great Depression (beginning in 1929), mills were already relocating out of the city for more labor-friendly environs in the South. Population continued to drop in the city as the Depression wreaked havoc nationally; massive job losses were caused by the further closing of one textile mill after another (Wolfbein 1944). The death blow came in 1938 with a massive hurricane that swept away whatever little industry still remained in the city.

© The Author(s) 2018
J.B. Hollander, *An Ordinary City*,
DOI 10.1007/978-3-319-60705-4_6

This shift in fortunes began a long slide in jobs and population that (while punctuated by periods of brief recovery) continued for over eight decades and even today seems to have hardly abated. Throughout the USA and abroad, this is a classic story of deindustrialization and is hardly remarkable: A major industrial city grows then faces some form of calamity and begins a multi-decade long weakening process. In the USA, the wide swath of territory from Maine across the Middle Atlantic up through Minnesota was named the Rust Belt by economic geographers to represent this deindustrialization. In this sense, New Bedford is just one of the many emptied-out locales—a prototype of a city contracting in jobs, people, and housing units. In this chapter, I will dive deeper and begin to examine the unique and novel story about how politicians, city planners, activists, and ordinary residents responded to the change their city faced.

The devastation that rocked New Bedford in the early twentieth century (the Great Depression and the Hurricane of 1938) paled in comparison to the long-term physical and social devastation that depopulation and abandonment has generated since then. Some details of those impacts are outlined in Chap. 1; here, I recount the history of how the city responded to this dramatic change. The basic facts are plain to see: from 1920 to 1980, the city lost 22,739 residents. In most of those decades, there was a fairly steady drop of 3% from the prior decade's population levels.

Before turning to the city's response to decline, I offer here a short elaboration of Chap. 1's overview of the major factors in New Bedford's twentieth-century decline. The city's reliance on textile and its rather sudden and precipitous decline in New England is widely regarded as the biggest driver for the New Bedford's decline (Wolfbein 1944; Koistinen 2002; Voyer et al. 2000). With whaling industries largely going out of business and fishing never accounting for more than 15% of the city's employment, it was the loss of textiles that really impacted employment levels. With southern wages "30–50 percent lower" than wages in New England, New Bedford firms had a hard time competing and either went out of business or relocated to the South (Koistinen 2002, p. 494).

> Traditional New England products lost out to new competition; fine goods yielded parts of the market to rayon and silk fabrics. Narrow calicoes, another regional specialty, were not in fashion. The new demand for industrial fabrics, particularly from the automobile industry, gravitated to the South. (Barkin 1981, p. 472)

Once textile industries began to see losses and eventually closures, it brought strain to the relationships between mill owners and unions. Labor battles raged for decades, with workers trying desperately to preserve the lifestyles they had enjoyed during the boom periods. As Koistinen (1999) points out, "leaders of the Northern textile unions were well aware that collective bargaining could compress the cost advantage of Southern firms by equalizing labor standards" (p. 167). This dilemma was addressed at the time through the creation of the New England Council, a body convened by the governors of the six New England states and operated by chamber of commerce and industry leaders (Koistinen 1999). They sought to promote innovation in the region as a response to the decline in textiles, specifically calling for support for banking, the service sector, communications, transportation, upgraded power systems, tourism, recreation, and better public perceptions of New England (ibid, p. 223).

Arguably this effort laid the successful groundwork for Greater Boston to make such adjustments (largely attributed to the partnerships that the New England Council made with Harvard and MIT) but the rest of New England, New Bedford in particular, did not make those kinds of investments in innovation and its economy continued to slide through the twentieth century.

The lack of attention of the New England Council on New Bedford is consistent with accounts of how city leaders viewed the ongoing crisis of decline: they did not appear active in formally responding to the changes underway. A few mayors and city counselors demanded wholesale demolition of "slums" over the course of the 1930s and 1940s, but little came of that kind of talk. As New Bedford's locational advantage waned, jobs, and then people, left in droves. After the war, GI Bill benefits also discouraged young people from staying in the city and pursuing mill employment, instead providing financial support to pursue higher education (Hartford 1996). City fathers undoubtedly tried to convince firms and individuals to stay, but the economic conditions were more favorable elsewhere and any official city action was not newsworthy; the efforts of the New England Council just had not been enough for New Bedford (Koistinen 1999).

But that changed when the federal government got into the city rebuilding business in the late 1950s. Originating with a series of Acts of Congress in the 1930s and 1940s that responded to a widespread sense that cities were in a state of physical decay, the broadly accepted goals of urban renewal were best articulated in the Housing Act of 1949. The Housing Act set aside federal resources to eliminate substandard, slum housing and replace it with "a decent home and a suitable living environment for every American family" (Housing Act of 1949; Hall 2000). By most accounts, they failed miserably (Gans 1962; Greer 1965; Anderson 1964a; Teaford 1990) at these lofty goals. Instead, one-million Americans were kicked out of their homes by federal officials and their houses demolished, and 90% of the displaced were relocated to other urban neighborhoods—in many cases overwhelming local housing supplies and generating new slums in what had been previously stable places (Anderson 1964b). The estimated $2.258 trillion of private investment in these renewal projects largely went to commercial, industrial, and high-rent residential projects (Doxiadis 1966). Out-of-town real estate developers pocketed the money and this, in turn, built a level of distrust with city officials around the ultimate goals of these federal urban renewal programs (Gittell 1989). Greer (1965) concluded that the results of urban renewal were precisely the opposite of the stated aims, in that after spending more than $3 billion in tax payer money, the federal government "has succeeded in materially reducing the supply of low-cost housing in American cities" (p. 3).

Beyond attempting to provide more affordable housing, urban renewal policies welcomed efforts by cities to decrease density in tenement-dominated neighborhoods. While the major federal renewal agencies, first the Urban Renewal Administration and then the US Department of Housing and Urban Development, gave some planning authority to local governments, they set out the principles and held a veto power over projects. Additionally, the manner in which these programs were developed built-in a power structure that regularly put the mayor and the city council in conflict (Gittell 1989). At a national level, these patterns are well documented. But a close look at the New Bedford urban renewal story reveals a different and more nuanced account. By demanding that cities decrease density and explore alternative uses for surplus residential lands, the urban renewal policies and programs appear to have helped the city manage depopulation. Certainly, there was a tremendous social and emotional cost to the renewal activities used in New Bedford and elsewhere (Fried 1966). But in reflecting on urban renewal's legacy, this chapter offers a unique and novel view of how government intervention into the physical form of the city during the 1960s and 1970s may have been helpful.

The Urban Crisis in New Bedford

In 1959, New Bedford's mayor, Francis J. Lawler, told the *Standard-Times* that New Bedfordians did not want urban renewal. Ironically, he then became the key figure in laying the groundwork for the city's involvement in this contested federal policy ("Urban Renewal" 1959, p. 6). First installed as mayor in 1953 upon the incarceration of the city's last mayor on a conspiracy conviction, Lawler himself had a $100 fine on his record for bookmaking. Coming from a career in insurance, the 38-year-old Lawler took the reins of the city with aplomb—but his popularity did not last and he was voted out of office less than one year later. In 1956, Lawler successfully ran for mayor and this time served for five years, effectively laying the groundwork for the city's urban renewal interventions.

After nearly a decade in public service, Lawler was interviewed by the *Standard-Times* in 1959 and he explained that his conversations over the years with residents and business owners has led him to conclude that urban renewal was not what New Bedford needed. The editors at the *Standard-Times* felt otherwise, and they ran a series that same year exposing their readers to the federal urban renewal programs, trying to make the case that New Bedford could benefit if the mayor and city leadership could get their act together.

Characterizing the city's problems as that of out-dated structures and abandoned buildings, the *Standard-Times* defined the problem facing New Bedford in very narrow terms: lack of a modern physical plant. Areas for renewal might include "rundown neighborhoods" that could be transformed into "competitive, attractive, tax-producing assets in the community" (Finn 1959b, p. 13).

These editors were drawing on the discourse of modernism to convince their readers that the past was bad and the future is good.[1] The promise of gleaming new streets, parks, and buildings was seductive. A 1959 article explained that urban renewal provides for "the demolition of slum areas and their replacement with modern sanitary housing, public buildings, or business structures" (Finn 1959a, p. 1). Who could argue with demolishing slums and replacing them with "modern sanitary housing"?

The editors' pleading appeared to work, as just two years after the *Standard-Times* series, Mayor Lawler was scrambling together a team to advance a proposal for federal urban renewal funding. The early discussions around urban renewal funding concentrated on removing slum housing and replacing it with modern facilities. The city also identified several projects around the South Terminal industrial area for renewal funding in hopes of attracting (and retaining) jobs. Thus, the thrust of the renewal program was to replace aging structures with newer ones and to attract (and retain) employment. City leaders saw new jobs as their best chance to attract more residents to the increasing number of empty and abandoned homes throughout the city.

In 1972, the Comptroller General of the United States published a report considering the impact of federal investments in New Bedford over the prior decade. The report authors assessed the results from urban renewal activities in the South Terminal, North Terminal, and West End, as well as concentrated code enforcement in several areas scattered throughout the city. Federal officials defined concentrated code enforcement as a:

> 3 year preventive program designed to arrest decline of an area where an urban renewal project is not warranted but where a concerted community effort is needed to conserve existing properties. Its principal objective is to restore the stability of neighborhoods by effective code enforcement and by the provision of adequate supporting facilities and services. (Comptroller General of the United States 1972, p. 48)

Preserving structures and preventing deterioration is admirable, but the concentrated code enforcement approach fails to address the very real underlying financial pressures that property owners are under due to falling rents and increasing maintenance expenses. There are several reasons why property owners in these so-called slums do a poor job of maintaining their properties. In a shrinking city (as New Bedford certainly was) the reason is largely because shrinking populations mean shrinking demand for housing, which translates into lower rents. Lower rents make it harder for investors to cover their costs to maintain properties and many will simply delay maintenance and care.

For New Bedford, over $700,000 in federal money was invested from 1967 through 1971 in concentrated code enforcement to effectively force owner-investors to care for properties for which they were facing declining rents and declining profits. As indicated in the aforementioned quote, some "facilities and services" were also made available to owners to attempt to change the investment equation and make rehabilitation of rental units more profitable. These efforts surely improved the quality of life for tenants in the targeted areas and improved the bottom-line for landlords, but it did little to alleviate the fundamental mismatch between the supply of housing and the diminishing demand from a shrinking population.

As the Comptroller's report explains, code enforcement is only appropriate when the conditions of a neighborhood have not degraded so much that urban renewal is necessary. When a place becomes so derelict and dilapidated, local renewal officials were directed by federal officials to initiate urban renewal. This entire analysis, dissection, and assessment process has been well criticized in the scholarly and popular literature (Jacobs 1961; Gans 1962; Metzger 2000). But the New Bedford case offers a new perspective. City leaders were, in fact, quite resistant to doing urban renewal in the first place (as explained above). When they were so pressured to move forward with a project, they focused on commercial and industrial reuse of residential areas instead of the more accepted projects that promoted residential reuse. After only a few years into its renewal program, New Bedford leaders quickly reversed course and demanded that federal monies go into historic preservation—helping to eventually change federal government policy in this area (McCabe and Thomas 1995).

Urban Renewal in Action: The South Terminal Project

Among the city's urban renewal efforts, the South Terminal was the most infamous. Eventually consisting of 197 acres, stretching north to south along the city's biggest waterfront fishing areas, the renewal zone went east to the Acushnet River and west to 1st and sometimes as far as 2nd Street in Downtown New Bedford (see Figs. 6.1 and 6.2). Predominantly a fishing zone, the neighborhood was also home to 203 dwellings and 114 business structures, all eventually demolished. City leaders embraced the concept of an expanded fishing area, along with a North-South connector road between the fishing area and Interstate 195. Their proposal to federal officials was unheard of at the time, as renewal projects elsewhere were aimed to upgrade housing quality, not to replace it with alternative uses (Martin 1965).

South Terminal was an economic development project. It was a job creation project. City leaders saw that employment and population were falling, and they called for an expansion of the South Terminal fishing area in order to facilitate and encourage job creation so as to reverse the employment and population trends. What these leaders did not say was that even if fishing did not grow as a result of the renewal project, alternative land uses for residential can make a lot of sense in a shrinking city. What you would not have heard, but was evident from the outcomes, was that the much maligned South Terminal project decreased the overall

Fig. 6.1 South terminal before urban renewal project, c. 1965 (photo credit: City of New Bedford)

number of housing units in New Bedford as well as housing density in the Downtown area, and aided in right-sizing the city. In this sense, the project met many of the federal renewal goals.

But there was a huge cost for this de-densification. Two-hundred forty-seven families were displaced from their homes and communities. The elderly and the lowest income among them were rehoused in two large housing complexes, Boa Vista and Harborview Towers, outside of the project boundaries (Gonsalves 2004). The others were forced to find new homes and establish new community connections, often pitting neighbors against each other in the search for new housing (Gittell 1999). In addition, the North-South limited access roadway (Route 18) that was a part of the South Terminal Project is infamous for the way it effectively

Fig. 6.2 South terminal after urban renewal project, c. 1967 (photo credit: City of New Bedford)

split the city in two, separating the downtown from the waterfront in particular. Like so much else about urban renewal nationally, it left New Bedfordians with unfulfilled promises and community malaise (Gittell 1999, p. 178).

Due to all the pain and suffering South Terminal created, and because of all the unjust and unfair practices that federal and local officials employed to develop the plan and execute, it is difficult to label it as a success or a model to follow. But it is useful to identify it as exemplary of smart shrinkage. It is the first of several examples I have found of the city trying to right-size and change the physical form of New Bedford to match a smaller population.

Another example is the United Front Homes project in New Bedford's West End. Notorious as one of the city's poorest neighborhoods, the West End was the Urban Renewal administration's dream neighborhood—full of poor residents, a high renter population, and complete with derelict and sub-standard dwellings. The history for this renewal project goes back to a string of riots that afflicted New Bedford and scores of other US cities in 1970. Rioting during this period has been heavily studied in the sociological and political science literatures, with strong consensus around civil rights, political liberation, and the expansion of economic opportunity as primary drivers of rioting (McAdam 1982). From my research, New Bedford appears to be no different.

In June 1970, a major non-profit organization in the city, the Urban Coalition, produced a report concluding:

> At this moment, New Bedford is, for a very large part of our population, an absolutely miserable city … a city where many can't make a decent living, can't get a decent home, can't get a decent education for their kids and can't find a decent place for their kids to play. (as quoted in Taylor 1970b, p. 35)

In response to these conditions, Louis A. Gomes brought together disparate community groups dedicated to improving housing quality in predominantly African-American neighborhoods (particularly the West End), forming the Black United Front. Under Gomes' leadership, the Black United Front claimed to represent the African-American community in its pursuit of its fair share of urban renewal funding.

It was an uphill battle for Gomes. As of 1970, out of the 1575 housing units either on the drawing board or under construction through federal urban renewal funding, only 170 were in the West End (Taylor 1970a,

p. 3). African-Americans in New Bedford faced entrenched racism and a stalwart status quo machine—particularly on the city council:

> Anti-black feeling in the council runs deep, Councilor William Saltzman, who was the largest vote-getter in last year's election, has said "I'll be damned if I'll knock out 500 white men's homes to integrate five Negro families. We'll build the housing where we want to build it. The beggars are not going to be the boss here." (Taylor 1970a, p. 3)

But city planners responded to the pressure from Gomes and the Black United Front, devising a plan to put the name "Black United Front" on a new urban renewal project. Earlier planning analysis identified portions of the West End as in need of concentrated code enforcement. City planners proposed to do some soft code enforcement, but HUD responded that these West End areas were "too far deteriorated to be treated by concentrated code enforcement and should come under urban renewal treatment" (Comptroller's Report 1972, p. 56). The federal government practically forced the city to carry out urban renewal in the West End.

While some code enforcement did occur during the renewal years, the only major renewal project ever to get accomplished in New Bedford outside the two fishing pier expansions was the planner's answer to the Black United Front, in the West End. In a zone of 12 acres, the city's renewal agency acquired derelict homes, demolished them, and then bid out to developers the opportunity to build new housing. With a series of problems in the bidding process, the city abruptly changed course in 1973 when faced with the rising political power of the Black United Front ("Black United Front gets $4.3m building loan" 1973, p. A-52).

The city quickly arranged to turn the now empty 12 acres over to Gomes and the Black United Front and helped arrange $4.3 million in funding from the Massachusetts Housing Finance Agency. The project consisted of 20, three-story buildings on a superblock of what had been 12 smaller blocks, bounded by Cedar and Chancery, Kempton and Court Streets. In total, 200 units of low and moderate income housing were built, primarily three-bedroom units, although a number of units had upwards of six bedrooms.

While exact figures are unavailable, judging by historic building patterns in the area there were likely 14 parcels in each original block, each hosting at least three-unit structures, resulting in over 500 housing units. The United Front Housing development resulted in 300 fewer housing

Fig. 6.3 Sketch of the proposed united front housing project (photo credit: SEB, LLC)

units, through a tight clustering of town-house style buildings arranged around a community center, day-care center, open space, and playgrounds (alternative land uses) (see Fig. 6.3).

In the late 2000s, the United Front Homes was widely regarded as a magnet for criminal activity and a failed urban design experiment (Anderson 2009). Interestingly, in trying to address the problems of the development, city leaders promoted an even further decrease in density. A major rehabilitation of the development was completed by the non-profit real estate developer Preservation of Affordable Housing (POAH), reducing the number of housing units down to 173 (Anderson 2009).

Focused on reducing housing density and changing residential uses to non-residential alternative uses, the United Front Homes project clearly exemplified some key principles of smart shrinkage. In fact, the city's five-year HUD comprehensive plan aimed for reducing density in many residential areas and urban renewal projects succeeded in a fairly drastic drop in 897 units up until 1971 alone (Comptroller's Report 1972).

As the urban renewal frenzy began to settle down, a prominent nonprofit historic preservation organization was formed and began a campaign to focus federal renewal dollars on rehabilitation. As I wrote in Chap. 1, the efforts of a group called the Waterfront Historic Area

League (WHALE) led to the 1996 designation of the New Bedford Whaling Historic Park, covering 34 acres at the heart of the city's historic center.

Looking Closely at Three Neighborhoods

There appears to be strong evidence from the historical record that the city of New Bedford's response to economic decline and depopulation from 1929 through 2000 resulted in lower housing densities and repurposing housing for other uses (whether intentional or not). In both the North and South Terminal urban renewal projects, as well as the United Front Homes project, that was certainly the case. But what about outside of those delineated project zones?

From my review of the historical evidence and interviews with former and current city officials, it seems that government policies and planning did little to address dense residential neighborhoods outside of those three renewal projects. With the exception of concentrated code enforcement, a vast majority of the city's neighborhoods experienced no direct city support or investment to address depopulation. And even the concentrated code enforcement, as I argue above, did little to alter the fundamental imbalance between the decreasing size of the population in New Bedford and the stable size of the housing stock.

To understand what happened in New Bedford outside of the urban renewal projects, I embarked on field research to study for myself the legacy of depopulation. In exploring the streets of New Bedford, I looked for addresses—145 Acushnet Avenue, 97 South 6th Street, 366 Pleasant Street—where houses and apartment buildings had once stood, and where today, as satellite images tell me, nothing remains.

A careful review of Sanborn Fire Insurance Maps over the last century has helped me to understand a pattern of decline seemingly imperceptible to the naked eye. The maps were designed to support fire insurance premiums and claims verification, but they are now an exquisite resource for studying how neighborhoods change. They include all major streets and building footprints for the aforementioned three neighborhoods for the years 1924, 1936, and 1975. Working with a team of graduate students, I digitized the maps and created figure-ground drawings to illustrate the changing density of housing in New Bedford as it emptied out. Figures 6.4, 6.5, and 6.6 show the three New Bedford study neighborhoods—South Central, Bullard Street, and Cove Street—over time, and where each shrunk. Through these maps, it is possible to witness how the physical form of the city accommodated a loss of 30,105 persons in 89 years and what the disappearance of tens of thousands of housing units looks like.

In studying the physical form of New Bedford from 1924 through 1975, several key patterns emerge.[2] This is a period where the city lost much of its manufacturing base and much of its population. Houses, as I've written before, tend to linger even in those circumstances—housing is quite durable and hardly disappears when a city begins to depopulate. But somehow, despite their study construction, tens of thousands of New Bedford houses have slowly disappeared and vacant land appears in its place. If the city government did not intervene in many of these places, who did?

What the Historic Maps Tell Us About a Shrinking City

The history of urban renewal in New Bedford is often told with mixed feelings: sadness for all the pain and misery is caused to those displaced, longing for the historic architecture and streetscapes it leveled, and hope that it was all worthwhile in the long-term interest of the city. The above account suggests that some of the public sector interventions may have helped New Bedford manage depopulation. To look further, let us turn to the buildings that appeared and disappeared during the 1924–1975 period in the three study area neighborhoods: South Central, Bullard Street, and Cove Street.

Figures 6.4, 6.5, and 6.6 provide a compelling picture of how South Central rose to become a major population center in the city by the mid-to-late 1920s (the 1924 map appears to show the peak of building density in South Central). Then, by 1936, a distinctive emptying-out appears throughout the neighborhood. Hardly any of the neighborhood's blocks appear to be untouched by this decline. But the 1936 map is most compelling in showing how a one-block wide by five-block long public housing development, Bay Village, replaced a densely developed cluster of homes on the eastern side of the neighborhood.

The 1975 South Central map shows the clearing away of more than eight blocks of densely developed housing in order to build the key North-South highway envisioned in the South Terminal urban renewal

WHAT THE HISTORIC MAPS TELL US ABOUT A SHRINKING CITY 115

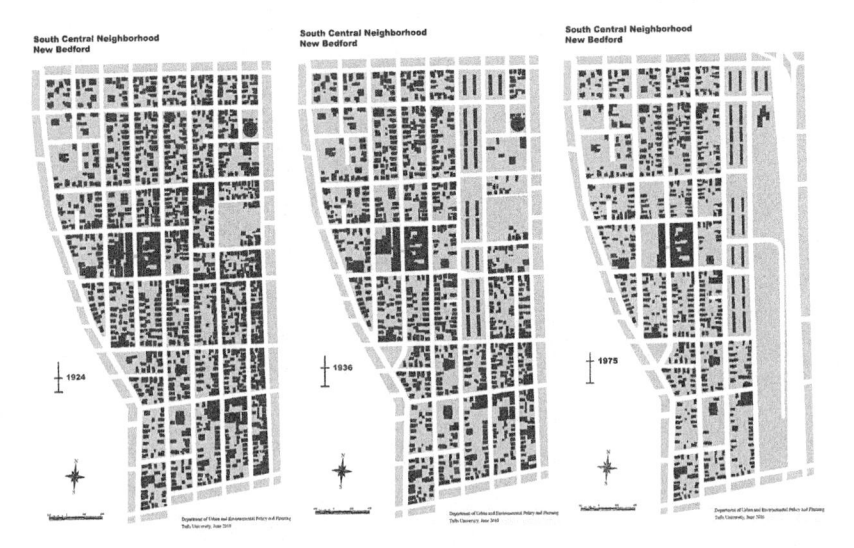

Fig. 6.4 Figure-ground drawings of South Central neighborhood 1924–1975, based on Sanborn Fire Insurance Maps

project. The fairly uniform thinning-out of the rest of the South Central neighborhood also continues to be evident in the 1975 map.

The Bullard Street maps are less stark, but also show a pattern of thinning-out. From 1924 to 1936, the neighborhood lost scores of homes but a clear pattern of new construction is also evident—particularly in the eastern portion of the neighborhood—making the overall shrinkage less dramatic than in South Central. By 1975, Bullard Street's decline is more pronounced with a loss of structures fairly evenly spread across the neighborhood.

For Cove Street, the story is different during this period. From 1924 to 1936, the neighborhood expanded its residential buildings, even adding an entire new block of housing to the South. Visually striking is the disappearance of one of the major mill buildings during this period, which is expected because the city was bleeding textile businesses. By 1975, the ten-story public housing complex named Tripp Towers was built on the site of the former mill, but not much else changed (physically) in Cove Street. Except for a few new buildings and just a handful of missing ones, the neighborhood managed massive population loss and the urban renewal period quite well. Given this small sample of three neighborhoods, the likely explanation is that Cove Street was simply a newer neighborhood,

Fig. 6.5 Figure-ground drawings of Bullard Street neighborhood 1924–1975, based on Sanborn Fire Insurance Maps

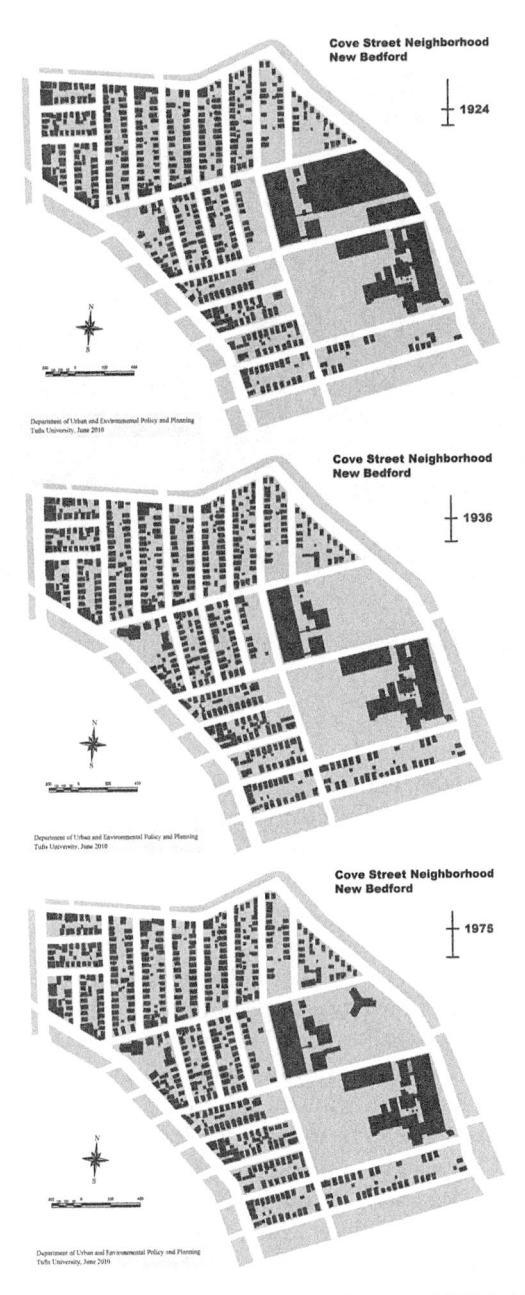

WHAT THE HISTORIC MAPS TELL US ABOUT A SHRINKING CITY 117

Fig. 6.6 Figure-ground drawings of Cove Street neighborhood 1924–1975, based on Sanborn Fire Insurance Maps

Fig. 6.7 Cove Street lot (photo credit: Erin Kizer)

with newer and higher quality housing stock than Bullard and South Central. As such, depopulation had little impact (during this period from 1924 to 1975) on the physical form of the neighborhood (Fig. 6.7).

* * *

From the start of the Great Depression in 1929 through 1975, the physical form of the city changed in sometimes drastic ways, some neighborhoods more than others. For those first few decades, city leaders did little to influence the emptying-out of neighborhoods of both people and structures. But then, with the advent of federal urban renewal funding, New Bedford got on board and developed a plan to remake the city after what had been almost three decades of depopulation. The plan involved converting large areas of residential uses into commercial and industrial uses, and a limited access highway (Route 18). These urban renewal projects had noticeable effect on the physical form of the city, as evidenced by the Sanborn maps of South Central shown in Fig. 6.4. But equally notable was how much the form of both Bullard Street and South Central changed outside the direct wrecking ball of urban renewal.

The City's HUD-mandated plans called for reducing density in the city and the Sanborn map analysis graphically shows how they managed to do that both directly and indirectly. Directly, the demolishment and lower density rebuilding strategy of urban renewal led to a net reduction in 897 housing units (Comptroller's Report 1972). Beyond the work of city officials, the general economic climate that inflicted New Bedford with first the collapse of the textile industry and then the Hurricane of 1938 appears from the Sanborn maps to have driven even further declines in density. The thinning-out of homes from South Central and Bullard Street houses raises many questions about how exactly that happened outside of city efforts. What has become of the vacant lots left behind? Is this process still going on, and what has been the policy and planning response in recent years?

In the next chapters, I offer a more detailed examination of those questions by employing a contemporary lens. Through a detailed review of policy and planning documents, I present an account of both governmental and non-governmental responses to decline from 2000 to 2011.

Notes

1. The city's urban renewal activities were central in advancing a preservationist perspective on the federal programs and ultimately helped create the first urban National Park in the city's Waterfront District built on the foundation of historic preservation (see discussion in Chap. 1).
2. As explained above, 1929 marked the beginning of New Bedford's economic and population decline due to the Great Depression. The 1924 map is useful in that it offers a view of the shape of the city only five years prior to its decline.

Bibliography

81st Congress of the United States. 1949. 81st Congress of the United States. 1949. Housing Act of 1949. In *United States Statutes at Large*, vol. 63. Washington, DC: United States Government Printing Office.

Anderson, Martin. 1964a. *The Federal Bulldozer: A Critical Analysis of Urban Renewal, 1949–1962*. Cambridge, MA: MIT Press.

———. 1964b. *The Federal Bulldozer: A Critical Analysis of Urban Renewal, 1949–1962*. Cambridge, MA: MIT Press.

Anderson, Charles. 2009. Renovation Will Construct New Housing, Reconnect United Front to Street Grid. *South Coast Today*, November 29. http://www.southcoasttoday.com/apps/pbcs.dll/article?AID=/20091129/NEWS/911290339.

Barkin, Solomon. 1981. Management and Ownership in the New England Cotton Textile Industry. *Journal of Economic Issues*. Social Science Premium Collection [ProQuest]. Web 23 January 2017.

Comptroller General of the United States. 1972. Impact of Federal Programs on Economic Development, Employment, and Housing in New Bedford, Massachusetts. B-159835, United States General Accounting Office.

Doxiadēs, Kōnstantinos Apostolou. 1966. *Urban Renewal and the Future of the American City*. Chicago, IL: Public Administration Service.

Finn, Bob. 1959a. Speed, Unity Here Vital for U.S. Aid on Building. *Standard-Times*, April 13.

———. 1959b. Thorough Planning Necessary Before City Can Qualify for Federal Urban Renewal Funds. *Standard-Times*, April 14.

Fried, Marc. 1966. Grieving for a Lost Home: Psychological Costs of Relocation. In *Urban Renewal: The Record and the Controversy*, ed. James Q. Wilson, 359–379. Cambridge, MA: MIT Press.

Gans, Herbert J. 1962. *The Urban Villagers: Group and Class in the Life of Italian-Americans*. New York, NY: The Free Press of Glencoe.

Gittell, Ross Jacobs. 1989. A Critical Analysis of Local Initiatives in Economic Revitalization. Order No. 9013286 Harvard University. Ann Arbor: ProQuest. Web 26 February 2017.

Gittell, Ross J., and J. Phillip Thompson. 1999. Inner-City Business Development and Entrepreneurship: New Frontiers for Policy and Research. In *Urban Problems and Community Development*, 473–520. Washington, DC: Brookings Institution Press.

Gonsalves, Jennifer White. 2004. Looking at the Urban Renewal Program of the 1960s Through the Lens of the South Terminal Redevelopment Project in New Bedford, Massachusetts. M.A. thesis. University of Rhode Island.

Greer, Scott. 1965. *Urban Renewal and American Cities: The Dilemma of Democratic Intervention*. Indianapolis, IN: Bobbs-Merrill Company, Inc.

Hall, Peter. 2000. *Cities of Tomorrow: An Intellectual History of Urban Planning and Design in the Twentieth Century*. Malden, MA: Blackwell Publishers.

Hartford, William F. 1996. *Where Is Our Responsibility?: Unions and Economic Change in the New England Textile Industry, 1870–1960*. Amherst: University of Massachusetts.

Jacobs, Jane. 1961. *The Death and Life of Great American Cities*. New York, NY: Random House.

Koistinen, David Joshua. 1999. Dealing with Deindustrialization: Economics, Politics, and Policy during the Decline of the New England Textile Industry,

1920–1960. Order No. 9930940 Yale University. Ann Arbor: ProQuest. Web 26 February 2017.

———. 2002. The Causes of Deindustrialization: The Migration of the Cotton Textile Industry from New England to the South. *Enterprise and Society*. ABI/INFORM [ProQuest]. Web 6 January 2017.

Martin, Roger. 1965. South Terminal Project Given Highest Priority. *Standard-Times*, May 19.

McAdam, Doug. 1982. *Political Process and the Development of Black Insurgency, 1930–1970*. Chicago, IL: University of Chicago Press.

McCabe, Marsha, and Joseph D. Thomas. 1995. *Not Just Anywhere: The Story of WHALE and the Rescue of New Bedford's Waterfront Historic District*. New Bedford, MA: Spinner Publications.

Metzger, John T. 2000. Planned Abandonment: The Neighborhood Life-Cycle Theory and National Urban Policy. *Housing Policy Debate* 11 (1): 7–40.

Taylor, F.B., Jr. 1970a. New Bedford Neglects Housing for Poor and Blacks. *Boston Globe*, July 16.

———. 1970b. Not Much Evidence of Reconciliation in New Bedford. *Boston Globe*, August 16.

Teaford, Jon C. 1990. *The Rough Road to Renaissance: Urban Revitalization in America, 1940–1985*. Baltimore, MD: Johns Hopkins University Press.

Urban Renewal. 1959. *Standard-Times*, May 6.

Voyer, Richard A., Carol Pesch, Jonathan Garber, Jane Copeland, and Randy Comeleo. 2000. New Bedford, Massachusetts: A Story of Urbanization and Ecological Connections. Environmental History. ProQuest SciTech Collection. Web. 11 July 2017.

Wolfbein, Seymour L. 1944. *The Decline of a Cotton Textile City: A Study of New Bedford*. New York, NY: Columbia University Press.

CHAPTER 7

Coming to Terms with Change: Contemporary Policy Responses

New Bedford faced particularly challenging conditions related to a regional and national trend of economic prosperity from 2000 to 2006 that was followed by a sudden and powerful economic collapse in the form of the foreclosure crisis and the Great Recession from 2007 to 2011. During this tumultuous decade, city planners continued to respond to depopulation in the same ways as in past decades. But not exactly the same. In this chapter, I offer a systematic examination of that government response to both (1) a legacy of depopulation, and (2) a boom and bust in the first decade of the twenty-first century.

House by house, block by block, the urban fabric of New Bedford has been shaped by nine decades of fairly consistent depopulation. Physical changes in the use and reuse of buildings and lots were affected by city and federal urban renewal efforts (as documented in Chap. 6), but what about contemporary urban planning and public policy? What actions and activities are today's city leadership taking to address decline? It is easy to look at the interventions of the 1950s through the 1980s and dismiss those planners as foolhardy or ignorant. It is easy to join the chorus of contempt for urban renewal and its destructive power. Much harder is to look in the proverbial mirror and examine how our enlightened urban planning and policy mechanisms work in a shrinking, postindustrial city. This chapter attempts to elucidate precisely what it is that local government activities do, and intend to do, in the face of ongoing depopulation.

© The Author(s) 2018
J.B. Hollander, *An Ordinary City*,
DOI 10.1007/978-3-319-60705-4_7

Given the city's long history of decline and recent spurt of growth, this chapter offers a glimpse into the thinking, meaning, and results of urban planning over the last decade in New Bedford.

READING CITY REPORTS FOR INSIGHT

About 15 years ago, I was working as an urban planner and was on a trip to Buffalo, New York—a city that has witnessed a 50% drop in its population over the last half-century. Strolling through the quiet downtown, I wondered about how odd it was that the city's recent plan had won a national planning award,[1] yet the city remained depressed and depressing. The irony was thick: a city which felt to me to be in disarray was a paragon of excellent planning. Something was wrong.

Years later, I worked with one of my graduate students and decided to probe further into this puzzle. Buffalo is unique in America in that not only is the city shrinking, but the entire region is also in decline. The more common morphology involves the well-documented hole-in-a-donut, where the center city is in decline and the surrounding suburbs are growing (Hollander et al. 2009). But Buffalo is different and my student, Bernard Cahill, and I decided to look closely at the region's plan: *Erie-Niagara Framework for Regional Growth*. The title was irresistible. Here, we had an entire region in decline and its primary tool for planning for the future was already ensconced in a seemingly futile attempt to reverse the entire process—instead of looking to a smart-shrinkage strategy for planning for decline.

Looking closely at the region's plan, we employed the social science research tool of content analysis (Hollander and Cahill 2011). A systematic and rigorous approach to understanding what a text is saying, content analysis has two main components: manifest and latent. Using manifest analysis, we essentially counted how many times a series of keywords (which we took from pre-existing literature) appeared in the plan. Then, using latent analysis, we examined what is meant (qualitatively) by the text. The results were extraordinary: the plan largely called for smart shrinkage, without saying so. The plan authors expressed a keen understanding of the demographic reality of a shrinking region and recommended the region find ways to retrofit itself to be smaller—all without actually using those words.

Given the piecemeal reuse pattern that appeared evident in New Bedford from the mapping analysis, focus groups, and interviews, I applied this same methodology to look at all of the New Bedford's planning and urban policy reports over the last decade. This approach allows for insight into what the city has been doing and what it wants to be doing. I complemented the content analysis with further interviews with city officials to be able to paint a complete picture. Together, these two sources help shed light on the puzzle that is New Bedford—its reused lots, its abandoned buildings, and its urban planning—in the face of decline.

A thorough review of planning and public policy activities in New Bedford over the boom and bust decade of the aughts resulted in 19 reports and plans covering a wide range of topics and geographies (see Table 7.1). The reports are written from 2002 through 2009 and are authored by a range of organizations, including consulting firms and non-profit organizations, all for the benefit of the city of New Bedford. One report was unavailable for review and thus excluded from the analysis.[2]

Adopting a similar approach to the one I used in the Buffalo research, I worked with a couple of graduate students to do both manifest and latent content analysis for each of the New Bedford reports. Using the same list of smart shrinkage-related keywords as I adopted in studying Buffalo, we also added the term "growth" to see how growing was emphasized in the reports.

In the first stage of the research, we looked broadly at the latent messages emerging from the reports. After reading through several of the reports, we determined key themes that emerged repeatedly and matched those with the broader research questions of this book.

Demographic Trends and Projections

The Buffalo plan neither acknowledged that the region was shrinking nor the compelling projections for future decline, though that very notion appears to undergird the plans set forth in the document. For the New Bedford plans, we began by looking at the first theme of how demographic trends are acknowledged and assessed.

Most of the plans largely ignored the city's past depopulation, but a few did directly engage in the negativity of that past as a basis for future planning. Two reports made a major focus of the negative dimensions of New Bedford's depopulation, another report emphasized it, and four others mentioned it. The rest of the reports ignored the challenges of past depopulation entirely.

The South Coast Rail Plan explains the challenge this way: "The historic cities of Fall River and New Bedford have been affected by nearly a

Table 7.1 New Bedford reports

Report #	Author, date, and title for New Bedford reports
1	BSC Group. (2008). Hicks-Logan-Sawyer Master Plan. Prepared for the City of New Bedford, MA
2	City of New Bedford. (2008). Downtown Action Plan
3	City of New Bedford. (October 14, 2008). Acushnet Avenue Corridor Vision Plan Community Meeting
4	City of New Bedford Planning Department. (2006). Fairhaven Mills Site Public Charrette
5	City of New Bedford Planning Department. (2008). 2008–2013 Open Space and Recreation Plan
6	FXM Economic Planning and Research. (2007). Economic Development Strategy for Downtown New Bedford, Part II: Measuring Success. Prepared for City of New Bedford Planning Department
7	Goody Clancy. (2005). Hicks-Logan-Sawyer Smart Growth Waterfront District: Vision Plan and Regulatory Strategy. Prepared for the City of New Bedford
8	HR&A Advisors Inc. (ND). New Bedford, Massachusetts, Market and Economic Analysis. Prepared for City of New Bedford
9	Johns, E. & Walega, R. (2008). Sustaining New Bedford. New Bedford Sustainability Task Force
10	Mass Development. (2008). City of New Bedford Upper Harbor District: Final District Development Plan. Prepared for the City of New Bedford
11	Muro, M., Schneider, J., Warren, D., McLean-Shinaman, E., Sohmer, R., & Forman, B. (2007). Reconnecting Massachusetts Gateway Cities: Lessons Learned and an Agenda for Renewal. Boston, MA: Mass INC; The Brookings Institute
12	New Bedford Economic Council. (2008). Creative Economy Task Force. Prepared for the City of New Bedford
13	New Bedford Economic Development Council. (2008). City of New Bedford Historic Mill Inventory
14	New Bedford Economic Development Council. (2008). Upper Harbor Vision Plan Community Meetings
15	RKG Associates, Inc. (2007). District Improvement Financing Plan for the Hicks-Logan-Sawyer Revitalization Area in New Bedford, MA. Prepared for the City of New Bedford, MA
16	South Coast Rail. (2009). South Coast Rail Economic Development and Land Use Corridor Plan
17	Southeastern Regional Planning and Economic Development District (SRPEDD). (2008). City of New Bedford Priority Development and Protection Areas
18	Utile, Inc. Architecture and Planning & FXM Economic Planning and Research. (2009). Downtown New Bedford Revitalization and Redevelopment Study. Prepared for the City of New Bedford, MA
19	Vanasse Hangen Brustlin (VHB). (2002). New Bedford/Fairhaven Harbor Plan. Prepared for the City of New Bedford and Town of Fairhaven

century of industrial disinvestment, while migration of population from the cities continues" (p. 23).

Turning to the future, few of the reports appear to be engaged in reality, largely skirting the projections for ongoing depopulation and shrinking employment for the city (see Chap. 1). An exception is the Downtown New Bedford Revitalization and Redevelopment Study (2009), which concludes that "little or no regional growth is forecast in population (support for residential and retail uses) or office using employment" (p. 55). More common is the denial that comes with reports like the South Coast Rail Plan, hinging future quality of life and investments on the "region's ability to shape the growth that's coming" (p. 6). This supposed new growth is hardly a reflection of the projections currently available (see Chap. 1) but end up framing much of the recommendations that follow.

None of the reports assess the future population and employment projections with any negativity—they all stay positive or neutral, upholding an unspoken rule referred to in Chap. 2 in that they do not admit to decline, as that is tantamount to admitting failure.

What the City Is Doing

After an open reading of each report, we developed a list of policies that were mentioned and categorized them according to conventional urban planning practice. The result is the list of policies in Table 7.2. In summary, the profile of activities matches closely with the work done in a typical twenty-first-century city, with a healthy mix of open space and park planning initiatives, job creation, housing rehabilitation, and sustainability efforts. New Bedford is embracing tourism and creative economy programs to try to improve economic conditions, but is also working to improve quality of life indicators by making pedestrian improvements to the city and emphasizing historic preservation.

At the top of the emphasis list are "major renovation/reuse of existing structures," "pedestrian improvements," "strategic investments," "land use management strategy," and "parks and open space." No huge surprises here, but a close look at the emphases is informative. The single most emphasized policy strategy was to renovate or reuse existing structures—an approach that can support smart shrinkage when a demand exists for alternative uses. The problem for New Bedford is that for many buildings, and in many neighborhoods, no such demand exists and even if it did, the publicly subsidized renovations have made matters worse. In

Table 7.2 Policy emphasis

Policy	Strength of policy emphasis
Major renovation/Reuse of existing structures	31
Pedestrian improvements	29
Strategic investments[a]	29
Land use management strategy	27
Parks and open space	27
Creative economy	22
Investment of public realm	21
Increased tourism	21
Management of abandoned structures/vacant lots/brownfields	20
Sustainability (Energy/Environment)	20
Increased investments/upgrades to facades, streets, services	20
Increase/Improve housing	19
Increased jobs	18
Historic preservation	18
New transportation	17
New construction	16
Zoning change	14
Transit-oriented development (TOD)	12
Regional planning	8

[a]Based on local assets, waterfront, regional connection area

a market analysis produced for the city, their consultants concluded "the data suggests that the new supply of renovated space is actually creating a surplus of available commercial and retail space" (H&RA Advisors, Inc. Undated, p. 35).

The Hicks-Logan-Sawyer Master Plan (2005) examined a largely industrial, moribund part of the city and strongly emphasized major renovation, rather than demolition. "It was clear from the community's feedback that a majority of those in attendance were in favor of a plan that would maintain as many existing structures and businesses as possible" (pp. 3–4). The plan goes on to develop several strategies for reusing and re-adapting former mill buildings for commercial and residential uses. What is noteworthy here is the distinct avoidance of demolition as a way to manage the glut of functionally obsolete structures in this neighborhood.

While not at the top of the emphasis list, the policy of "Management of Abandoned Structures/Vacant Lots/Brownfields" did get a relatively high score as 9 of 18 reports at least mentioned it. The city's 2008 Open

Space and Recreation Plan expressed the goal that "as the City of New Bedford acquires vacant parcels of land it is systematically looking to place court games and family play areas at these sites" (p. 71). The 2008 Sustaining New Bedford report ended up calling for the city to "convert several empty lots into community gardens for residents" (p. 68). While different reports viewed the "management" of vacant lots differently, it is hard for the city to ignore the real estate realities that they face in finding economically viable new uses for these lots. Whereas a more stable or growing city could use vacant lots as part of a broader economic strategy to manage growth, create clusters, or generate new synergies, such options are more challenging for New Bedford.

Several years ago, I did research on how New Bedford addressed its commercial and industrial abandoned buildings. That work resulted in a chapter in a book I published in 2009 called *Polluted and Dangerous*. One of the most interesting stories I told in that chapter is how the city, under the leadership of Mayor Fred Kalisz, convened a task force to help slot new uses into the dozen or so large abandoned and commercial/industrial buildings in the city.

This slotting process was a political disaster for the mayor as not all property owners were notified that their land and building's future use was being decided for them. The task force was disbanded and the slotting process went quiet. But the notion that the city can support a series of new uses, and that the job of public policy and planning is to slot those new uses into abandoned sites, was a clever one.

In today's real estate and economic climate, the slotting concept is fraught with even greater challenges. How can city leaders be certain that there is enough demand for new uses to match the scale and scope of abandonment and vacancy in the city? In my review of planning in the city over the last decade, it appears that much of the real efforts the city has undertaken have largely avoided slotting and have been more realistic about demand.

However, there are exceptions. The highly emphasized policies of "Land Use Management Strategy" and "Strategic Investments" reveal a very different set of assumptions about what kind of demand is out there. One report exploring financing options for the Hicks-Logan-Sawyer neighborhood emphasized city efforts to "transform an older, blighted industrial area that consists of almost 100 acres improved with more than two million square feet of building area situated on over a mile of riverfront, into a sustainable, mixed-use redevelopment district"

(RKG Associates 2007, p. 6). Here, city leaders are planning for the possible, not the probable. This kind of policy aims to create demand out of thin air. Well, maybe not exactly out of thin air. A Mass, Inc. and Brookings Institution report identified New Bedford and other similarly situated postindustrial cities in Massachusetts as well placed to receive the new kind of "smart growth" real estate investments that are so popular today (Muro et al. 2007, p. 29).

Under this policy approach, New Bedford is opening its doors for bold visionaries to rebuild the city with new mixed-use, pedestrian-oriented, transit-supported neighborhoods. Planning for the possible, not the probable. It is an idea my colleague, Julian Agyeman, has been talking a lot about. The modern city planning profession was born more than 100 years ago out of visionary thinking by Burnham, Olmstead, Tugwell, MacKaye, and others. Those early planners used an emerging suite of analytical tools, reasoning, and design to paint exquisite pictures of what the future could hold; plans that the American Planning Association today celebrates as "landmark" like the Plan of Chicago, Central Park in New York City, and Yellowstone National Park. As the profession evolved and grew, the planning function became increasingly ensconced within the routine administrative functions of local government. Somewhere in the middle of the twentieth century, a concern for predictability, risk avoidance, and conservatism impacted the very heart and soul of planning, and we went from planning for the possible to planning for the probable.

This thinking by Dr. Agyeman is beginning to suggest room for a return to planning for the possible. As New Bedford comes to terms with its demographic realities, opportunities still remain for the city to attempt wholesale land-use transformation of parts of the city to engage less with the real estate market demands but with generating new demand. An example Dr. Agyeman has studied is the High Line in New York City. Today considered the second most popular tourist attraction in the city and a major real estate value boost for the surrounding blocks, the High Line was just a dream (and an untested one at that) at its inception. An elevated subway line had been abandoned for decades and was a blight on the neighborhood. Under the leadership of Joshua David and Robert Hammond, a band of activists and power brokers put the deal together to turn the eyesore into a beautiful park. There is excitement within New Bedford City Hall to plan for the possible and to create the next High Line in this quiet corner of Southeastern Massachusetts.

Why the City Is Doing It

Part of the reason that city leaders are attempting to attract visionary land-use transformations is that some leaders themselves are bold and visionary. But a look at the actual reasons given in the reports provides a more complex, multi-faceted answer to the question: why is the city doing what it is doing?

Fourteen of the 18 reports had either a major or minor focus on economic development as a rationale for city action, all of the others but one mentioned it (see Table 7.3). No other rationale was so prevalent. Quality of life improvements (score of 27) and safety (score of 18) paled in comparison to economic development's score of 45.

In a downtown development report, the authors wrote a commonly expressed sentiment: "expansion of economic activity in Downtown New Bedford will be required to fill vacant and underutilized space" (FXM Economic Planning and Research 2007, p. 8). Why should the city act?

Table 7.3 Reasons for policies

Report #	Economic development	Quality of life improvements	Safety	Historic preservation	Healthy environment
1	3	2	0	3	0
2	1	2	1	0	0
3	3	3	1	0	0
4	3	3	2	3	0
5	1	2	0	0	0
6	3	0	1	1	0
7	3	2	0	0	1
8	3	0	1	0	0
9	0	1	0	0	2
11	3	3	1	0	0
12	1	3	0	1	0
13	3	0	0	3	0
14	3	2	2	3	2
15	3	0	0	0	0
16	3	1	0	0	0
17	3	2	1	3	0
18	3	0	0	0	1
19	3	1	0	1	1
	45	27	10	18	7

0—Not mentioned; 1—Mentioned; 2—Emphasized; 3—Major/main focus

The answer provided: to generate new economic activity to fill up an emptied-out city. In many ways, this motivation stands in complete opposite to a smart-shrinkage strategy which would aim to address an emptied-out city using other tools, focusing more on improving quality of life.

Only four reports used quality of life as a major or minor focus as a rationale for city action, though nine other reports either mentioned or emphasized it. A quality of life motivation for action opens up a more creative set of solutions for the emptied-out city problem. Rather than just trying to "fill vacant and underutilized space," a motivation of improving quality of life would direct city energies toward adaptive and creative reuse or reengineering of vacant and underutilized space. Examples include more demolition of derelict structures to make way for open space and agricultural activities, more renovations of offices to accommodate housing or artists' studios, and more reconfiguration of blocks and street networks to meet the infrastructure needs of a smaller city.

It is worth noting the safety and historic preservation motivations were mentioned and emphasized in several reports, just to a much lesser extent than economic development and quality of life. Historic preservation has such a rich history itself in New Bedford that it appears to stand alone as a *raison d'être* for many of the reports. For five of the reports, historic preservation was a major or minor focus for justifying city action, making the case that New Bedford's historic urban fabric is a national cultural artifact in and out of itself and ought to be preserved for broader societal betterment.

What Words Did They Use

By looking at how the city engages with demographic patterns, what the city does regarding policies and planning, and why the city does what it does, some key ideas seem to emerge. The city draws largely on an economic development and growth strategy to do both smart shrinkage and smart growth. This conclusion can now be tested further by applying manifest analysis and actually counting the number of times each report uses a pre-determined set of words. Here, the focus is primarily on what it is that the city is doing to respond to decline.

As with my research in Buffalo, I drew directly on an early and important book in the shrinking cities literature, *Shrinking Cities: Volume 2 Interventions* (Oswalt 2006). The book was the third book in a series on shrinking cities published by the German Federal Cultural Foundation as part of their Shrinking Cities Project.[3] The book series is the result of an international design competition and traveling exhibition by the same name to bring the issue of urban shrinkage to the attention of large segments of the general public in a number of postindustrial countries around the globe. In the book, various strategies for responding to shrinkage are divided into four categories: deconstruction, reevaluating, reorganizing, and imagining. A short explanation of each is offered next, based on my research with Bernard Cahill (Hollander and Cahill 2011):

Deconstructing
The term "deconstructing" can misleadingly imply only the demolition of the built environment when in fact it has a much more nuanced and complex meaning. More accurately, deconstructing describes strategies to change the physical composition of a shrinking city or region in order to address the imbalance of surplus infrastructure for ever fewer people, a process or policy prescription known in some academic circles as "rightsizing."

For Schilling and Logan (2008), the strategy of "rightsizing" primarily means "stabilizing dysfunctional markets and distressed neighborhoods by more closely aligning a city's built environment with the needs of existing and foreseeable future populations by adjusting the amount of land available for development" (p. 453). To this end, Schilling and Logan propose a smart-shrinkage approach for shrinking cities that incorporates as its key component the conversion of abandoned or vacant properties into what they call "green infrastructure."

Reevaluating
Unlike deconstructing strategies, different types of reevaluating strategies may or may not include manipulation of the built environment, resulting in some overlap. Urban agriculture and the reinterpretation of existing infrastructure are good examples of ideas that straddle the two concepts (Lauinger 2006), while renewable energy generation (Schwarz 2008, 79) and interim uses are stricter forms of reevaluating involving fewer physical changes (Overmeyer 2006; Rosenfeld 2006). The focus of much of reevaluating involves the changes in the use and activities that happen at vacant or abandoned buildings or land.

Reorganizing
Reorganizing is focused on the changes that can be made to the organization and functioning of municipal government to more effectively address

the issues faced by shrinking cities and regions. It therefore has less to do with changes to the built environment and more to do with the management structure of communities and policy processes. Examples include changes in municipal zoning and land-use changes, raising taxes (Lauinger 2006, 570), or focusing on small neighborhood-level initiatives (Gratz 1994). The Relaxed Zoning Overlay tool, first introduced in my book *Sunburnt Cities* (2011) and later expanded on in a paper (Pantalone and Hollander 2012), is a good example of how a more flexible and dynamic zoning system provides potentially improved options for shrinking places.

Imagining

Of the four different concepts discussed here, imagining is perhaps the most self-explanatory and hardest to operationalize. As one might suspect from the term itself, imagining entails the realization or creation of a new image for the future of their community by the residents of a shrinking place. This effort is underpinned by the unique role played by collective symbolism found in a place's history and culture.

Popper and Popper (1999) have written extensively on the role of metaphors as an envisioning or "reenvisioning" tool to help citizens conceptualize a future vision for their region by injecting shared cultural symbolism into the public planning conversation.

Identity in shrinking places can also be strengthened or recreated through other forms of group activities in the community, such as city day, harvest festivals, and parades. As with industrial heritage museums, many of these activities can likewise activate much-needed economic activity and draw the attention of future "investors, tourists, and subsidizing bodies" (Bittner 2006, p. 795).

For the manifest analysis, we attempted to dig deeper into my hypothesis that the city was applying smart shrinkage by using the categories from *Shrinking Cities: Volume 2 Interventions*. These single-word categories are organized into chapters by theme, as explained above: deconstructing, reevaluating, reorganizing, and imagining. My search indicators for the quantitative measurement of smart-shrinkage keywords and phrases were collected from the essays in each of these chapters as well as from outside materials compatible within these categories, borrowing liberally from the work I did in Buffalo. The only difference was that in this project, we also included the keyword "growth"—attempting to measure, if only coarsely, how frequently growth-oriented policy discussions were used in New Bedford.

To conduct the manifest analysis, we searched the 18 New Bedford reports for the existence and frequency of these keywords and phrases indicative of smart-shrinkage strategies. Once this data was gathered, we then undertook another latent analysis of the keywords and phrases in context of the reports to discern if they were being used in a manner consistent with smart shrinkage.

This two-pronged method was possible because we conducted the content analysis manually, without the aid of computer software. While this allows for some human error, such as overlooked words or phrases, by examining "the power of words in a 'key-word-in-context' ... list to see how the word is used in a sentence," (Gaber and Gaber 2007, p. 110) we were in a better position to understand the intent behind words such as "decline." For example, while the word "decline" alone might suggest that planners are embracing smart shrinkage, it is also just as likely that in context the word is instead being used as a descriptor of current conditions to justify the implementation of strategies anticipating future growth. The results of the analysis were tabulated to graphically demonstrate the existence and frequency of such words and phrases.

What the Numbers Show

For each of the five categories, I present next the total sum of how many times relevant keywords appeared and how many times that appeared in a context that was relevant to smart decline, see Table 7.4.

Deconstructing

Deconstruction is not a major element of the New Bedford reports. That much, I suspected. But, Table 7.4 shows that deconstruction keywords do appear in all of the reports and in some cases are related to a smart-shrinkage policy orientation. The biggest deconstruction word count came for the term "infrastructure," with 133 counts, 13 of those relevant to smart shrinkage. These counts were spread out among all of the reports, each having at least one use of the word "infrastructure." Thirteen instances of infrastructure were relevant to smart shrinkage, a pretty high percentage as compared to other terms. For the term "connections" all but one of the 103 mentions of the word are irrelevant to smart shrinkage.

"Restoration" was the only other keyword that had any sizable number of appearances relevant to smart decline, with eight. The other keywords in Table 7.4 relevant to smart shrinkage had just a handful of references,

Table 7.4 Word counts

Deconstruction keywords	Total mentions	Mentions relevant to smart shrinkage
Infrastructure	133	13
Connections	103	1
Rehabilitation	54	1
Renovation	38	2
Restoration	36	8
Converted/convert/converting	26	3
Compact/compact development	26	5
Conversion	20	3
Redesign	19	
Evolve	15	0
Reconstruct(ion)	11	0
Housing stock	8	2
More compact city/compact core/compact center	6	1
Expansion of River ways, Watersheds, Parkland	3	2
Reduce infrastructure	1	1
Dismantling/Dismantled	1	0

See Appendix A for a total list of all keywords for each category

Reevaluating keywords	Total mentions	Mentions relevant to smart shrinkage
Recreational	172	22
Alternative	130	1
Reuse	116	13
Vacant	104	19
Agricultural	30	7
Agriculture	20	4
Reinvestment	13	0
Networks	12	2
Urban sports/sports	8	1
		69

Reorganizing keywords	Total mentions	Mentions relevant to smart shrinkage
Reform	22	0
Engagement	11	1
Transferable development rights	10	3

(continued)

Table 7.4 (continued)

Reorganizing keywords	Total mentions	Mentions relevant to smart shrinkage
Citizen involvement/citizen participation	7	0
Regional economy	4	0
Competitive position	3	0
Regional connectivity	2	2
Microfinance/microenterprise	1	0
Regional linkages	1	0

Imagining keywords	Total mentions	Mentions relevant to smart shrinkage
Vision	176	3
Cultural	132	34
Heritage	67	21
Conceptual(ize)	29	3
Reenvisioning/envisioning/envision	27	3
Heritage tourism	9	5
		69

Growth	Total mentions	Mentions relevant to smart shrinkage
Growth[a]	305	0
Smart growth	66	0
Economic growth	13	0
New growth	12	0
Population growth	9	0
Job growth	6	0
Residential growth	5	0
Industrial growth	3	0
Housing growth	1	0

[a]Phrases that include the word "growth" are counted again here

certainly nothing dramatic. When it comes to calling for making major physical alterations to the built environment in New Bedford, it appears from these counts that the only popular option is changing infrastructure, and that other concepts are largely absent from the reports.

Reevaluating

Of the 13 reevaluating keywords, only 9 appeared in any of the reports—with "recreational" and "alternative" showing up most frequently, followed by "reuse" and "vacant." Though not many key words appeared, those four were quite prevalent, each appearing more than a hundred times and three of the words (recreational, reuse, and vacant) each having substantial numbers of appearances relevant to smart shrinkage.

The planning reports were seriously engaged with reevaluating New Bedford to explore new uses and new thinking about existing infrastructure. The heavy appearance of these keywords relevant to smart shrinkage supports the notion that planning in New Bedford has included a reinterpretation of how land ought to be used in the face of shrinkage.

The appearance of those four heavily counted keywords is spread fairly evenly throughout the 18 reports, with a particularly strong appearance of "vacant" in the city of New Bedford Historic Mill Inventory (2008) and the Downtown New Bedford Revitalization and Redevelopment Study (2009)—not surprisingly given the topics of those two reports.

In total, the reevaluating keywords had 69 appearances in the reports where they were relevant to smart shrinkage. While there were 16 deconstruction keywords which appeared in the reports, there were only 44 words that were relevant to smart shrinkage. This suggests that reevaluating is a much more prevalent category for New Bedfordian smart-shrinkage planning than deconstruction. Repurposing land and buildings instead of rebuilding them was a practice which I was able to partially observe in my absorption analysis presented in the next chapter, for I saw was whether buildings disappeared or not and then was able to note how the newly vacant land was reevaluated for a new use.

Reorganizing

With its 13 keywords, reorganizing seems to be well suited for policy and planning reports in a shrinking city, with its calls for rightsizing government and removing onerous rules. This was not the case in New Bedford. While words like "reform" and "engagement" each received a handful of mentions in the reports, the reorganizing keywords only had a total of six appearances relevant to smart shrinkage.

Planning in New Bedford has been focused on matters outside local government organization and policy innovation, mentioning words that have been the touchstone for twenty-first-century urban reform like "citizen involvement" and "regional linkages" less than five times.

This is not to suggest that the reports showed no evidence of reorganizing, but it was largely a silent portion of the city's strategy for addressing policy problems and certainly played no role in how the city is approaching smart shrinkage.

Imagining

Imagining was different. Six of the category's seven keywords appeared in the reports. The keyword "vision" was the single most common word we tracked, with 176 appearances. "Cultural" and "heritage" also had substantial numbers of mentions. More important, imagining keywords had precisely the same number—69—of smart shrinkage relevant keyword appearances as reevaluating.

Most of the imagining keywords appear throughout the 16 reports, but it is the Hicks-Logan-Sawyer Vision Plan that dominates the word "vision" with 76 counts. As a vision plan, that is certainly of no surprise, but the important point is how the rethinking of an entire neighborhood reflects a broader smart-shrinkage approach. It demonstrates the need to connect the culture and heritage of a whole neighborhood to a new vision, a new thinking about the future. City planners here chose to reimagine their future.

Growth

The research I did in Buffalo did not include a set of growth keywords, but we couldn't resist just running these numbers to see how often the city's plans spoke to growth and especially how the shrinkage keywords compared. The results were not very surprising, the word "growth" itself generated 305 mentions, across almost all the reports—just three of them (the Downtown Action Plan, Acushnet Avenue Corridor Vision Plan, and the Upper Harbor Vision Plan) did not use the word "growth" at all.

We selected eight types of growth to also include in the analysis and found that "smart growth," "economic growth," and "new growth" were the most frequently mentioned phrases. "Population growth" was only mentioned nine times, "housing growth" only once.

Together, the appearance of these configurations of "growth" dwarfed any other individual shrinkage-related keyword—substantially. The word "growth" was used, but perhaps not overused. Planning reports called for growth but also clearly for smart shrinkage. The absence of "population growth" and "housing growth" from most reports in remarkable. Given the power of local politics to be driven by a growth machine, it is also notable that "job growth" had just six mentions and "industrial growth" only three. New Bedford's planning has been engaged in the discourse of growth, but this analysis reveals a distinctly even-handed treatment of plans to reverse the city's long-standing shrinkage.

Voices from the Field

In the previous chapter, I reported on extensive interviews I conducted with community leaders, residents, and local officials to paint a picture of how the city has changed over the last eight decades. During those interviews with current and former local officials, I also asked about the contemporary policy response to depopulation—what was the city doing? The content analysis of 16 city reports provided some evidence, and this section offers additional perspective from the people in positions of power.

Just as the city reports placed much emphasis on the notion of renovating and reusing existing structures, my interviews revealed a similar theme, specifically concerned with upgrading and investing in housing structures. City and community leaders viewed housing as a key issue for addressing a myriad of social and economic challenges within residential neighborhoods of New Bedford. One leader of a non-governmental organization (NGO) active in New Bedford said:

> We don't see housing as a means in itself, we see it as part of neighborhood revitalization. ... We bought a home, evicted a couple that was dealing drugs. I was back in the neighborhood and someone said "the neighborhood has never been so quiet, thanks so much!" It shows that you could really make a difference.

Over the last decade, City Hall has made a major effort to partner with these community development organizations to rejuvenate the housing stock with the aim of affecting broader change in neighborhoods. When speaking with a city official, the NGO leader explained a typical neighborhood intervention effort where they "worked with a couple of non-profits, acquired 8–10 abandoned-foreclosed [properties]—the majority of them were turned into homeowner [owner-occupied]." It is a model that is common in New Bedford and beyond: renovate a dilapidated rental property and make it owner-occupied.

Community leaders I spoke to believed that it is a model that works: "When non-profits like us come in and do something, it really makes a difference." City leaders feel that it's a sensible investment of limited public dollars. For many derelict rental structures, the rents are so low that a major renovation does not make financial sense: the costs of renovation cannot be recouped through rent in a reasonable amount of time. For that reason, the city of New Bedford, working with state and federal funding partners, put in a subsidy to these housing renovation projects "to make the numbers work" as one city official put it.

Also related to maintaining and strengthening housing conditions is a major city push to enhance building code enforcement, to track abandoned properties, and to go after scofflaw landlords. After the foreclosure crisis and Great Recession, a senior city official explained that "the first thing we did was to identify every distressed property" and they helped "move individuals, make financial institutions pay for relocations." Taking a very hands-on role in protecting and preserving the city's housing stock was in response to a set of dire conditions: "we saw properties being mined [for copper], we insisted that people had to secure buildings according to code—I wanted to secure the buildings, from an arson standpoint, a crime standpoint. It's far too dangerous. 'If you won't do it, we will and lien the building,'" city officials said to owners of abandoned properties.

In recent years, code enforcement has not been a priority for City Hall. "Eight to ten years ago we had a housing division that did inspections, that division doesn't even exist anymore," explained a city official. But that has changed and a new vacant property registration ordinance and more resources toward code enforcement are reenergizing code enforcement.

The new ordinance requires that owners of vacant buildings register and pay a fee. The longer their buildings are in an uncared for status, the higher the fee, and it goes up to $1500. "Investors are coming in and basically mothballing the properties [after the property goes through foreclosure] we are saying 'what is your plan? If you're going to sit on these properties, you are going to have to pay,'" said a city official.

Arguably, even better than penalties is when the city relies on its network of citizen activists, like Ken Resendes, a citizen activist in the Bullard Street neighborhood. "I can get info from Ken. He says 'it is vacant,' I try to track it. We have June, in inspectional services, through [their] attorneys, they provide her with a list of auction properties." City officials are not very optimistic in protecting housing from decay and abandonment, and the scale of the problem is daunting. By the time they hear about a foreclosure, the building has likely been vacated and abandoned for weeks, if not months. A common refrain in my interviews was "It's hard to be proactive," though everyone wants to be.

The city's hyper-focus on supporting the renovation and rehabilitation of residential structures is aimed to stimulate broader investment in surrounding properties and the surrounding neighborhood. That's the aim, but evidence is weak to prove it really accomplishes that goal. An equally dubious city strategy articulated in the interviews was echoed loudly in the reports: economic development. The recruitment and retention of firms through public subsidy and planning efforts is intended to change the larger economic conditions in New Bedford so as to generate increased demand for housing in the neighborhoods. In theory this sounds wonderful, in practice results are mixed. City officials expressed little understanding of the potential pitfalls of economic development, and instead seem keen on positioning the city for job growth and all of its associated economic benefits. One city leader felt that "we've never in fifty years been better positioned for job creation and real growth."

New Bedford does economic development through two main strategies: firm attraction and retention, and big development projects. For attracting firms, the city's economic development arm collected research on where New Bedford's economic strengths are, then they:

> summarized those studies and sent them to 250 business and education and NGO leaders, a report per month. ... What are our authentic attributes for job growth? We finally teased out five to six key sectors we are going after: renewables, life sciences, marine science and technology, creative economy and tourism, hi-tech back office. ... We have this ocean highway right here. ... We have a hell of a product here! (City official)

Current strategies are aimed to bring in and retain jobs for middle-income workers. City officials have developed a diagram that they have taken on the road to talk about the kinds of people they want to fill these new jobs. Those people are not the poor. One city leader explained that those people—the unemployed, the indigent, the undereducated—account for 7.5% of the population, and that there's little he could do for them. Then, there's the rich, but "they'll be OK wherever they live." He's most worried about those squeezed between the rich and the poor—the middle group.

Middle-income New Bedfordians, "this is what we're talking about. People like me, like Jerry here"—the same city official pointed to his 20-something-year-old intern. Both of them were middle-class white guys. This is "the population that we are really targeting, because money is scarce. It breaks my fucking heart, but are we going to reach them [the poor]?" This city official doesn't think so, and he instead would let other parts of the city help them, such as human service agencies or charitable organizations.

While I found little validation of this viewpoint in other interviews, the policies speak for themselves. The retention and recruitment of firms for which the poor are not qualified to work at does little for them. Facets of urban theory support this approach. If you can further repopulate New Bedford's middle class by squeezing out the poor, it can lead to an overall more attractive climate for capital investment.

If all this tax-payer funding works to retain and recruit new firms, the results can bode very well for homeowners and existing businesses. There seems little in this economic development policy, however, for the 7.5% that can't be "reached."

Another facet of economic development emphasized during my interviews was planning and public investment around large development projects. When asked about how this approach can address long-standing trends of depopulation, a city leader responded: "We are not working towards one homerun project that would save us." Instead, they are focusing on several home runs—a train station to connect the city by rail to Boston, a new casino, and staging grounds for the construction of a major (and controversial) offshore wind project near Cape Cod.

In one interview, a city official mocked a previous mayor who invested his entire economic development strategy on the building of an aquarium that ultimately was never built. "Frankly it is a strategy built on the back of despair," continued the same official. Today's city leaders have several aquarium-style projects that they are supporting and investing in. No matter the actual public dollars going in, each one of them represents a significant amount of City Hall's human resources and energy going into these large development projects with uncertain potential outcomes.

The former Fairhaven Mills complex is one such example. Sitting on almost four acres on Coggeshall Street, the complex was partially demolished in the early 2000s and then completely demolished. By 2009, construction was underway to bring a suite of new retail businesses to the site, including a supermarket and restaurants. "You're going to see an evolution of urban life at the Fairhaven Mills complex, that's where the future is going to be" (long-time resident).

In the Harbor area, city officials are betting heavily on an expanded suite of uses (beyond fishing) that could open up opportunities for large-scale city transformation. "We've introduced recreational, boating, ferry—we can accommodate more than just the fishing industry." The Harbor initiative is part of the larger plan to downgrade the highway (Route 18) and turn it into an ordinary, low-speed road.

When I asked city leaders if it is possible to plan for a future that does not include economic growth, they all said no. They argued for a continuation of the strategies employed over the last several decades to promote the city as a product for investors. Unfortunately, few investors are buying that argument, and the employment picture continues to remain weak.

This leads to the last set of policies that city leaders discussed as a type of back-up plan in case their jobs and population figures continue to decline: smart shrinkage. While I have been familiar with New Bedford for many years, it was an article in June 2009 in *The New York Times* that got me excited. In the midst of the Great Recession, the story turned to a novel policy solution, noting that then Mayor Scott Lang was experimenting with embracing smart shrinkage. To address the growing foreclosure crisis, he was ordering residential structures to be demolished. The article went on to explain why that was a big deal: "Mr. Lang hopes the demolitions make room for small parks, community gardens or parking lots. 'It might make sense to open up a little air, allow some green space, create a little more of a recreational-type pattern,' he said."

City leaders in New Bedford are doing more than just knocking down derelict buildings—they are acting purposefully to imagine lower housing densities and finding new uses for where residential uses had been. They are doing some form of smart shrinkage.

This city strategy begins with realistic understanding of past and project demographic change and turns to the question of how to reduce the number of housing units in low-demand residential districts. One long-time city official ruminated on the current conundrum:

> 130,000 [people is what New Bedford] was built for, today we're trending downward. As much as we'd like otherwise. Statistically, it's supposed to be in the low 90s, so we need to take that into account when we look at the number of [housing] units we have. We've seen large scale conversion of mills into housing. (City official)

That same city employee went on to express real concern for the conversion of mills into housing, given the trends underway. Despite this attitude, nobody wants to repeat the mass clearances on the urban renewal period discussed in Chap. 6. For New Bedford leaders, the problem is a pragmatic one: "Some of the housing stock [in New Bedford] is substandard—it wasn't built particularly well, it might be best … [to have] some demolitions, create green space and large lots. It's a last resort only when it's not economically feasible to rehab." This city official felt that when a home needs to be demolished because of health and safety concerns, it is best to take advantage of that opportunity and reduce total density, as Mayor Lang explained to *The New York Times*. The example that city officials shared with me was at a parcel that was improved by two triple-decker homes. Both homes had fallen into disrepair while being let out to low-income tenants. The owner had become delinquent on city taxes and the properties eventually came into city ownership. The city renovated one of the buildings, demolished the other, and built off-street parking (a small parking lot) and a small grassy plot where the second structure had stood.

A similar approach has been used elsewhere in the city, according to a city official: "We've demolished some properties and rebuilt on the lot and usually lower density" with off-street parking, some grass, and maybe a side yard. To reduce housing density, the city will tear down two three-unit triple-deckers and build a modest single-family home with a driveway and a yard. While the catalytic effect on the surrounding properties and larger neighborhood is unknown, the takedown of two surplus housing units is clearly accomplished. In terms of supply and demand, that may accomplish more than a simple housing rehab program that fixes up homes using public subsidy. New Bedford officials are remarkably aware of that fact, more so than their city reports seem to suggest.

"Who would think that a garden would get people so excited. We might not have enough plots next year!" Thus commented a community activist regarding a new garden in her neighborhood on the site of a former factory, instituted through a city-run community gardening program. The city is actively involved in facilitating alternative uses for residential properties as demand for housing continues to shrink. Instead of just hoping that some of the city's housing stock is retrofitted for non-housing uses, the city is attempting to support this transition.

The first use city officials described in my interviews was permanent supportive housing for people with disabilities, where state-funded non-profits provide housing and services in structures that had previously been used for private housing. This is the kind of use that is hard to find a location for—the "not in my backyard" outcries usually come from neighbors in wealthy suburban locations, so inner cities are usually a more welcome locale. The precise impacts on a community of these supportive housing facilities is tough to measure, but the concerns typically revolve around negative property value impacts. For a shrinking city—where the alternative could be an empty house, a drug house, a vacant lot, or worse—supportive housing has been recognized by city officials as a desirable option.

Another option considered by the city is to allow abutters to take over vacant lots and incorporate them into their own properties. There are a number of costs and hurdles for owners to go through, but the benefits can be substantial. Generally, abutter would simply take over the vacant lot next door for their own purposes, attempting to obtain a legal interest through adverse possession; the abutter lot program is a legal improvement on the more common procedure. Either way, abutters have proven to be effective stewards of vacant land, as also evidenced in the analysis of current uses of vacated land in the three case study neighborhoods in Chap. 6. Abutters use vacant lots for parking, gardens, ancillary buildings, extended yards, and even, in one case, a tree farm.

While practices of reducing density and actively finding new uses for vacant sites is not in widespread use (confirmed by the analysis of reports), the general approach is a powerful one and wholly consistent with smart shrinkage. While calling for new jobs and housing rehabilitation elsewhere, the city is also fully cognizant of the very real disconnect between the number of people who live in the city and the size of the housing stock.

The Contours of Today's Smart Shrinkage and Growth

Smart shrinkage and smart growth are most certainly weapons in New Bedford's suite of tools it has been employing over the last decade to address a myriad of challenges in the city. With regard to addressing the problem of depopulation, the answer offered here is tentative to be sure. Many city officials do not view depopulation as the problem and they are correct in that view: as outlined in Chap. 2, depopulation is caused by a number of important factors. The decline in New Bedford's employment base has meant that the city's residential neighborhoods are far less desirable to live in than in the past. Therefore, city leaders have attempted to reverse this process to attract and retain more firms to make the residential neighborhoods more desirable. They are also working on housing rehabilitation and renovation to make the housing stock more attractive. In addition, they are enforcing building codes and going after dead-beat landlords.

In my review of city reports, I found a wide range of other policies in place in New Bedford to improve the pedestrian experience, parks and green spaces, the creative economy, tourism, transportation, sustainability, historic preservation, and more. When viewed through the lens of smart shrinkage, those official city documents were also calling for a more right-sized infrastructure, improved land-use policies, more recreational and agriculture uses, and a cultural/heritage reimaging of what kind of a city New Bedford is and can be.

Together the reports and interviews tell a story of a city government trying to play the conventional economic development game of chasing industry and betting on big "game-changing" projects, while also investing money and time in a genuine effort to decrease the city's housing density and find new non-housing uses for formerly residential structures and land. In the history of urban studies in the USA, such smart-shrinkage activities have never been so well documented, though I suspect the strategies employed by the city are not that uncommon.

Neither Youngstown's famous plan for a "smaller, better Youngstown" nor the Detroit Future City plan have been implemented on the ground, and certainly the result has not been documented. Flint, Michigan, and Cleveland, Ohio, have been active in pushing the edges of what it means to plan for sustainability in the face of depopulation, but these findings from New Bedford are different. Here, we can see a substantial policy initiative that differentiates the city from what has been empirically shown in fellow shrinking Rust Belt cities, validated both through interviews and through a content analysis (the reason is less about New Bedford being an innovative city and more about the smart-shrinkage lens I employed to study the city's actions). Mapping results from the sixth chapter began to show a real thinning out of the three case study neighborhoods. In the next chapter, those maps will be updated with 2010 data and even more compelling patterns appear. Not only has the city of New Bedford supported and administered a version of smart shrinkage and smart growth programs, but it appears from the data in the next chapter that it has actually been effective on some level in implementing them.

Notes

1. The City of Buffalo's (2004) Queen City in the twenty-first century: Buffalo's Comprehensive Plan Won the Congress for New Urbanism's Charter Award in 2009.

2. The excluded report was #10. In addition, two reports (#6 and #12) could not be searched electronically so they were removed from the manifest content analysis but included in the latent content analysis (see Table 7.1 for details on each excluded report).
3. Described in Chap. 3.

Bibliography

Bittner, Regina. 2006. Post-Fordist Production of Space. In *Shrinking Cities, Volume 1: International Research*, ed. Philipp Oswalt, 572–581. Ostfildern, Germany: Hatje Cantz Verlag.

City of Buffalo. 2004. *Queen City in the 21st Century: Buffalo's Comprehensive Plan*. Buffalo, NY: Office of Strategic Planning.

FXM Associates. 2007. *Economic Development Strategy for Downtown New Bedford, Part II: Measuring Success*. Mattapoisett, MA: FXM Associates.

Gaber, John, and Sharon Gaber. 2007. *Qualitative Analysis for Planning & Policy: Beyond the Numbers*. Chicago, IL: American Planning Association.

Gratz, Roberta Brandes. 1994. Each Town Its Own Face. *The Wall Street Journal*, September 8.

Hollander, Justin B., and Bernard Cahill. 2011. Confronting Population Decline in the Buffalo, New York, Region: A Close Reading of the Erie-Niagara Framework for Regional Growth. *Journal of Architecture and Planning Research* 28 (3): 252–267.

Hollander, Justin B., Karina Pallagst, Terry Schwarz, and Frank J. Popper. 2009. Planning Shrinking Cities. *Progress in Planning* 72 (4): 223–232.

Lauinger, Holger. 2006. Urban Agriculture. In *Shrinking Cities, Volume 2: Interventions*, ed. Philipp Oswalt. Ostfildern, Germany: Hatje Cantz Verlag.

Muro, Mark, John Schneider, David Warren, Eric McLean-Shinaman, Rebecca Sohmer, and Benjamin Forman. 2007. *Reconnecting Massachusetts Gateway Cities: Lessons Learned and an Agenda for Renewal*. Boston, MA: MassINC.

Oswalt, Philipp. 2006. *Shrinking Cities. Interventions*. Hatje Cantz Verlag.

Overmeyer, Klaus. 2006. Vacant Lots as Incubators? Interim Uses in Shrinking Cities. In *Shrinking Cities, Volume 2: Interventions*, ed. Philipp Oswalt, 324–329. Ostfildern, Germany: Hatje Cantz.

Pantalone, Stephen, and Justin B. Hollander. 2012. Relaxed Zoning Overlay. *Zoning Practice* 28 (9): 1–7.

Popper, Deborah E., and Frank J. Popper. 1999. The Buffalo Commons: Metaphor as Method. *Geographical Review* 89 (4): 491–510.

RKG Associates. 2007. *District Improvement Financing Plan for the Hicks Logan Sawyer Urban Revitalization Area in New Bedford, MA*. Durham, NH: RKG Associates.

Rosenfeld, Elske. 2006. What is Art Up to in Disused Buildings? In *Shrinking Cities, Volume 2: Interventions*, ed. Philip Oswalt, 355–361. Ostfildern, Germany: Hatje Cantz Verlag.

Schilling, Joseph, and Jonathan Logan. 2008. Greening the Rust Belt: A Green Infrastructure Model for Right Sizing America's Shrinking Cities. *Journal of the American Planning Association* 74 (4): 451–466.

Schwarz, Terry. 2008. The Cleveland Land Lab Experiments for a City in Transition. In *Cities Growing Smaller*, ed. Cleveland Urban Design Collaborative, 72–84. Cleveland, OH: Kent State University.

CHAPTER 8

Urban Absorption

I learned a lot about New Bedford by talking to residents and community leaders, but looking at some very old maps and walking the streets helped as well. The Sanborn Fire Insurance maps presented in Chap. 6 provide a compelling view of how policy responses during the urban renewal period (and prior) coincided with physical changes in the form of the three study neighborhoods. In this chapter, I go further by bringing in more current mapping data to better correspond with the more contemporary policy responses described in Chap. 7.

More than just updating the data, the ability to examine existing conditions provides a unique opportunity to triangulate this mapping data with a ground-truthing exercise: if the maps tell us that a structure had been at the corner of Forest Street and Acushnet Avenues but has vanished in the latest map, then direct observation of conditions at that corner can reveal quite a lot about how the city has adjusted to depopulation.

This chapter offers just such a mix of mapping results with direct observation to explore a compelling new idea in the world of shrinking cities: urban absorption. How do cities with population loss absorb the loss of structures into their urban fabric? What becomes of the vacant lots left behind when a structure is removed?

During the summer of 2010, I worked with a team of graduate students to edit the 1975 figure-ground drawings (see Figs. 6.4, 6.5, and 6.6) based on a close examination of satellite imagery presented on Google Earth. We edited the 1975 maps based on any additions, major alternations, or removal of structures observed in the Google Earth satellite data. These new maps for 2010 are presented alongside the historical maps to ease comparison (Figs. 8.1, 8.2, and 8.3).

With the 2010 maps, the trajectory of each neighborhood appears in even starker focus than was apparent by only looking up through 1975 (as presented in Chap. 6). Figures 8.1, 8.2, and 8.3 provide a compelling picture of how each neighborhood grew, reached full build-out, and then began to thin out. Beginning with South Central, it is clear from the maps that the neighborhood rose to become a major population center in the city by the mid- to late 1920s (e.g., the 1924 map appears to show the peak of building density in South Central). Then, by 1936, a distinctive emptying out appears, and hardly any of the neighborhood's blocks appear to be untouched by this decline.

The 1975 South Central map is the first view of urban renewal efforts described in Chap. 4, continuing a thinning-out pattern since 1924. The 2010 maps show a fairly uniform, though modest, thinning out of the rest of the South Central neighborhood since 1975, accompanied by even more modest new construction. The result in that the neighborhood is dramatically less dense than it was at its peak in 1924.

The Bullard Street maps are less obvious but show a distinct pattern of thinning out. As discussed in Chap. 4, 1924–1975 was a period of general thinning out, and that pattern continues in the 2010 map, though more subtly. For all but a couple of city blocks in the neighborhood, there is a noticeable loss of at least two or three structures from 1975 to 2010—not nearly to the degree seen during the same period in South Central, but worthy of note.

Although nothing as substantial as what occurred in Bullard Street or South Central, the 2010 map shows continued slow thinning out of buildings. Except for a few new buildings and just a handful of missing ones, the neighborhood managed massive population loss and the urban renewal period quite well.

Overall, the maps suggest that most of the physical changes in the study neighborhoods took place around the middle of the last century, but a general thinning out has been slowly at work since the Great Depression. The aim of this research is not to measure in precise details the location, rate, or spread of this thinning out process. Rather, these maps are intended to illustrate a broad pattern at work where structures have disappeared and been replaced by empty spaces on the maps. As any cartographer knows, there is no such thing in the real world as an empty space. All spaces are used in one way or another and the maps cannot fully capture that information.

8 URBAN ABSORPTION   153

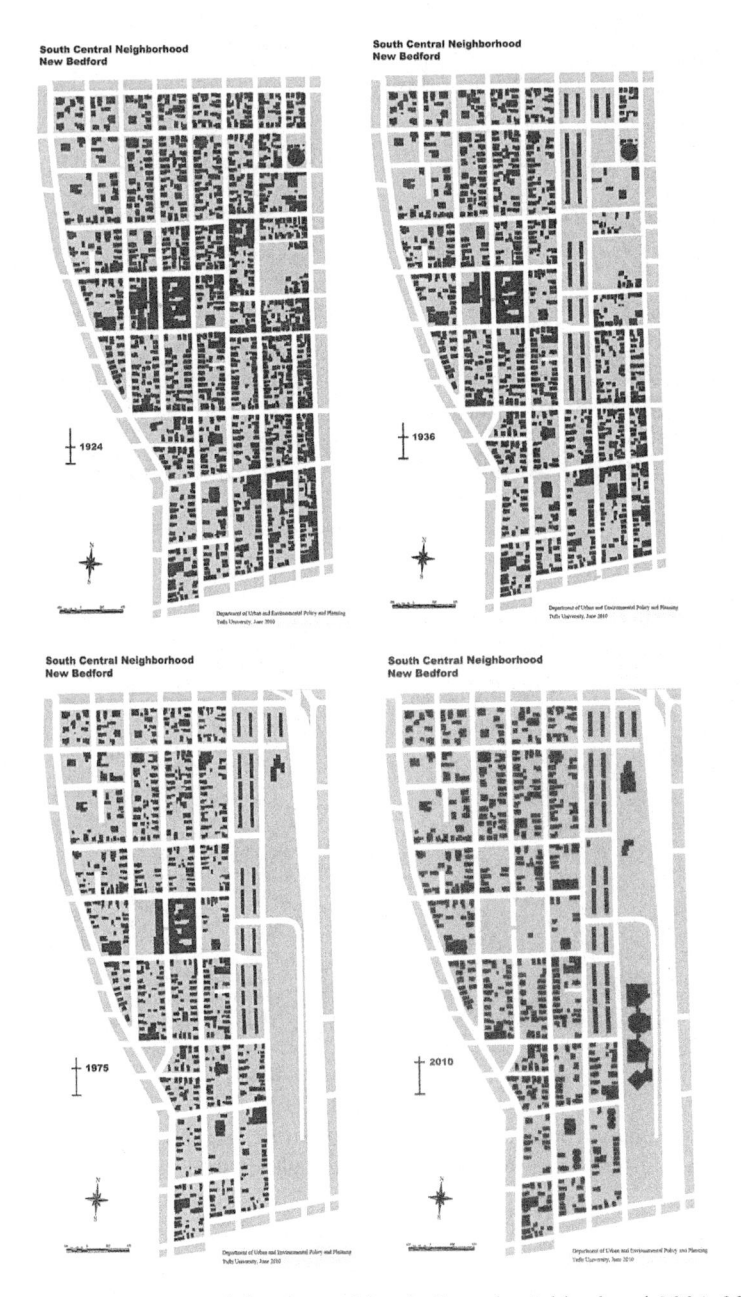

Fig. 8.1 Figure-ground drawings of South Central neighborhood 1924–2010, based on Sanborn Fire Insurance Maps and Google Earth

154 8 URBAN ABSORPTION

Fig. 8.2 Figure-ground drawings of Bullard Street neighborhood 1924–2010, based on Sanborn Fire Insurance Maps and Google Earth

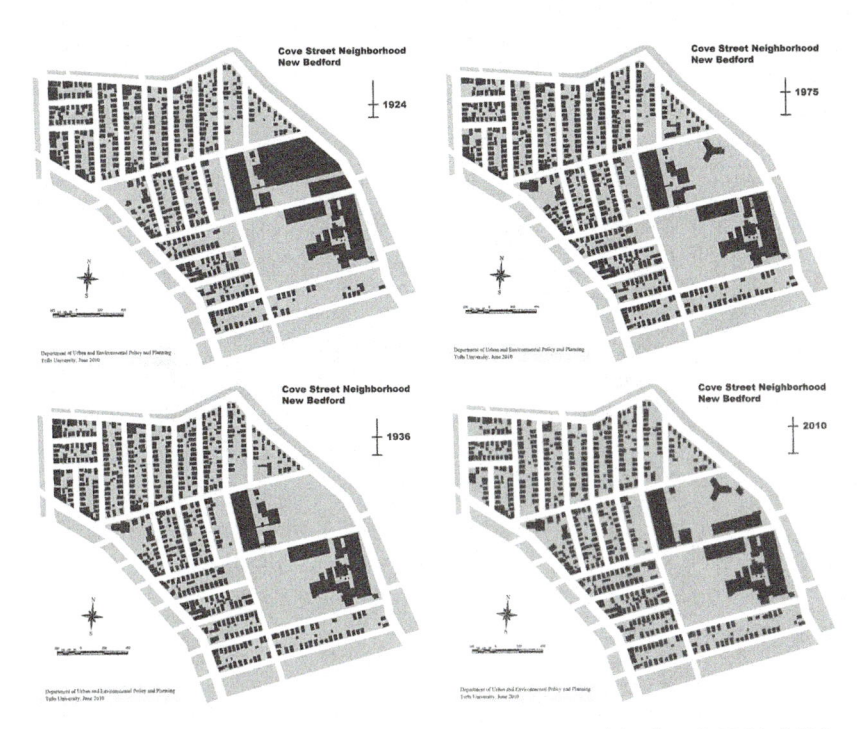

Fig. 8.3 Figure-ground drawings of Cove Street neighborhood 1924–2010, based on Sanborn Fire Insurance Maps and Google Earth

In the fall of 2010, again working with my trusted graduate students, we began to obtain answers to the question of what has become of those empty spaces. Are they really empty after all?

The first step was to look closely at the maps (Figs. 8.1, 8.2, and 8.3) and look for all instances where a structure existed at one point in time but, as of 2010, no longer existed. For the three study neighborhoods, we found well over 100. To make the field research more meaningful, we matched our records with those provided to us from the city of New Bedford's Assessors Office. The Assessor's Office maintains records on property ownership on a parcel basis, not on a building basis. That is, a single-family home on a 5000 square foot lot is categorized by the Assessor's Office by the address of the lot and an accompanied parcel ID number.[1]

In many cases, we found that there were multiple structures associated with a single lot.[2] We went forward with the analysis focusing on these

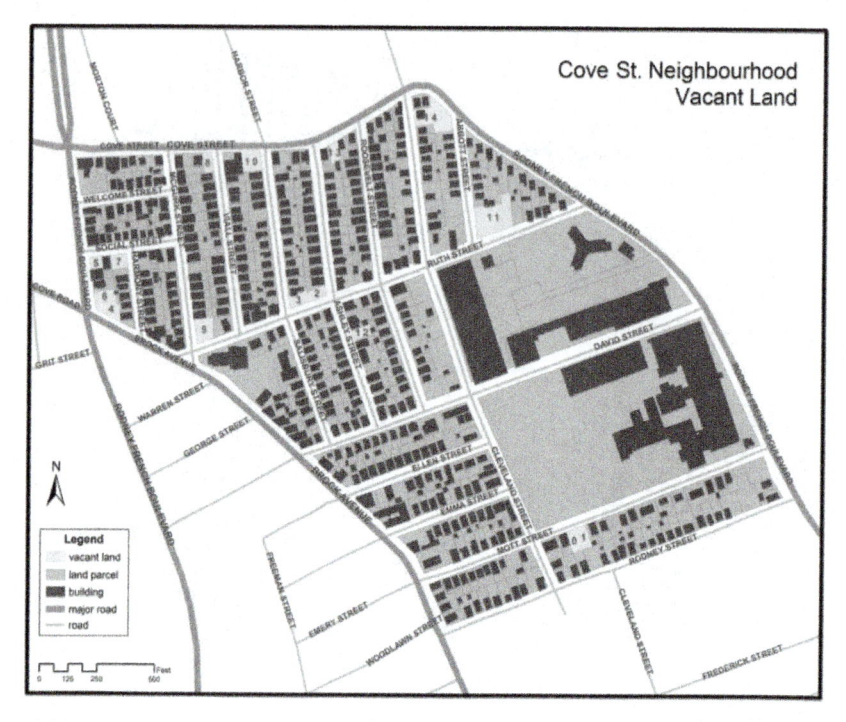

Fig. 8.4 Map indicating Cove Street parcels on which a structure had previously existed, but by the 2010 map had vanished

parcels as the key unit of study. A total of 75 parcels met this criteria, having at some point since 1924 hosted a structure that, as of 2010 was no longer present. South Central had 36 parcels, North End had 24, and Cove Street had 15. Figure 8.4 illustrates how we did this for one of the neighborhoods, Cove Street. This map was an essential tool for the on-the-ground work to follow.

Next, we went into the field to do a windshield survey intent on uncovering what had happened at each of these 75 parcels. The aforementioned maps clearly show that some buildings that disappear are replaced by new structures. The process that results in that kind of rebuilding is interesting, useful, and very well documented in the literature.[3] What is entirely unknown (and the motivation for this phase of the research) is what becomes of those parcels which do not get rebuilt. That same literature presented in Chap. 2 hints that those 75 parcels will likely be vacant lots, the worst kind of liability on a depressed neighborhood as they are settings for drug deals, dumping grounds, and a sign of malaise sending a message to prospective investors: stay away! But here we decided to find out for ourselves whether they are all vacant and abandoned lots, bringing down the neighborhoods. It was hardly what the interviews and focus groups told us, but we had to see for ourselves.

The windshield survey meant driving up and down each of the three neighborhoods looking for those parcels identified above (using the map in Fig. 8.4 for each neighborhood), taking a photograph of each, and then capturing in notes the general conditions and use of the parcel. We took special care to observe if and how the parcel was being reused or absorbed back into the life of the neighborhood.

The parcels of interest are highlighted in yellow and numbered in Fig. 8.4. Accompanying this guide was a list of all the parcels and space to make notes about the use, condition, and other comments on each. I compiled all the results and through an open reading of the notes generated a coding system to make sense of the field observations. Tables 8.1, 8.2, and 8.3 show the results of the field research for all three neighborhoods. In addition to general notes about the condition of the lot, I developed codes for active use (1 = yes, 0 = no, 2 = partially)[4] and for those lots in active use, codes for type of use (1 = parking, 2 = extension of abutting use [non-parking], 3 = passive green space, 4 = park/gardens, 5 = other).

Most surprising about these tables is the extent to which so many of these lots are in an active use and have been reused for a new use that does not require a new structure. This is the heart of what it means for a city to effectively shrink, and here is strong evidence that three neighborhoods in New Bedford have adjusted themselves to new uses as the population has fallen for nine decades. Table 8.4 provides summary statistics on the total number of lots where a structure was lost, the percentage that have been at least partially reused, and the percentage that have been fully reused. Nothing in the literature on cities and abandonment would have led me to have expected such overwhelming absorption. Instead, in Chap. 2, I wrote that knowledge to-date on how cities adjust to decline is largely a sad story of devastation and disaster. These numbers tell a very different story (see Table 8.4).

In the North End neighborhood, almost 92% of those lots where a structure was lost have been partially absorbed back into the urban fabric—87.5% have been fully absorbed through a complete reuse. Thirteen of Cove Street's 15 lots where a structure had been present have been partially reused, though only 10 have been fully reused. Lastly, South Central

Table 8.1 Cove Street neighborhood

Cove Street neighborhood	General notes	Active use (1 = yes, 0 = no, 2 = partially) (yes means that the area is actively being used for some use, including passive green space—the key is that it is being cared for and protected)	Type of use (1 = parking, 2 = extension of abutting use (non-parking), 3 = passive green space, 4 = park/gardens, 5 = other)	Address	Owner (PP = private property held by individual, NB = owned by New Bedford)	Acreage
Lot 0	Overgrown with bushes/brambles. No connection to other buildings	0	–	82 MOTT ST	PP	0.098
Lot 1	Overgrown with bushes/brambles. No connection to other buildings	0	–	78 MOTT ST	NB	0.098
Lot 2	Park, trees with a fence lining the area, benches, Christmas lights on central tree	1	4	RUTH ST	NB	0.07
Lot 3	Park, trees with a fence lining the area, benches, Christmas lights on central tree	1	4	99 RUTH ST	NB	0.09

8 URBAN ABSORPTION 159

Lot 4	Fenced-in grass lot, does not seem to be used for anything	2	3	982–986 BROCK AVE	PP	0.13
Lot 5	Parking lot for car repair shop	1	1	SE W RODNEY FRENCH BLVD	PP	0.06
Lot 6	Fenced-in grass lot, does not seem to be used for anything	2	3	48 W RODNEY FRENCH BLVD	NB	0.09
Lot 7	Grass patch	1	3	1 HARMONY ST	NORTH AMERICAN TRUST	0.1
Lot 8	Roped off parking lot	1	1	SS COVE ST	PP	0.08
Lot 9	Ruth Street Neighborhood Common with swings, slide, benches, picnic table. Park was established by the Cove Street neighborhood organization	1	4	NS RUTH ST	NB	0.15
Lot 10	Fenced-in parking lot and car sales lot for J.M. auto sales	1	1	SS COVE ST	PP	0.15

(*continued*)

Table 8.1 (continued)

Cove Street neighborhood	General notes	Active use (1 = yes, 0 = no, 2 = partially) (yes means that the area is actively being used for some use, including passive green space—the key is that it is being cared for and protected)	Type of use (1 = parking, 2 = extension of abutting use (non-parking), 3 = passive green space, 4 = park/gardens, 5 = other)	Address	Owner (PP = private property held by individual, NB = owned by New Bedford)	Acreage
Lot 11	Abandoned lot, pavement used for parking	2	1	NS RUTH ST	DAVID STREET LLC	0.47
Lot 12	Used as a driveway for an adjacent house	1	1	ES ASHLEY ST	NB	0.08
Lot 13	Parking lot for first base café	1	1	SS COVE ST	PERZENTZ RICHARD F "TRUSTEE"	0.08
Lot 14	Parking lot for boat/Jet Ski/car dealer	1	1	ES CLEVELAND ST	PP	0.36

Table 8.2 North End neighborhood

Cove Street neighborhood	General notes	Active use (1 = yes, 0 = no, 2 = partially) (yes means that the area is actively being used for some use, including passive green space—the key is that it is being cared for and protected)	Type of use (1 = parking, 2 = extension of abutting use (non-parking), 3 = passive green space, 4 = park/gardens, 5 = other)	Address	Owner (PP = private property held by individual, NB = owned by New Bedford)	Acreage
Lot 0	Used by the neighboring house with a no trespassing and no parking signs. Grass with some cement	1	2	90 BEETLE ST	PP	0.09
Lot 1	Overgrown area	0		369 COGGESHALL ST	PP	0.04
Lot 2	Parking lot for Rite Aid	1	1	1229 ACUSHNET AVE	PJC REALTY MA INC	0.28
Lot 3	Parking lot for empty building space	2	1	1183 ACUSHNET AVE	MEDEIROS ELIZABETH "TRUSTEE"	0.14

(continued)

162   8   URBAN ABSORPTION

Table 8.2 (continued)

Cove Street neighborhood	General notes	Active use (1 = yes, 0 = no, 2 = partially) (yes means that the area is actively being used for some use, including passive green space—the key is that it is being cared for and protected)	Type of use (1 = parking, 2 = extension of abutting use (non-parking), 3 = passive green space, 4 = park/gardens, 5 = other)	Address	Owner (PP = private property held by individual, NB = owned by New Bedford	Acreage
Lot 4	Parking lot for Rite Aid	1	1	WS ACUSHNET AVE	P J C REALTY CO INC	0.16
Lot 5	Parking lot which is fenced in, used by Auto recondition specialist	1	1	ES N FRONT ST	PP	0.06
Lot 6	Parking lot for a church, there is no separation in the parking lots which was indicated on the map	1	1	236 N FRONT ST	ROMAN CATHOLIC BISHOP OF	0.13
Lot 7	Parking lot not attached to anything	1	1	SS SAWYER ST	NB	0.05

8 URBAN ABSORPTION 163

Lot 8	Parking lot for royal café	1	1	225 SAWYER ST	CARVALHO ANTONIO C "TRUSTEE"	0.1
Lot 9	Parking lot for Pentecostal assembly	1	1	ES N FRONT ST	PP	0.1
Lot 10	Parking lot not attached to anything	1	1	SS SAWYER ST	NB	0.27
Lot 11	Parking lot not attached to anything	1	1	NS BEETLE ST	NB	0.21
Lot 12	"outdoor storage" area which seems to be used for storage, mostly trash from neighbors and New Bedford Iron Works	1	5	NS BEETLE ST	N B WIRE & IRON WORKS INC	0.1
Lot 13	Fenced-in, paved lot being used for plants and storage	1	5	WS HOWARD ST	COSTA HENRIQUE R "TRUSTEE"	0.12
Lot 14	Parking lot for Our Lady of Perpetual Hope Church	1	1	ES HOWARD ST	ROMAN CATHOLIC BISHOP OF	0.19
Lot 15	Parking lot for Our Lady of Perpetual Hope Church	1	1	247 N FRONT ST	ROMAN CATHOLIC BISHOP OF	0.12

(continued)

Table 8.2 (continued)

Cove Street neighborhood	General notes	Active use (1 = yes, 0 = no, 2 = partially) (yes means that the area is actively being used for some use, including passive green space—the key is that it is being cared for and protected)	Type of use (1 = parking, 2 = extension of abutting use (non-parking), 3 = passive green space, 4 = park/gardens, 5 = other)	Address	Owner (PP = private property held by individual, NB = owned by New Bedford)	Acreage
Lot 16	Parking lot for Our Lady of Perpetual Hope Church	1	1	70 HOWARD ST	ROMAN CATHOLIC BISHOP OF	0.16
Lot 17	Parking lot for a church, there is no separation in the parking lots which was indicated on the map	1	1	ES N FRONT ST	ROMAN CATHOLIC BISHOP OF	0.29
Lot 18	Parking lot for construction firm next door	1	1	394 N FRONT ST	LUROB REALTY CORP	0.06
Lot 19	Parking lot for Belleville Auto	1	1	319 BELLEVILLE AVE	DEMELO LIBERIO "TRUSTEE"	0.14
Lot 20	Parking lot for visitors to the North End	1	1	ES ACUSHNET AVE	NB	0.15

Lot 21	Parking lot for visitors to the North End	1	1	ES ACUSHNET AVE	COCHRANE JAMES R JR	0.1
Lot 22	Rocky area covered in shrubbery, there is sign indicating that the vacant lot is part of the Vacant Lot Restorative Initiative by the city of New Bedford	0	—	ES ACUSHNET AVE	NB	0.08
Lot 23	Parking lot for Belleville Auto	1	1	WS BELLEVILLE AVE	NB	0.11

166   8 URBAN ABSORPTION

Table 8.3 South Central neighborhood

Cove Street neighborhood	General notes	Active use (1 = yes, 0 = no, 2 = partially) (yes means that the area is actively being used for some use, including passive green space—the key is that it is being cared for and protected)	Type of use (1 = parking, 2 = extension of abutting use (non-parking), 3 = passive green space, 4 = park/gardens, 5 = other)	Address	Owner (PP = private property held by individual, NB = owned by New Bedford)	Acreage
Lot 0	Fenced-in parking lot for fire department personnel only	1	1	137 PURCHASE ST	NB	0.16
Lot 1	Parking lot possibly for adjacent church	1	1	191 PURCHASE ST	ROMAN CATHOLIC BISHOP OF	0.21
Lot 2	Parking lot for Benji's Jewelry	1	1	224 COUNTY ST	ROMAN CATHOLIC BISHOP OF	0.12
Lot 3	Parking lot for Benji's Jewelry	1	1	NS ROCKLAND ST	ROMAN CATHOLIC BISHOP OF	0.06
Lot 4	Overgrown area which is fenced in. What looks like an old garden box. Lot is connected to an open area in back of country street	0	–	WS S SECOND ST	PP	0.09

8 URBAN ABSORPTION 167

Lot 5	Paved lot	0	—	88 ACUSHNET AVE	PP	0.1
Lot 6	Overgrown area which is fenced in. What looks like an old garden box. Lot is connected to an open area in back of country street	0	—	WS S SECOND ST	PP	0.28
Lot 7	Cape Verdean American Veterans Memorial Square, grass area with flags	1	4	ES COUNTY ST	NB	0.4
Lot 8	Sandy lot which neighbors used for cars and a pop-up van	1	1	WS ACUSHNET AVE	NB	0.09
Lot 9	Fenced-off overgrown area	0	—	145 ACUSHNET AVE	NB	0.08
Lot 10	Overgrown area with shrubbery, brambles and thickets	0	—	WS ACUSHNET AVE	CRUZ DEVELOPMENT CORPORATION	0.17
Lot 11	Open, grassy area	1	3	113 GRINNELL ST	PP	0.08
Lot 12	Open, grassy area	1	3	111 GRINNELL ST	PP	0.08
Lot 13	Grassy area with bushes, empty	1	3	WS ACUSHNET AVE	PP	0.13
Lot 14	Parking lot not connected to any building	1	1	SS RUSSELL ST	INTERNATIONAL CHURCH	0.18
Lot 15	Parking lot dedicated to Antonio Ramos	1	1	WS PLEASANT ST	INTERNATIONAL CHURCH	0.41

(*continued*)

Table 8.3 (continued)

Cove Street neighborhood	General notes	Active use (1 = yes, 0 = no, 2 = partially) (yes means that the area is actively being used for some use, including passive green space—the key is that it is being cared for and protected)	Type of use (1 = parking, 2 = extension of abutting use (non-parking), 3 = passive green space, 4 = park/gardens, 5 = other)	Address	Owner (PP = private property held by individual, NB = owned by New Bedford)	Acreage
Lot 16	School bus yard	1	5	435 PURCHASE ST	PP	0.39
Lot 17	Fenced-in grassy area seemingly connected to adjacent house with a hammock and stone bench	1	2	ES PLEASANT ST	PP	0.09
Lot 18	Our Lady of Assumption parking lot	1	1	39 S SIXTH ST	ROMAN CATHOLIC BISHOPS OF	0.24
Lot 19	Paved church parking lot	1	1	97 S SIXTH ST	ST JOHN BAPTIST CHURCH	0.06
Lot 20	Paved church parking lot	1	1	41 WING ST	ST JOHN THE BAPTIST OF NB	0.06
Lot 21	Serenity Garden on 1/3 of the lot, the rest was open grass	1	4	ES S SIXTH ST	NB	1.75

Lot 22	Paved, fenced-in area with a white building	0	—	WS PURCHASE ST	NB	1.69
Lot 23	Paved, fenced in, overgrown area with a sign saying "future site of the Wilder-Bailey Memorial Community Center"	0	—	491 PURCHASE ST	PORTUGUESE CHURCH OF THE	0.14
Lot 24	Parking lot not connected to any building	1	1	ES S SIXTH ST	PP	0.1
Lot 25	Parking lot for Albert Cordio Accountin	1	1	382 COUNTY ST	PP	0.04
Lot 26	Basketball courts and a park built in 1939. Dedicated to Joseph Monte who was a POW	1	4	SS CANNON ST	NB	0.73
Lot 27	Playground Park with a jungle gym and benches. Dedicated to Kenneth L Pires. "Thanks to the generous and loving spirit of the community"	1	4	WS ACUSHNET AVE	NB	0.14

(continued)

Table 8.3 (continued)

Cove Street neighborhood	General notes	Active use (1 = yes, 0 = no, 2 = partially) (yes means that the area is actively being used for some use, including passive green space—the key is that it is being cared for and protected)	Type of use (1 = parking, 2 = extension of abutting use (non-parking), 3 = passive green space, 4 = park/gardens, 5 = other)	Address	Owner (PP = private property held by individual, NB = owned by New Bedford	Acreage
Lot 28	Playground Park with a jungle gym and benches. Dedicated to Kenneth L Pires. "Thanks to the generous and loving spirit of the community"	1	4	WS ACUSHNET AVE	NB	0.22
Lot 29	Parking lot for an abandoned building and the surrounding houses	1	1	181 ACUSHNET AVE	FAMILIA FAMILY LLC	0.4
Lot 30	Fenced-off overgrown area	0		WS ACUSHNET AVE	PP	0.19

Lot 31	Overgrown open area with two garden boxes. Religious candles and ribbons on trees	2	5	215 ACUSHNET AVE	PP	0.12
Lot 32	Lot with mud and asphalt	0	—	NS PURCHASE ST	PP	0.07
Lot 33	Parking lot for Veteran Association Hall	1	1	WS PURCHASE ST	PP	0.08
Lot 34	Empty grass lot next door to Headstart	1	3	366 PLEASANT ST	NB	0.05
Lot 35	Empty grass lot next door to Headstart	1	3	SS WALNUT ST	NB	0.06

Table 8.4 Lot summary

Neighborhood	Total # of lots	Lots where a structure was lost		Lots partially reused[a]		Lots fully reused[a]	
		#	%	#	%	#	%
South Central	479	36	7.5%	27	75.0%	26	72.2%
Cove Street	467	15	3.2%	13	86.7%	10	66.7%
North End	491	24	4.9%	22	91.7%	21	87.5%

[a]Among lots where a structure was lost

Table 8.5 Lot uses

Type of use (1 = Parking, 2 = Extension of abutting use [non-parking], 3 = Passive green space, 4 = Park/gardens, 5 = Other)	
New uses for lots	
Parking	40
Extension of abutting use (non-parking)	2
Passive green space	8
Park/Garden	8
Other	4
Outdoor storage	
School bus yard	
Religious sanctuary	
	$n = 62$

has witnessed a remarkable 27 of its 36 lots reused or reabsorbed at least partially, with 26 being fully reused.

It is hard to ignore the dominance of parking as a new use in the three neighborhoods, representing 40 of the 60 lots that were either partially or fully reused. Passive green space ($n = 8$) and formal parks or gardens ($n = 8$) were the next most common uses, followed by non-parking abutter extensions and several "other" uses including outdoor storage and a religious sanctuary (Table 8.5).

The photographic evidence supports these results, with scores of examples of lots being converted to parking, gardens, parks, or side lots (see Figs. 8.5, 8.6, 8.7, 8.8, 8.9, 8.10, 8.11, 8.12, 8.13, and 8.14). A quick tour through South Central helps tell this urban absorption story.

8 URBAN ABSORPTION   173

Fig. 8.5 South Central vacant lot (photo credit: Erin Kizer)

Walking north on Second Street, with the sound of cars whizzing along Route 18 to the right, the regular pattern of triple-deckers along the left side of the street is interrupted—midblock—by two open parcel (lots 4 and 6). Lot 4 is a mere 0.09 of an acre and is owned by a private property owner (according to the city of New Bedford Assessor's Office). Lot 6 includes a Second Street lot, but is also attached from the back of the lot to another lot on Acushnet Avenue, and is also owned by a private owner and comprises 0.3 acres. Both Lots 4 and 6 were improved by structures along Second Street at the time of the 1975 Sanborn maps. For that back lot portion of Lot 6 along Acushnet Avenue, the last map showing a structure there was from 1936. Both lots appear to fit the expected condition of vacant lots in shrinking cities: overgrown, surrounded by a barbed wire fence, and uncared for (see Fig. 8.5). I classified these two lots as such, indicating that the land is not in an active use state. A closer look reveals something more compelling—evidence of a roughly 30 feet by 30 feet raised garden bed (see Fig. 8.6). That too

Fig. 8.6 South Central vacant lot (photo credit: Erin Kizer)

is in disrepair but portends the kind of absorption seen elsewhere in the neighborhood.

Two blocks north along Acushnet Avenue, we come upon Lot 8, halfway between Grinnell Street and Wing Street. City Assessor's records indicate that the parcel is currently owned by the city of New Bedford, and a look at past Sanborn maps show that a structure was present in 1975. The 0.9 acre lot is covered with sand and shows signs of being cared for (see Fig. 8.7). When we visited, a pop-up trailer and private automobile were parked there.

Still going further along Acushnet another block and making a left onto Bedford Street, one block down we come to Lot 16. I have to go back to 1924 Sanborn maps to see evidence of a structure there. Today, the 0.4 acre lot is owned by a private party and is used as a school bus parking yard (see Fig. 8.8).

This brief tour of South Central illustrates some of the key trends presented earlier: while not all, a vast majority of lots where structures were removed have been reabsorbed into the city's urban fabric. Through pri-

8 URBAN ABSORPTION 175

Fig. 8.7 South Central vacant lot (photo credit: Erin Kizer)

marily parking uses, but other uses, as well, the typical vacant lot has been repurposed to help contribute to neighborhood well-being.

What remains unclear is the precise process by which this occurs. While I did interview dozens of New Bedford residents and asked them about how the process occurred, it turns out that much of the documented absorption has occurred over decades, and residents I interviewed had little if any direct knowledge of how existing uses came to be. The exceptions to this are the city parks that have been built in recent years.

Relying on interviews I conducted with long-time residents, local officials, legal records, and even a news story in the *Standard-Times*, I was able to piece together one such story of absorption on Cove Street. Lot 9 is located on the North side of Ruth Street, at the intersection with McGurk Street. The lot was improved by two triple-decker residential structures, last appearing in Sanborn maps in 1975. As property values continued to fall in the 1970s and 1980s, each structure received fewer and fewer investments from its owners, and each continued to fall into disrepair. Fire partially consumed each and with a

Fig. 8.8 South Central bus lot (photo credit: Erin Kizer)

strong neighborhood push, city government funds were spent demolishing each structure in the 1980s.

In 1997, a non-profit organization, Community Action for Better Housing, Inc. purchased the parcel for $110,000. The next year, the non-profit sold the lot to the city on the condition that the parcel be used for a park. In 1999, the park was dedicated as the Ruth Street Neighborhood Common, made possible by the Cove Street Neighborhood Association with support from Catholic Social Services (Hartnett 2008) (see Fig. 8.9). Here, neighborhood activism was the key ingredient, with political pressure applied on the mayor and city councilmen allowed for a vacant lot to be absorbed into the neighborhood as an asset.

Because legal research helped uncover some of the details and specifics of the history of the Ruth Street park, I next undertook a thorough review of the legal histories of all formerly improved lots in Cove Street in the hopes of uncovering other patterns and trends. The review meant going to the Bristol County Registry of Deeds to trace property transfers back three owners. This kind of title research involved identifying the book and

Fig. 8.9 Cove Street garden (photo credit: Erin Kizer)

page numbers of current lots, and then following that record back to the prior sale (another book and page) and then again, and again.

The results of the title search were interesting but shed little light on the absorption process. In doing this research, I had a couple working hypotheses that the following might correlate with absorption patterns: (1) recorded demolition liens, and (2) recorded tax liens or city foreclosures. For the small sample of properties I examined in Cove Street, none of these hypotheses turned out to bear out much evidence.

Only two of the parcels had a demolition lien attached to the property records, one (lot 0) was recorded in 1993 and the other (lot 7) was recorded in 1992 (see Table 8.6). Today, lot 0 is one of the very few uncared for sites in Cove Street, featuring overgrown bushes and brambles, and owned by a private party (see Fig. 8.10). Lot 7 is a slightly different story. Now owned by the city of New Bedford, the lot is a well-groomed grassy patch, with a clearly articulated pathway laid diagonally across the rectangular parcel (see Fig. 8.11). Both sites were legally demolished,

Fig. 8.10 Cove Street vacant lot (photo credit: Erin Kizer)

but each contributes very differently to the quality of the Cove Street neighborhood.

Turning to the next possible relationship, I looked at those parcels in Cove Street which had tax liens placed against them or were foreclosed by the city. A total of nine had a tax lien placed on them during the period I reviewed and five of those were eventually foreclosed by the city (see Table 8.6). All of those city foreclosures occurred between 1996 and 2007, and all but one remain today in city ownership. The single exception appears to be an example of the application of the little used side-lot abutters program, which provides an easy mechanism for the city to convey at little cost its real property interest in land to an abutter for the purposes of lot expansion. This is what seems to have happened to Lot 12 on Ashley Street. The parcel was improved by a structure as recently as 1975 (based on the Sanborn maps) and was sold several times from 1979 until 1996 from one private party to another. Then, in 1996, due to failure to pay taxes the city foreclosed on the property and held it until the lot

Fig. 8.11 Cove Street vacant lot (photo credit: Erin Kizer)

was conveyed from the city to a private party in 2010 for $1899. As indicated in Fig. 6.viii, the parcel is actively used as a driveway for an abutting private home. The new owner installed a chain link fence with a sliding driveway door, crushed stones along the driveway, and arranged for professional quality landscaping around the remainder of the lot.

For the four lots on Cove Street that were foreclosed by the city and remain in city ownership, one is overgrown with bushes, but the other three are being cared for and maintained. With such a small sample, it's hard to establish any strong relationships here, but what seems clear is that both city-owned and privately owned lots are being reused effectively—with the tax lien and foreclosure process appearing to have very little weight in determining current uses.

With the title evidence, mapping results, interviews, and field observations taken all together, they help to elucidate the process of urban absorption in New Bedford. A real and tangible change has happened in the three study neighborhoods. They lost structures yet instead of

Fig. 8.12 South Central garden (photo credit: Erin Kizer)

being burdened by the conventional vacant lot syndrome, these neighborhoods are thriving. The explanation lies in how individual lots have been reused and repurposed by private property owners and, in some cases, city action. This reuse and repurposing has not followed any kind of grand plan or vision but has largely been implemented based on pragmatic considerations.

A group of neighbors needed additional space for their community garden, so they spent a weekend and turned a trash strewn lot into a communal space (see Fig. 8.12). An owner of a triple-decker apartment building wanted to provide off-street parking for his tenants (see Fig. 8.13), and an immigrant from the Azores wanted a place to grow grapes and expand her garden (see Fig. 8.14).

But the rate and pattern of urban absorption varied across the three neighborhoods. A question emerges as to whether the differences between the neighborhoods are meaningful. The methods I employed make such an assessment difficult. However, a possible explanation is that Cove

Fig. 8.13 South Central parking lot (photo credit: Erin Kizer)

Street is simply a newer neighborhood, with newer and higher quality housing stock than Bullard and South Central. As such, depopulation had a more modest impact (during this period from 1924 through 2010) on the physical form of the neighborhood.

Whatever the reason for a differential rate of absorption, the fact is that each neighborhood did manage to successfully absorb a vast majority of their vacant lots. And while the timing and legal circumstances of demolitions, tax liens, and city government foreclosures may have played a part, they do not appear to have had a determinative role in the absorption process.

Instead, it seems from this analysis that the city government was largely absent from helping these three neighborhoods manage their depopulation. Research reported earlier in the book tells a different story, but together these pieces weave together a tale of a moderately active but largely ineffective local policy and planning operation. The effects of city intervention on urban absorption was around code enforcement, the filing

Fig. 8.14 South Central garden

of tax liens (as well as the threat of doing so), and the filing of demolition liens. The city's intervention did not impact on charting new uses for vacant lots, except for the very few public parks and handful of abutter lots the city helped create. Instead, it was the actions of hundreds of individuals, investors, and neighbors who took matters into their own hands and identified a new use that made sense for them—one that they could help to protect and maintain, and ultimately one where they could contribute to creating stability and high quality of life in their neighborhood. In the face of decades of a mix of decline and growth, the physical legacy of change can be seen through this urban absorption model—a window of sorts to view change in an ordinary city.

Table 8.6 Summary of results—Cove Street title searches

Lot number/ reference number	Address	Tax liens	City of NB foreclosure	Demolish date	Sale lien	Sale date	Sale date	Ref/last owner before transfer/ sale date/$	Last sale price	Current owner (PP = private property held by individual, NB = owned by new Bedford)/date of acquisition	Property notes	Active use (1 = yes, 0 = no, 2 = partially)	Type of use	Acreage
14 74/ Lot 0	(SS MOTT ST) 82 MOTT ST	1991, 1995		1993		1976	1983	1988	$205,000	PP	Overgrown with bushes/brambles. No connection to other buildings	0		0.098
14 75/ Lot 1	78 MOTT ST	1995, 1997	1997			1936 1980	N/A	1983	$0	NB	Overgrown with bushes/brambles. No connection to other buildings	0		0.098
15,143/ Lot 2	(NS Ruth St) 85, 87, 89 RUTH ST	2006	2007			1954 1970	1978	1984	$0	NB	Park, trees with a fence lining the area, benches, Christmas lights on central tree	1	4	0.07

(continued)

Table 8.6 (continued)

Lot number/ reference number	Address	Tax liens	City of NB foreclosure	Demolish date	Sale lien date	Sale date	Sale date	Ref/last owner before transfer/ sale date/$	Last sale price	Current owner (PP = private property held by individual, NB = owned by new Bedford)/date of acquisition	Property notes	Active use (1 = yes, 0 = no, 2 = partially)	Type of use	Acreage
15,148/ Lot 3	99 RUTH ST	2006	2007		1981	1982	1985	1987	$0	NB	Park, trees with a fence lining the area, benches, Christmas lights on central tree	1	4	0.09
15,199/ Lot 4	(NS BROCK AVE) 982–986 BROCK AVE				1971	1977	1978	1984	$185,000	PP	Fenced-in grass lot, does not seem to be used for anything	2	3	0.13
15 42/ Lot 5	28/SE W RODNEY FRENCH BLVD				1942	1942	New Bedford Wholesale Tire for $10,600. 1972	1980	$100	PP	Parking lot for car repair shop	1	1	0.06

15 44/ Lot 6	48 (50) W RODNEY FRENCH BLVD	1992	1997		1944 1977 1984	1985	$100	NB	Fenced-in grass lot, does not seem to be used for anything	2	3	0.09
15 45/ Lot 7	(WS Harmony St) 1 HARMONY ST	1990		1992	1975 1984 1988	1988	$210,000	NB	Grass patch	1	3	0.1
15 62/ Lot 8	SS COVE ST				1960 Auto Parts 1972	Church of First Born 1986	2011	$100	PP	Roped off parking lot	1	1	0.08
15 77/ Lot 9	(McGurk St) NS RUTH ST (133 William St)				1974; 1988 1983; 1985	1990	Community Action for Better, Housing, Inc, 1997	$1	NB	Ruth Street Neighborhood Common	1	4	0.15
15 89/ Lot 10	SS COVE ST (82 & 70-78 Cove St)	1981		1978	1977 1981	Church of First Born 1987	2002	$100	PP	Fenced-in parking lot and car sales lot for J.M. auto sales	1	1	0.15
16,103/ Lot 11	NS RUTH ST	1981			1962; 1980 1979; 1980		2001	$1,200,000	PP	Abandoned lot, pavement used for parking	2	1	0.47
16,118/ Lot 12	ES ASHLEY ST	1996	1996		1979; 1988 1986	1996	2010	$1899	PP	Used as a driveway for an adjacent house	1	1	0.08

(continued)

Table 8.6 (continued)

Lot number/ reference number	Address	Tax liens	City of NB foreclosure	Demolish lien	Sale date	Sale date	Sale date	Ref/last owner before transfer/ sale date/$	Last sale price	Current owner (PP = private property held by individual, NB = owned by new Bedford)/date of acquisition	Property notes	Active use (1 = yes, 0 = no, 2 = partially)	Type of use	Acreage
16 2/ Lot 13	SS COVE ST				1937	1976	1989	2002	$277,000	PP	Parking lot for first base café	1	1	0.08
16 62/ Lot 14	ES CLEVELAND ST					1883	1928	2008	$105,000	PP	Parking lot for boat/Jet Ski/ car dealer	1	1	0.36

Notes

1. The Assessor's Office also maintains records as to whether a parcel is improved by a structure and whether that structure is in a derelict condition.
2. This may have been due to a number of possible factors, including that lots can be merged.
3. See Chaps. 2 and 3.
4. In the abandoned property research literature, the concept of active use is important as a means by which vacant lots are protected and maintained, see Chap. 2. Here, active use is defined as any use which requires a human presence on at least a weekly basis to care for the parcel. This can go far in preventing and discouraging dumping and other illegal activities, as well as to send a more inviting message to prospective investors.

Bibliography

Hartnett, Ken. 2008. A Tale of Two Parks in the City's South End. *Standard-Times*, August 24.

CHAPTER 9

Conclusion

This is not just a book about New Bedford—instead, it is an effort to understand how a city manages change. Throughout the preceding chapters, I have begun to offer evidence about how that happened in one post-industrial port city in New England. Part of what I hoped to uncover was an answer to the question: Who manages change in cities anyhow? That responsibility rests with a lot of people and a lot of organizations, both public and private. For New Bedford, there were substantial efforts by city officials during the urban renewal era to de-densify the city. In my review of contemporary city action, there appears to have been some hybrid version of a smart-shrinkage and smart-growth policy in place to better promote the reuse of vacant land and to come to terms with ongoing depopulation, while also addressing the issues surrounding new population and development. Those policies were embedded within a broader government strategy to increase employment and drive growth. But, nevertheless, city planning activities did partially attempt to manage decline in certain areas.

As the interviews, mapping analysis, and follow-up field observations confirmed, the city has effectively right-sized its built form to match a smaller population. What I cannot assert here is the existence of a clear causal link between city action and today's conditions. In some areas, the city's policies have proven to be abject failures. In others, the city government seems to have been successful. What matters is that New

Bedford—and by that, I mean city officials, community leaders, business interests, and residents—has *managed* demographic change through a mix of diverse policies strategies, including smart shrinkage and smart growth.

But questions remain about whether the city's actions have resulted in positive outcomes for the people of New Bedford. Few residents I interviewed had much to say that was positive about the city, echoing the findings from Rory Nugent's (2009) *Down at the Docks*. Most were just frustrated by the decreasing economic standing of residents in their neighborhoods; in other words, they were sick of their middle-income neighborhoods being turned into poor neighborhoods. The lower-income residents I interviewed told a different, but complementary, story. They were frustrated by quality of life issues in their neighborhoods, calling for more police protection.

But together, these two populations of residents agreed that nobody wanted New Bedford to become a poorer city than it is. Nobody wanted home prices or rents to fall further, which is a typical response to further economic and population decline. To prevent further destabilization, the people I spoke to during this research saw real opportunity to manage decline through smart shrinkage, though support was hardly universal.

With people so unhappy, it may be a bit odd to suggest that the city managed its decline well. I proffer here that such rightsizing was rarely intentional and certainly not part of a grand, well-thought-out plan. Instead, the rightsizing process appears to have been a natural response by individuals, businesses, and government agencies to a very bad condition: economic and population decline. What resulted in New Bedford, and what I observed in the city, is hardly ideal. But the adaptive and resilient character of the city is certainly noteworthy. I began this book by emphatically stating that New Bedford is a great city. Certainly that is a subjective judgment, but the evidence presented here shows that despite a regular record of job loss and fairly steady stream of population loss, the physical adjustment of the built environment (both purposeful and not) has worked to help make the city smaller. A smaller city, maybe worse in some ways, but not as bad as it could have been if hundreds of demolished homes had never been reused or absorbed back into the urban fabric.

In order to assess in a philosophical sense, whether the changes that occurred in New Bedford were good, just, and right, it is useful to return to the five normative propositions I introduced in Chap. 3.

1. Smart shrinkage and growth planning processes must include and explicitly recognize multiple voices.
   It is clear from the historical review of city policies during the urban renewal era (and subsequent ones), that this proposition was not fully realized. Practically none of the city's policies were labeled as "smart" but many policies functioned nevertheless according to smart growth or smart shrinkage policies, as illustrated in the report analyses. Some of those more recent planning efforts have been more effective in recognizing multiple voices and have included broad citizen outreach.
   Looking forward, it is crucial that cities learn from the New Bedford experience and do more than outreach, so that they can go further to engage multiple voices. My own Open Neighborhood Project offers important lessons on how to tap into high-tech tools, alongside other more conventional approaches to bring multiple voices into deliberation.
2. Smart shrinkage and growth planning processes should be political and deliberative in nature.
   The city's mid-twentieth-century experiences of slum clearance were largely grounded in modernism and resulted in the kinds of "mistakes" planners love to vilify. But today's planning in New Bedford has been very much bottom-up and explicitly political. Today's postmodern planning practice values quality of life and the lived experiences of residents, rather than a singular objective aim of economic growth.
3. Smart shrinkage and growth planners should be cognizant of differential communication techniques and should provide information that enables citizens to recognize and challenge power imbalances and structures of domination.
4. Smart shrinkage and growth planning processes must be transparent and value different types and sources of information.
   For these two propositions, the research in this book has shown a failure on the part of the city of New Bedford to practice a just form of smart shrinkage or smart growth. The labeling of city reports as "growth" plans during periods of decline belies the demographic reality under which the city is operating. In Chap. 6, I demonstrated the lack of substantial engagement by the city with the realities of depopulation, thereby robbing citizens and other non-governmental

bodies of the discursive space to debate and guide future city action around depopulation. The city can do more to follow the guidance offered in this normative proposition by sharing key demographic information and analysis directly with citizens and engaging in a conversation around the choices the city faces in the future.

5. Smart shrinkage and growth planning processes should be regional in scope, but local in control and implementation.
The ongoing South Coast planning effort in the Greater New Bedford region aims to extend commuter rail from Boston to New Bedford. Several key city plans and scores of interviews touched on this broader regional context for New Bedford's future demographic change. Nevertheless, more needs to be done by the city to explore the kinds of partnerships available to prepare the city for a role in the region, both with the rail extension and without it. Much planning has been invested into the rail extension, but the city ought to consider the possibility of future depopulation (with or without the rail). While the South Coast region has exploded in population in recent decades, regional planning has borne little impact on how the city manages decline.

As New Bedford continues to prepare for an unknown future, this proposition reminds the city's planners of the need to maintain a regional viewpoint.

Limitations and Recommendations for Future Research

With any research endeavor, I needed to make key decisions about how to focus the inquiry to fit into reasonable amounts of time and resources. In doing so, there are always trade-offs between depth and breadth, between details and big pictures, and between personal intimacy and distant observer status. This research could have gone further into the history of New Bedford, studying the personal lives of those impacted by the city's initial decline or those who were displaced by urban renewal. Future research ought to explore those perspectives and attempt to uncover the meaning that people living in the early stages of decline make of the changes they face.

Likewise, the decision to focus in on the three study neighborhoods limited the research and excluded the trajectories and experiences of other parts of the city. While somewhat representative, the three neighborhoods are distinct, and future research could take a broader view and collect statistics and interview a broader set of stakeholders throughout the city's neighborhoods to paint a more complete picture of the city's changes.

Finally, the urban absorption mapping and analysis suffered from several methodological weaknesses that could be improved upon in future research. The time-series Sanborn fire insurance maps could be measured more quantitatively, bringing in elaborate GIS mapping and spatial analysis. Future research might explore the spatial correlations between vacancy, reuse, and neighborhood quality indicators (like crime, teenage pregnancy rates, and literacy attainment). In that same sense, very little evidence is available to fairly measure residents' overall sense of happiness, and surveys could be administered to track those attitudes over time to assess what the effect of city policies have been for New Bedford.

Policy Recommendations

There are a number of key policy implications of the research from this book. First, the work presented here shows that city planning can be effective in expanding the urban absorption process that appears to be largely driven by private market actors. Whether through adopt-a-lot programs, community gardens initiatives, or the construction of city parks, there is a documented role for local governments to support urban absorption, and the evidence reviewed in this research suggests that city government can do more. Local conditions must be studied in other cities and through the repetition of the mapping, direct observation, and interview methods used here; other cities can gain a handle on how they too may be able to support urban absorption processes.

I began this book by introducing the power of protection and maintenance to help cities manage vacant and abandoned properties. The research on New Bedford confirms that value of cities, states, and the federal government continuing to invest heavily in the protection and maintenance of vacant and abandoned properties. That means major code enforcement initiatives and city energies devoted to demolition of derelict structures and supporting the programming of new uses for that land.

On a related note, it is critical that state and federal authorities remain vigilant about how cities building stock may exceed their populations in such a way that contributes to vacancy and abandonment. That means that states and the federal government should monitor these patterns of disequilibrium and tie funding formulas for demolition to such imbalances. For example, if a city's population falls over time and its building stock remains steady, that should trigger public support for demolition and reuse planning. Unfortunately, much state and federal funding for cities is tied to population levels and as those levels dip, so does the money. Just the opposite is needed to address the challenges of shrinking cities.

For a city as historic as New Bedford, lessons about preservation abound from this study. Demolishing every old building in the city would literally eradicate the city's historic urban fabric. But leaving derelict structures to rot causes serious problems, as well. A compromise solution is needed, again grounded in local conditions, for cities attempting to balance preservationist goals with broad quality of life goals for residents. I recommend that other cities follow New Bedford's example by designating key zones as historic districts (like the National Park in Downtown) but allowing residential neighborhoods to more freely adjust to falling population levels through active demolition and repurposing.

To Shrink a City?

> The study of depopulation is essentially the study of failure. The primary definition of a city, its very reason for existence, is its population, and those cities that fail to hold or increase their populations are in a very real way failures as cities. (Phillipps 2008)

The historian Jeremy Phillipps is wrong: depopulation does not equal failure. I began this book by declaring that a city on the bottom of all Massachusetts rankings of city performance is actually a wonderful place. In the years that I have been studying the city, I have grown increasingly fond of how well it has managed both its growth and its decline, how beautiful its waterfront is, how bustling its businesses are, and how hardy its people are.

In fact, the primary purpose of a city is not to maintain its population. Populations rise and fall. People come and go. Jeremy Phillips requires us to consider a much harder question—if the purpose of a city is not to maintain its population, then what is its purpose? As the normative propositions above suggest, the purpose of the city is to be just and to offer a high quality of life to those residents who do not leave.

Here, implications for other comparable cities become clear. Cities invest heavily in maintaining their populations, recruiting new industry, and trying to grow. But the New Bedford case illustrates that another path exists. Cities do not need to be bound by the judgments of those who deride them as failures, instead opportunities exist for ordinary cities to learn from the lessons presented herein and manage demographic change. The ideas of smart shrinkage and smart growth are not abstract or inaccessible. They are, above all, pragmatic solutions to a pragmatic problem: how to manage change for a city outside the limelight—not some kind of urban catastrophe like Detroit, or a wunderkind city like San Francisco, but for an ordinary city like New Bedford.

Bibliography

Nugent, Rory. 2009. *Down at the Docks*. New York, NY: Pantheon.
Phillipps, Jeremy. 2008. Living on Past Glories and Future Dreams the Effects of Depopulation on Early Modern Urban Development in the Former Castle Town of Kanazawa. *European Journal of East Asian Studies* 7 (2): 263–294.

Appendix A

Comparing New Bedford with other US cities helps to illustrate why it makes an ideal subject for a book about ordinary cities. Using US Census data, I compiled demographic data for all US cities which had a population of between 75,000 and 125,000 in 1970 ($n = 144$). These medium-sized cities are in every region of the USA and spread across 35 states (see Fig. A.1). California is the host to most of these cities, with 28 of them, but otherwise they tend to be clustered in the Northeast (25%) and Midwest (24%).

In 1970, New Bedford had a population of 101,759, where this group of cities averaged 101,690. In the decades that followed, 17 lost more than 20% of their population and 57 grew by more than 20% (by 2010). That meant that half the cities stayed roughly the same over 40 years, either growing or declining by not more than 0.5% per year, on average.

New Bedford fits that profile precisely; the city experienced a net decline in population of 6.6% but essentially maintained level population for four decades (see Table 1.1 for details of New Bedford's population change).

The city's historic pattern of depopulation did show up in Census data on vacancy, where in 2010, New Bedford, 9.7% of the city's housing units were classified as "other" vacant—a designation that connotes an abandoned building status. Similarly, the mean other vacancy rate in the 144 cities was 8.8%. Overall vacancy also tracked closely between

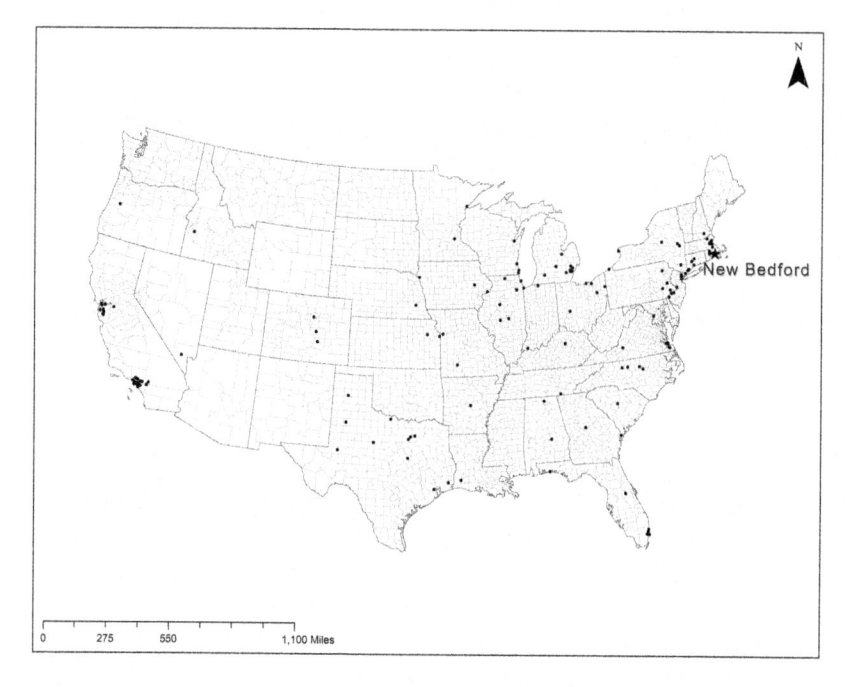

Fig. A.1 Map of cities included in typicality analysis

New Bedford and the 144 cities, with 25.6% in New Bedford and 27% samplewide.

Across race, ethnicity, and age, New Bedford also represents a typical city of its size: New Bedford's Black population was lower, 6.4%, than the full sample, 16.7%, but its Hispanic population was quite close to the full group of cities, 18% compared with 21%. For the 144 cities, those under age comprise 23.2% of the population, where those over 65 years are 12.30%; in New Bedford the percent under 18 is exactly the same as the sample, where the older demographic was very close, 14.6%.

Using conventional methods of central tendency, the city of New Bedford is typical of cities of its size in the USA, across many dimensions of size, population change, vacancy, ethnicity, and age.

To probe this question of "ordinariness" a bit more, I loaded all of the above variables for both 1970 and 2010 into the SAS statistical software package. SAS Proc RobustReg was used to obtain both classical Mahalanobis distance measure and a robust version.

APPENDIX A   199

Treating all of the 144 cities as a single cloud of data, I asked how far each city was from the center of the multivariate cloud of data points while simultaneously accounting for the cloud scatter. Both a multivariate mean and a robust version of the multivariate mean (accounting for outliers) were computed. This approach also generates both a classical covariance matrix and a robust version from which Mahalanobis distance measures are produced.

For both 1970 and 2010, I included population, number of households, number of housing units, mean income, rental rate, home ownership rate, vacancy rate, "other" vacancy rate, poverty rate, unemployment rate, land area, percent female, percent male, percent white, percent African-American, percent Hispanic, and percent foreign-born (details about each variable are in Table A.1 below).

Table A.1 Variables used in typicality analysis

Variable	Definition	Census table
1970POP	Total population	T1 Total Population
1970HH	Total households	T14 Total Occupied Households
1970HU	Total housing units	T107 Housing Units
1970%OHU	% Occupied housing units	T109 Occupancy Status
1970RENT	Tenure (% Rent) of OHU	T108 Tenure
1970OWN	Tenure (% Owned) of OHU	T108 Tenure
1970VAC	% Vacant housing units of Total	T109 Occupancy Status
	% Vacant Housing Units (other)	T111. Vacant Housing Units by Type of
1970VAC2	Total vacant year-round housing units	Vacancy for Year-Round Housing Units
1970MEAN	Mean household income	T85 Average Family Income
		T98 Poverty Status of Unrelated Individuals
1970POV	% People of all ages in poverty	by Age
1970UNEM	% Unemployed of 16+ population in civilian labor force	T56 Unemployment Rate
1970LA	Land area in square miles	T3 Land Area (Sq. mile)
1970PSM	Persons per square mile	T2 Population Density (Per sq. mile)
1970FEM	% Female	T4 Sex
1970MALE	% Male	T4 Sex
1970WHITE	% White (a)	T12 Race
1970AFR	% African-American (a)	T12 Race
1970HIS	% Hispanic or Latino of any race (b)	T13 Spanish Origin
1970FOR	% Foreign born	T132 Nativity by Citizenship Status

(*continued*)

Table A.1 (continued)

Variable	Definition	Census table
1970 < 18	% < Age 18	T8 Age (Short Version)
1970 > 64	% > Age 64	T8 Age (Short Version)
1980POP	Total population	T1
1980HH	Total households	T19 Households by Household Type
1980HU	Total housing units	
1980%OHU	% Occupied housing units	T82 Occupancy Status
1980RENT	Tenure (% Rent) of OHU	T81 Tenure
1980OWN	Tenure (% Owned) of OHU	T81 Tenure
1980VAC	% Vacant housing units of Total % Vacant Housing Units (other)	T82 Occupancy Status
1980VAC2	Total vacant year-round housing units	T83 Vacancy Status
1980MED	Median household income in 1979 Dollars	T53 Median Household Income
1980POV	% People of all ages in poverty	T100 Poverty Status in 1971 (short version)
1980UNEM	% Unemployed of 16+ population in civilian labor force	T40 Unemployment Rate for Civilian Population
1980LA	Land area in square miles	
1980PSM	Persons per square mile	
1980FEM	% Female	T3 Sex
1980MALE	% Male	T3 Sex
1980WHITE	% White (a)	T12 Race
1980AFR	% African-American (a)	T12 Race
1980HIS	% Hispanic or Latino of any race (b)	T13 Race by Spanish Origin Status
1980FOR	% Foreign born	T119 Nativity and Place of Birth
1980 < 18	% < Age 18	T7 Age (Short Version)
1980 > 64	% > Age 64	T7 Age (Short Version)
1990POP	Total population	T1
1990HH	Total households	T16 Household Type
1990HU	Total housing units	T72 Housing Units
1990%OHU	% Occupied housing units	T74 Occupancy Status
1990RENT	Tenure (% Rent) of OHU	
1990OWN	Tenure (% Owned) of OHU	
1980VAC	% Vacant housing units of Total % Vacant Housing Units (other)	T74 Occupancy Status
1990VAC2	Total vacant year-round housing units	T75 Vacancy Status by Type of Vacancy
	Median household income in 1989	T43 Median Household Income in 1989
1990MED	Dollars	Dollars

(continued)

Table A.1 (continued)

Variable	Definition	Census table
1990POV	% People of all ages in poverty	T93 Poverty Status in 1989 by Age Group
1990UNEM	% Unemployed of 16+ population in civilian labor force	T29 Unemployment Rate for Total Population 16 Years and Over
1990LA	Land area in square miles	T3 Land Area (sq. miles)
1990PSM	Persons per square mile	T2 Population Density (per sq. mile)
1990FEM	% Female	T6 Sex by Age
1990MALE	% Male	T6 Sex by Age
1990WHITE	% White (a)	T12 Race
1990AFR	% African-American (a)	T12 Race
1990HIS	% Hispanic or Latino of any race (b)	T13 Race by Spanish Origin Status
1990FOR	% Foreign born	T110 Nativity by Citizenship Status
1990 < 18	% < Age 18	T7 Age (Short Version)
1990 > 64	% > Age 64	T7 Age (Short Version)
2000POP	Total Population	T1
2000HH	Total Households	T20 Households by Household Type
2000HU	Total Housing Units	T157 Occupancy Status
2000%OHU	% Occupied housing units	T157 Occupancy Status
2000RENT	Tenure (% Rent) of OHU	T156 Tenure
2000OWN	Tenure (% Owned) of OHU	T156 Tenure
2000VAC	% Vacant housing units of Total % Vacant Housing Units (other)	T157 Occupancy Status
2000VAC2	Total vacant year-round housing units	T158 Vacancy Status
2000MED	Median household income in 1999 Dollars	T93 Median Household Income in 1999 Dollars
2000POV	% People of all ages in poverty	
2000UNEM	% Unemployed of 16+ population in civilian labor force	T73
2000LA	Land area in square miles	T4 Land Area (Sq. miles)
2000PSM	Persons per square mile	T3 Population Density (per sq. mile)
2000FEM	% Female	T5 Sex
2000MALE	% Male	T5 Sex
2000WHITE	% White	
2000AFR	% African-American	
2000HIS	% Hispanic or Latino of any race	
2000FOR	% Foreign born	T201 Nativity by Citizenship Status

(continued)

Table A.1 (continued)

Variable	Definition	Census table
2000 < 18	% < Age 18	T6 Sex by Age
2000 > 64	% > Age 64	T6 Sex by Age
2010POP	Total Population	T1
2010HH	Total Households	T58 Households by Household Type
2010HU	Total Housing Units	T68 Housing Units
2010%OHU	% Occupied housing units	T70 Occupancy Status
2010RENT	Tenure (% Rent) of OHU	T69 Tenure
2010OWN	Tenure (% Owned) of OHU	T69 Tenure
2010VAC	% Vacant housing units of Total % Vacant Housing Units (other)	T70 Occupancy Status
2010VAC2	Total vacant year-round housing units	T71 Vacancy Status
2010MED	Median household income in 2009 dollars	
2010POV	% People of all ages in poverty	
2010UNEM		
2010LA	Land area in sq. miles	T2 Population Density (per sq. mile)
2010PSM		

Figure A.2 shows the distribution of the 144 cities across the 1970 variables. A low Mahalanobis value suggests that the city is close to the center of the group (e.g., Brockton, Massachusetts, has a 1.78 score) where a high value means the city is very atypical (e.g., Fort Lauderdale's 9.34 value). A robust Mahalanobis measure provides an additional score that mitigates the impact of outliers. When the Mahalanobis and robust versions are close, within roughly ±20%, we can view the near agreement as a value/location estimate not affected by its position in the variable space by other cities. New Bedford registered a 3.77 Mahalanobis distance and a 4.16 robust distance, well within a 20% difference. In Fig. A.2, New Bedford is positioned well within the core group of cities using 1970 data, validating my analysis above which labels the city as typical.

Leverage Diagnostics

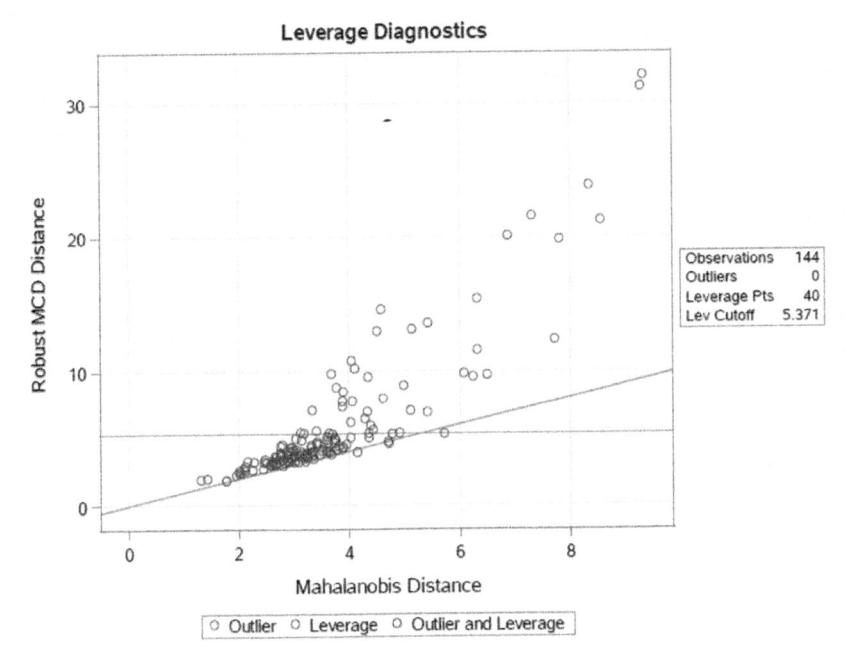

Observations	144
Outliers	0
Leverage Pts	40
Lev Cutoff	5.371

Fig. A.2 Mahalanobis distances for 144 cities, 1970

Running the same analysis for the 2010 data, I observed similar results (see Fig. A.3). Like the 1970 data, New Bedford is clustered tightly among the bulk of the cities in the sample, with a Mahalanobis distance of 2.41 and a robust distance of approximately 2.41. Where New Bedford was ranked 73 of 144 cities regarding its robust distance from the cloud center and distribution in 1970 data, it's ordinariness was even more pronounced in the 2010 data where it ranked 14th. Put another way, based on 2010 data, New Bedford is among the top 10% of cities with the most typical demographic and land use characteristics: just a normal American city.

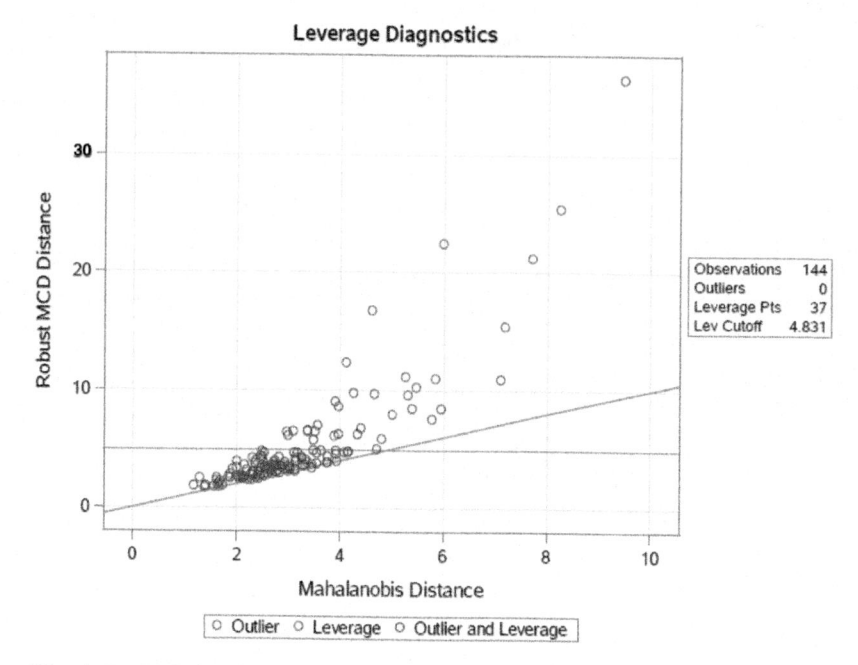

Fig. A.3 Mahalanobis distances for 144 cities, 1970

Appendix B

Table B.1 Reports used in content analysis

Rpt 1	BSC Group. (2008). Hicks-Logan-Sawyer Master Plan. Prepared for the City of New Bedford, MA	http://www.newbedford-ma.gov/Planning/HLS/HLS.html
Rpt 2	City of New Bedford (2008). Downtown Action Plan	http://nbedc.org/wp-content/uploads/2008 downtown action plan.pdf
Rpt 3	City of New Bedford. (October 14, 2008). Acushnet Avenue Corridor Vision Plan Community Meeting	http://www.newbedford-ma.gov/Planning/Acushnet%20Ave%20Community%20Report.pdf
Rpt 4	City of New Bedford Planning Department. (2006). Fairhaven Mills Site Public Charrette	http://www.newbedford-ma.gov/Planning/Fairhaven%20Mills%20Charette%20Report.pdf
Rpt 5	City of New Bedford Planning Department. (2008). 2008–2013 Open Space and Recreation Plan	http://www.newbedford-ma.gov/Planning/2008%20Open%20Space%20&%20Recreauon%20Plan.pdf
Rpt 6	FXM Economic Planning and Research. (2007). Economic Development Strategy for Downtown New Bedford Part II: Measuring Success. Prepared for City of New Bedford Planning Department	http://www.mdf.org/documents/EconomicDevelopmentStrategyfordowntownNewBedford.pdf

(*continued*)

Table B.1 (continued)

Rpt 7	Goody Clancy. (2005). Hicks-Logan-Sawyer Smart Growth Waterfront District: Vision Plan and Regulatory Strategy. Prepared for the City of New Bedford	http://commpres.env.state.ma.us/publications/sgta05/nbed report June05.pdf
Rpt 8	HR&A Advisors Inc. (ND). New Bedford, Massachusetts, Market and Economic Analysis. Prepared for City of New Bedford	http://www.newbedford-ma.gov/Planning/HRAsNewBedfordMarketEconomicAnalysis.pdf
Rpt 9	Johns, E. & Walega, R. (2008). Sustaining New Bedford. New Bedford Sustainability Task Force	http://www.newbedford-ma.gov/Mayor/PressReleases2008/Sustaining New Bedford.pdf80pg
Rpt 10	Mass Development. (2008). City of New Bedford Upper Harbor District: Final District Development Plan. Prepared for the City of New Bedford	NA
Rpt 11	Muro, M., Schneider, J., Warren, D., McLean-Shinaman, E., Sohmer, R., & Forman, B. (2007). Reconnecting Massachusetts Gateway Cities: Lessons Learned and an Agenda for Renewal. Boston, MA: Mass INC; The Brookings Institute	http://www.brookings.edu/~/media/Files/rc/reports/2007/02regionsandstates muro/massgateways.pdf
Rpt 12	New Bedford Economic Council. (2008). Creative Economy Task Force. Prepared for the City of New Bedford	http://nbedc.org/wp-content/uploads/creative-economy.pdf
Rpt 13	New Bedford Economic Development Council. (2008). City of New Bedford Historic Mill Inventory	http://www.fasttracknewbedford.com/resources/Supporting%20Documents/2008 NB-MillInventory-UpperHarbor-Hicks-etc.pdf
Rpt 14	New Bedford Economic Development Council. (2008). Upper Harbor Vision Plan Community Meetings	http://nbedc.org/wp-content/uploads/city of new bedford upper harbor vision plan.pdf

(continued)

Table B.1 (continued)

Rpt 15	RKG Associates, Inc. (2007). District Improvement Financing Plan for the Hicks-Logan-Sawyer Revitalization Area in New Bedford, MA. Prepared for the City of New Bedford, MA	http://www.fasttracknewbedford.com/resources/Supporting%20Documents/HLS Financing.pdf
Rpt 16	South Coast Rail. (2009). South Coast Rail Economic Development and Land Use Corridor Plan	http://southcoastrail.eot.state.ma.us/downloads/3%20-%20South%20Coast%20Rail%20Corridor%20Plan%20-%20Low%20Resolution.pdf
Rpt 17	Southeastern Regional Planning and Economic Development District (SRPEDD). (2008). City of New Bedford Priority Development and Protection Areas	http://www.newbedford-ma.gov/Planning/priority/priority protection.html
Rpt 18	Utile, Inc. Architecture and Planning & FXM Economic Planning and Research. (2009). Downtown New Bedford Revitalization and Redevelopment Study. Prepared for the City of New Bedford, MA	http://www.newbedford-ma.gov/Planning/downtown 2009 study.html
Rpt 19	Vanasse Hangen Brustlin (VHB). (2002). New Bedford Fairhaven Harbor Plan. Prepared for the City of New Bedford and Town of Fairhaven	http://response.restoration.noaa.gov/bookshelf/1667 nb fair harborplan.pdf

Appendix C

Table C.1 Themes used in latent content analysis

Themes	Theme definitions
Pos. assessment of past decline	Discussion expressing a notion of perceived population gain to date
Negative assessment of past decline	Acknowledgment of population decline to date
Acknowledgment of public disinvestment	Acknowledgment of public disinvestment to date
Neutral/positive projections of future population	Projection of future population growth/hopeful sentiment of the future draw of New Bedford
Major renovation/reuse of existing structures	Discussion regarding recommendations to renovate or reuse existing structures for planning purposes
Management of abandoned structures/vacant lots/brownfields	Discussion recommending addressing abandoned structures, vacant lots, and brownfields
Land Use Management Strategy	Discussion regarding strategy of future land use, including suggested land use modifications
Pedestrian improvements	Discussion of future city involvement in improving sidewalks, cross-walks, or other factors like signage or lighting that enhances the pedestrian realm and pedestrian connectivity throughout the city

(*continued*)

Table C.1 (continued)

Themes	Theme definitions
Investment of public realm	Discussion focused on enhancing public spaces for the purpose of tying together diverse land use (i.e., streets, sidewalks, parks, other public-shared spaces). This differs from pedestrian improvements as those are focused on creating a safe and connective pathway for those on foot. This also differs from facade improvements, as that category relates to the esthetic look of the landscape along with the city investment in upkeep and city-wide services
Creative economy	Discussion of investing in those industries that have their origin in individual creativity, skill, and talent, which have a potential for wealth and job creation through the generation and exploitation of intellectual property (from rpt 13, appendix, p 134). "Creative economy businesses encompass both innovative companies and cultural organizations" (Rpt 18, p 58, taken from Creative Economy Association of the North Shore)
New transportation	Discussion of the desire to invest in new modes of transportation (i.e., commuter rail) or transportation infrastructure (major highway improvements, port development, dedicated bike trails, etc.)
Increased tourism	Discussion of an intent to focus development in the city with tourism as a major industry
Strategic investments (based on local assets, waterfront, regional connection area)	Discussion of focusing future industry around local assets that make New Bedford district from other gateway cities (i.e., waterfront development, incubator space development, marine science focus, etc.)
Increased jobs	Discussion regarding the need to bring jobs to the city
Zoning change	Discussion regarding a need to modify local zoning, or mention of recent success due to modified zoning regulations/special permits
New construction	Discussion expressing an intent to building new buildings
Sustainability (energy/environment)	Discussion regarding a future city in which energy use is either reduced thereby reducing emissions and/or some amount of energy is generated from renewable technologies. Discussion regarding a future dedicated to improving the natural environment, air quality, water quality, ecology, level of toxins, and so on would also fall under this category

(continued)

Table C.1 (continued)

Themes	Theme definitions
Parks and open space	Discussion of a plan to investment in creating parks and open space
Regional planning	Discussion of the need and positive potential related to planning regionally
TOD	Discussion of future city focus on transit-oriented development
Increased investments/ upgrades to facades, streets, services	Discussion expressing a need to further invest in the physical upkeep of streetscapes, building facades, and city services
Increase/improve housing	Discussion of a future with an increased number of residential units or improved housing quality of current units
Economic development	Discussion regarding the intent to enhance the community by increasing the amount of economic activity
Quality of life improvements	Discussion suggesting that investment in the city is for the purpose of improving the quality of life for the residents by enhancing city services (broadband, educational programs, etc.) which contribute to overall well-being
Safety	Discussion expressing a need to improve vehicle and pedestrian safety, general perceived street safety, or increase police presence (Rpt 4, p 8 and Rpt 6 p iii)
Historic preservation	"Discussion focused on the premise that the preservation of the historic built environment can be a critical vehicle to new development", or discussion highlighting the value of the historic tax credit (paraphrased from Rpt 4, p 11)
Healthy environment	Expressed "interest in improving the environment and enhancing public health" (Hollander, 2009)

Appendix D

Table D.1 Keywords used in manifest content analysis

Agricultural
Agriculture
Alternative
Citizen involvement
Compact/compact development
Competitive position
Conceptual(ize)
Connections
Conversion
Converted/convert/converting
Cultural
Dismantling/dismantled
Economic growth
Engagement
Evolve
Expanded land use
Expansion of river ways, watersheds, parkland
Green industry(ial)/land use
Growth
Heritage
Heritage tourism
Housing growth
Housing stock
Industrial growth

(*continued*)

Table B.1 (continued)

Infrastructure
Innovative land use
Interconnections
Job growth
Market/marketing (the region)
Microfinance/microenterprise
More compact city/compact core/compact center
Networks
New forms
New growth
Population growth
Purchase of development rights
Reconstruct(ion)
Recreational
Redesign
Reduce infrastructure
Reenvisioning/envisioning/envision
Reform
Regional connectivity
Regional economy
Regional greenways
Regional linkages
Rehabilitation
Reinvestment
Renovation
Repositioning
Residential growth
Restoration
Restoration of infrastructure
Reuse
Service bundling/combination of service
Smart growth
Support for volunteers
Transferable development rights
Urban sports/sports
Vacant
Vision

Bibliography

81st Congress of the United States. 1949. 81st Congress of the United States. 1949. Housing Act of 1949. In *United States Statutes at Large*, vol. 63. Washington, DC: United States Government Printing Office.

Accordino, John, and Gary T. Johnson. 2000. Addressing the Vacant and Abandoned Property Problem. *Journal of Urban Affairs* 22 (3): 301–315.

Agyeman, Julian. 2013. *Introducing Just Sustainabilities: Policy, Planning, and Practice*. London: Zed Books.

Alanen, A.R., and J.A. Eden. 2014. *Main Street Ready-Made: The New Deal Community of Greendale*. Wisconsin: Wisconsin Historical Society.

Allmendinger, Philip. 2009. *Planning Theory*. 2nd ed. Basingstoke: Palgrave Macmillan.

Altman, Alex. 2009. Detroit Tries to Get on a Road to Renewal. *Time Magazine*, March 26.

Anderson, Martin. 1964a. *The Federal Bulldozer: A Critical Analysis of Urban Renewal, 1949–1962*. Cambridge, MA: MIT Press.

———. 1964b. *The Federal Bulldozer: A Critical Analysis of Urban Renewal, 1949–1962*. Cambridge, MA: MIT Press.

Anderson, Charles. 2009. Renovation Will Construct New Housing, Reconnect United Front to Street Grid. *South Coast Today*, November 29. http://www.southcoasttoday.com/apps/pbcs.dll/article?AID=/20091129/NEWS/911290339.

Anderson, Michelle. 2012. Dissolving Cities. *Yale Law Journal* 121: 1364–1447.

Angotti, Tom. 2008. *New York for Sale: Community Planning Confronts Global Real Estate*. Cambridge, MA: MIT Press.

Armborst, Tobias, Daniel D'Oca, and Georgeen Theodore. 2006. However Unspectacular. In *Shrinking Cities. Volume 2: Interventions*, ed. Philipp Oswalt, 324–329. Ostfildern, Germany: Hatje Cantz.

Arnstein, Sherry R. 1969. A Ladder of Citizen Participation. *Journal of the American Institute of Planners* 35 (9): 216–224.

Ballon, Hilary, and Kenneth T. Jackson. 2008. *Robert Moses and the Modern City: The Transformation of New York*. New York, NY: W.W. Norton.

Barkin, Solomon. 1981. Management and Ownership in the New England Cotton Textile Industry. *Journal of Economic Issues*. Social Science Premium Collection [ProQuest]. Web 23 January 2017.

Bear, William C., and Christopher B. Williamson. 1988. The Filtering of Households and Housing Units. *Journal of Planning Literature* 3 (2): 127–152.

Beauregard, Robert A. 2003. *Voices of Decline: The Postwar Fate of U.S. Cities*. 2nd ed. New York, NY: Routledge.

———. 2009. Urban Population Loss in Historical Perspective: United States, 1820–200. *Environment & Planning A* 41 (3): 514–528.

———. 2013. Chapter 10. Strategic Thinking for Distressed Neighborhoods. *The City After Abandonment*. doi:10.9783/9780812207309.227.

Bellah, Robert N. 1985. *Habits of the Heart: Individualism and Commitment in American Life*. Berkeley, CA: University of California Press.

Bellah, Robert N., Richard Madsen, William M. Sullivan, Ann Swidler, and Steven M. Tipton. 1985. *Habits of the Heart: Individualism and Commitment in American Life*. Berkeley, CA: University of California Press.

Benhabib, Seyla. 1996. *Democracy and Difference: Contesting the Boundaries of the Political*. Princeton, NJ: Princeton University Press.

Bertron, Cara, and Donovan Rypkema. 2012. Historic Preservation and Rightsizing. Accessed March 23, 2017. http://www.achp.gov/achp-rightsizing-report.pdf.

Bier, Thomas. 2001. *Moving Up, Filtering Down: Metropolitan Housing Dynamics and Public Policy*. Washington, DC: Brookings Institution, Center on Urban and Metropolitan Policy.

Bittner, Regina. 2006. Post-Fordist Production of Space. In *Shrinking Cities, Volume 1: International Research*, ed. Philipp Oswalt, 572–581. Ostfildern, Germany: Hatje Cantz Verlag.

Blakely, Edward J., and Ted K. Bradshaw. 1994. *Planning Local Economic Development: Theory and Practice*. Thousand Oaks, CA: SAGE Publications.

Bluestone, Barry, and Bennett Harrison. 1982. *The Deindustrialization of America: Plant Closing, Community Abandonment and the Dismantling of Basic Industry*. New York, NY: Basic Books, Inc.

Boston Sunday Globe. 1973. Black United Front Gets $4.3m Building Loan. *Boston Sunday Globe*, March 28.

Bradbury, Katharine L., Anthony Downs, and Kenneth A. Small. 1981. Forty Theories Of Urban Decline. *Journal of Urban Affairs* 3 (2): 13–20. doi:10.1111/j.1467-9906.1981.tb00007.x.

———. 1982. *Urban Decline and the Future of American Cities.* Washington, DC: Brookings Institution.

Brindley, Tim, Yvonne Rydin, and Gerry Stoker. 1996. *Remaking Planning.* 2nd ed. New York, NY: Routledge.

Bruegmann, Robert. 2006. *Sprawl: A Compact History.* Chicago, IL: University of Chicago press.

BSC Group. 2005. *Hicks-Logan-Sawyer Master Plan.* Boston, MA: BSC Group.

Buff, Rachel Ida. 2008. The Deportation Terror. *American Quarterly.* Arts and Humanities Database [ProQuest]. Web 8 January.

Burnett, Kim. 2003. Strengthening Weak Market Cities: A 10-Step Program for CDCs. *Shelterforce* 131 (September/October). Accessed May 29, 2013. http://www.shelterforce.com/online/issues/131/weakmarkets.html.

California Department of Finance. 2015. E-1 Population Estimates for Cities, Counties, and the State. Accessed January 11, 2016. http://www.dof.ca.gov/Forecasting/Demographics/Estimates/E-1/.

Caro, Robert A. 1974. *The Power Broker: Robert Moses and the Fall of New York.* New York, NY: Knopf.

Chapple, Karen. 2015. *Planning Sustainable Cities and Regions: Towards More Equitable Development.* New York, NY: Routledge.

Chudacoff, Howard P. 1981. *The Evolution of American Urban Society.* Upper Saddle River, NJ: Prentice Hall.

City of Buffalo. 2004. *Queen City in the 21st Century: Buffalo's Comprehensive Plan.* Buffalo, NY: Office of Strategic Planning.

City of New Bedford. 2007. *2008–2013 Open Space and Recreation Plan.* New Bedford, MA: City of New Bedford Planning Department.

———. 2008a. *New Bedford Historic Mill Inventory.* New Bedford, MA: New Bedford Economic Development Council.

———. 2008b. *Sustaining New Bedford.* New Bedford, MA: Sustainability Task Force.

City of Youngstown. 2005. *Youngstown 2010 Citywide Plan.* Youngstown, OH: City of Youngstown.

Clark, David. 1989. *Urban Decline: The British Experience.* London: Routledge.

Comptroller General of the United States. 1972. Impact of Federal Programs on Economic Development, Employment, and Housing in New Bedford, Massachusetts. B-159835, United States General Accounting Office.

Crossney, Kristen B., and David W. Bartelt. 2005. Residential Security, Risk, and Race: The Home Owners' Loan Corporation and Mortgage Access in Two Cities. *Urban Geography* 26 (8): 707–736.

———. 2006. The Missing Link: An Assessment of the Legacy of the Home Owners' Loan Corporation. *Housing Policy Debate* 16 (3/4): 547–574.

Cunningham-Sabot, E., and S. Fol. 2007. Schrumpfende Städte in Westeuropa: Fallstudien aus Frankreich und Grossbritannien. *Berliner Debatte Initial* 1: 22–35.

Dear, Michael, and Steven Flusty. 1998. Postmodern Urbanism. *Annals of the Association of American Geographers* 88 (1): 50–72.

Deng, Lan. 2013. Building Affordable Housing in Cities After Abandonment: The Case of Low-Income Housing Tax Credit Developments in Detroit. In *The City After Abandonment*, ed. Margaret Dewar and June Manning Thomas, 41–63. Philadelphia: The University of Pennsylvania Press.

Dewar, Margaret. 1998. Why State and Local Economic Development Programs Causes so Little Economic Development. *Economic Development Quarterly* 12 (1): 68–87.

Dewar, Margaret, and June Manning Thomas. 2013. *The City After Abandonment*. Philadephia: University of Pennsylvania Press.

Dewar, Margaret, Matthew Weber, Eric Seymour, Meagan Elliot, and Patrick Cooper-McCann. 2015. Learning from Detroit: How Research on a Declining City Enriches Urban Studies. In *Reinventing Detroit: The Politics of Possibility*. New Brunswick, NJ: Transaction.

Downs, Anthony. 1975. Using the Lessons of Experience to Allocate Resources in the Community Development Program. In *Recommendations for Community Development Planning: Proceedings of the HUD/RERC Workshops on Local Urban Renewal and Neighborhood Preservation*. Chicago: Real Estate Research Corporation.

Doxiadēs, Kōnstantinos Apostolou. 1966. *Urban Renewal and the Future of the American City*. Chicago, IL: Public Administration Service.

Doyle, James. 2003. *City of Pawtucket, Rhode Island Comprehensive Community Plan*. Pawtucket, RI: City of Pawtucket.

Duany, Andres, and Emily Talen. 2002. Transect Planning. *Journal of the American Planning Association* 68 (3): 245–266.

Dunn, Christine E. 2007. Participatory GIS—A People's GIS? *Progress in Human Geography* 31 (5): 616–637.

Egan, Timothy. 2005. Ruling Sets Off Tug of War Over Private Property. *The New York Times*, July 30.

Fainstein, Susan S. 2010. *The Just City*. Ithaca: Cornell University Press.

Fausset, Richard. 2009. Empty Florida Homes May Return to Nature. *Los Angeles Times*, April 16.

Fernandez Agueda, B. 2009. Urban Planning in Industrial Cities: The Reversibility of Decay. Presentation at City Futures Conference, Madrid, June 4–6.

Finn, Bob. 1959a. Speed, Unity Here Vital for U.S. Aid on Building. *Standard-Times*, April 13.

———. 1959b. Thorough Planning Necessary Before City Can Qualify for Federal Urban Renewal Funds. *Standard-Times*, April 14.

Fishman, Robert. 1982. *Urban Utopias in the Twentieth Century: Ebenezer Howard, Frank Lloyd Wright and Le Corbusier.* Cambridge, MA: MIT Press.
Forester, John. 1996. Argument, Power and Passion in Planning Practice. In *Explorations in Planning Theory*, ed. Seymour Mandelbaum, Luigi Mazza, and Robert Burchell, 241–262. New Brunswick, NJ: Center for Urban Policy Research.
Freeman, L. 2006. *There Goes the Hood.* Philadelphia: Temple University Press.
Fried, Marc. 1966. Grieving for a Lost Home: Psychological Costs of Relocation. In *Urban Renewal: The Record and the Controversy*, ed. James Q. Wilson, 359–379. Cambridge, MA: MIT Press.
Frieden, Bernard J., and Lynne B. Sagalyn. 1991. *Downtown, Inc.: How America Rebuilds Cities.* Cambridge, MA: MIT Press.
Friedmann, John. 1987. *Planning in the Public Domain: From Knowledge to Action.* Princeton, NJ: Princeton University Press.
Frug, Gerald E. 1999. *City Making: Building Communities without Building Walls.* Princeton, NJ: Princeton University Press.
FXM Associates. 2007. *Economic Development Strategy for Downtown New Bedford, Part II: Measuring Success.* Mattapoisett, MA: FXM Associates.
———. 2009. *Downtown New Bedford Economic Revitalization and Development Study.* Mattapoisett, MA: FXM Associates.
Gaber, John, and Sharon Gaber. 2007. *Qualitative Analysis for Planning & Policy: Beyond the Numbers.* Chicago, IL: American Planning Association.
Gans, Herbert J. 1962. *The Urban Villagers: Group and Class in the Life of Italian-Americans.* New York, NY: The Free Press of Glencoe.
German Federal Cultural Foundation. 2006a. In *Shrinking Cities, Volume 2: Interventions*, ed. Philipp Oswalt. Ostfildern, Germany: Hatje Cantz Verlag.
———. 2006b. In *Shrinking Cities, Volume 1: International Research*, ed. Philipp Oswalt. Ostfildern, Germany: Hatje Cantz Verlag.
Gittell, Ross Jacobs. 1989. A Critical Analysis of Local Initiatives in Economic Revitalization. Order No. 9013286 Harvard University. Ann Arbor: ProQuest. Web 26 February 2017.
Gittell, Ross J., and J. Phillip Thompson. 1999. Inner-City Business Development and Entrepreneurship: New Frontiers for Policy and Research. In *Urban Problems and Community Development*, 473–520. Washington, DC: Brookings Institution Press.
Glaeser, Edward. 2009. Bulldozing America's Shrinking Cities. *New York Times*, Economix blog. June 16. Accessed February 10, 2012. http://economix.blogs.nytimes.com/2009/06/16/bulldozing-americas-shrinking-cities/.
Glaeser, Edward, and Joseph Gyourko. 2005. Urban Decline and Durable Housing. *Journal of Political Economy* 113 (2): 345–375.
Gonsalves, Jennifer White. 2004. Looking at the Urban Renewal Program of the 1960s through the Lens of the South Terminal Redevelopment Project in New Bedford, Massachusetts. M.A. thesis. University of Rhode Island.

Gonzalez, George A. 2009. *Urban Sprawl, Global Warming, and the Empire of Capital.* Albany, NY: SUNY Press.

Gordon, Eric, Steven Schirra, and Justin Hollander. 2011. Immersive Planning: A Conceptual Model for Designing Public Participation with New Technologies. *Environment and Planning B: Planning and Design* 38 (3): 505–519. doi:10.1068/b37013.

Gratz, Roberta Brandes. 1994. Each Town Its Own Face. *The Wall Street Journal,* September 8.

———. 2009. Demolition a Wrong Answer for Imperiled Neighborhoods. *Citiwire.net,* June 18. http://citiwire.net/columns/demolition-a-wrong-answer-for-imperiled-neighborhoods/.

Greenlees, Janet. 2016. Workplace Health and Gender among Cotton Workers in America and Britain, C.1880s–1940s. *International Review of Social History.* Social Science Premium Collection. Web 23 January 2017.

Greer, Scott. 1965. *Urban Renewal and American Cities: The Dilemma of Democratic Intervention.* Indianapolis, IN: Bobbs-Merrill Company, Inc.

Grossmann, Katrin, Caterina Cortese, Annegret Haase, and Iva Ticha. 2012. How Urban Shrinkage Impacts on Patterns of Socio-Spatial Segregation: The Cases of Leipzig/Germany, Ostrava/Czech Republic and Genova/Italy. Presentation at Urban Affairs Association 42nd Annual Conference, Pittsburgh, PA, April 18–21.

Guerrieri, Veronica, Daniel Hartley, and Erik Hurst. 2012. Very Local House Price Dynamics. *American Economic Review: Papers & Proceedings* 103 (3): 120–126.

Haase, Dagmar. 2013. Shrinking Cities, Biodiversity and Ecosystem Services. In *Urbanization, Biodiversity and Ecosystem Services: Challenges and Opportunities.* Netherlands: Springer.

Haase, Dagmar, Sven Lautenbach, and Ralf Seppelt. 2010. Modeling and Simulating Residential Mobility in a Shrinking City Using an Agent-Based Approach. *Environmental Modelling & Software* 25 (10): 1225–1240.

Hackworth, J. 2014. The Limits to Market-Based Strategies for Addressing Land Abandonment in Shrinking American Cities. *Progress in Planning* 90: 1–37.

Hall, Peter. 1997. Modeling the Post-Industrial City. *Futures* 29 (4–5): 311–322.

———. 2000. *Cities of Tomorrow: An Intellectual History of Urban Planning and Design in the Twentieth Century.* Malden, MA: Blackwell Publishers.

Harper, Thomas L., and Stanley M. Stein. 1996. Postmodernist Planning Theory: The Incommensurability Premise. In *Explorations in Planning Theory,* ed. Seymour Mandelbaum, Luigi Mazza, and Robert Burchell, 414–429. New Brunswick, NJ: Center for Urban Policy Research.

Harrington-Davis, B. 2010. Residents Have Their Say on Vision for Acton's Kelley's Corner, Acton Beacon, July 2.

Hartford, William F. 1996. *Where Is Our Responsibility?: Unions and Economic Change in the New England Textile Industry, 1870–1960.* Amherst: University of Massachusetts.

Hartnett, Ken. 2008. A Tale of Two Parks in the City's South End. *Standard-Times*, August 24.
Harvey, David. 1973. *Social Justice and the City*. Baltimore, MD: John Hopkins University Press.
———. 1996. *Justice, Nature and the Geography of Difference*. London: Blackwell.
———. 2003. Social Justice, Postmodernism and the City. In *Designing Cities: Critical Readings in Urban Design*, ed. Alexander R. Cuthbert, 101–115. Malden, MA: Blackwell Publishing.
Healey, P. 1996. The Communicative Work of Development Plans. In *Explorations in Planning Theory*, ed. Seymour Mandelbaum, Luigi Mazza, and Robert Burchell, 263–288. New Brunswick, NJ: Center for Urban Policy Research.
Henderson, Steven R. 2015. State Intervention in Vacant Residential Properties: An Evaluation of Empty Dwelling Management Orders in England. *Environment and Planning C: Government and Policy* 33 (1): 61–82.
Hobbs, Frank, and Nicole Stoops. 2002. *Demographic Trends in the 20th Century*. Washington, DC: U.S. Census Bureau.
Hoch, Charles. 1996. A Pragmatic Inquiry about Planning and Power. In *Explorations in Planning Theory*, ed. Seymour Mandelbaum, Luigi Mazza, and Robert Burchell, 30–44. New Brunswick, NJ: Center for Urban Policy Research.
Hollander, Justin B. 2009. *Polluted and Dangerous: America's Worst Abandoned Properties and What Can Be Done About Them*. Burlington, VT: University of Vermont Press.
———. 2010. Moving Towards a Shrinking Cities Metric: Analyzing Land Use Changes Associated with Depopulation in Flint, Michigan. *Cityscape: A Journal of Policy Development and Research* 12 (1): 133–151.
———. 2011. *Sunburnt Cities: The Great Recession, Depopulation and Urban Planning in the American Sunbelt*. London: Routledge.
Hollander, Justin B., and Bernard Cahill. 2011. Confronting Population Decline in the Buffalo, New York, Region: A Close Reading of the Erie-Niagara Framework for Regional Growth. *Journal of Architecture and Planning Research* 28 (3): 252–267.
Hollander, Justin B., and Jeremy Nemeth. 2011. The Bounds of Smart Decline: A Foundational Theory for Planning Shrinking Cities. *Housing Policy Debate* 21 (3): 349–367.
Hollander, Justin B., Karina Pallagst, Terry Schwarz, and Frank J. Popper. 2009. Planning Shrinking Cities. *Progress in Planning* 72 (4): 223–232.
Hollander, Justin B., Colin Polsky, Dan Zinder, and Dan Runfulo. 2010. The New American Ghost Town: Foreclosure, Abandonment and the Prospects for City Planning. *Land Lines* 23 (2): 2–7.
Hoover, Edgar M., and Raymond Vernon. 1962. *Anatomy of a Metropolis: The Changing Distribution of People and Jobs within the New York Metropolitan Region*. Cambridge, MA: Harvard University Press.

Howard, Ebenezer. 1902. *Garden Cities of To-morrow, etc.* London: Swan Sonnenschein & Co.

Howe, Elizabeth. 1995. Introduction: Part II—Ethical Theory and Planning Practice. In *Planning Ethics: A Reader in Planning Theory, Practice and Education*, ed. Sue Hendler, 123–140. New Brunswick, NJ: Center for Urban Policy Research.

Hoyt, Homer. 1933. *One Hundred Years of Land Values In Chicago; The Relationship of the Growth Of Chicago to The Rise in Its Land Values, 1830–1933.* Chicago, IL: University of Chicago Press.

HR&A Advisors Inc. (undated). New Bedford, Massachusetts, Market and Economic Analysis. Prepared for City of New Bedford.

Hughes, Mark A., and Rebekah Cook-Mack. 1999. The City Needs a Fresh Approach to Dealing with Vacant Property. *The Philadelphia Inquirer*, May 23.

Hutson, Malo André. 2015. *The Urban Struggle for Economic, Environmental and Social Justice: Deepening Their Roots*. London: Routledge.

Immergluck, D. 2012. Distressed and Dumped Market Dynamics of Low-Value, Foreclosed Properties during the Advent of the Federal Neighborhood Stabilization Program. *Journal of Planning Education and Research* 32: 48–61.

Innes, Judith Eleanor, and David E. Booher. 2010. *Planning with Complexity: An Introduction to Collaborative Rationality for Public Policy*. Milton Park, Abingdon, Oxon and New York, NY: Routledge.

Jackson, Kenneth T. 1985. *Crabgrass Frontier: The Suburbanization of the United States*. New York, NY: Oxford University Press.

Jacobs, Jane. 1961. *The Death and Life of Great American Cities*. New York, NY: Random House.

Jargowsky, Paul A. 1997. *Poverty and Place: Ghettos, Barrios, and the American City*. New York, NY: Russell Sage Foundation.

Johnson, M.P., J. Hollander, and A. Hallulli. 2014. Maintain, Demolish, Re-purpose: Policy Design for Vacant Land Management Using Decision Models. *Cities* 40 (Part B): 151–162.

Keenan, Paula, Stewart Lowe, and Sheila Spencer. 1999. Housing Abandonment in Inner Cities-The Politics of Low Demand for Housing. *Housing Studies* 14 (5): 703–716.

Kelling, George L., and James Q. Wilson. 1982. Broken Windows – The Police and Neighborhood Safety. *The Atlantic*, March 1.

Kelo, Susette, et al. 2005. *v. City of New London, Connecticut, et al.*, 125 S. Ct. 2655.

Koistinen, David Joshua. 1999. Dealing with Deindustrialization: Economics, Politics, and Policy during the Decline of the New England Textile Industry, 1920–1960. Order No. 9930940 Yale University. Ann Arbor: ProQuest. Web 26 February 2017.

———. 2002. The Causes of Deindustrialization: The Migration of the Cotton Textile Industry from New England to the South. *Enterprise and Society*. ABI/INFORM [ProQuest]. Web 6 January 2017.

Kowarik, Ingo, and Stefan Körner. 2005. *Wild Urban Woodlands New Perspectives for Urban Forestry*. Berlin: Springer.

Kvale, Steinar. 2007. *Doing Interviews*. London: Sage.

Langdon, Philip. 2005. NOTE FOR SALE. *Planning* 71 (4): 12–15.

Lauf, Steffen, Dagmar Haase, Ralf Seppelt, and Nina Schwarz. 2012. Simulating Demography and Housing Demand in an Urban Region under Scenarios of Growth and Shrinkage. *Environment and Planning B: Planning and Design* 39 (2): 229–246. doi:10.1068/b36046t.

Lauinger, Holger. 2006. Urban Agriculture. In *Shrinking Cities, Volume 2: Interventions*, ed. Philipp Oswalt. Ostfildern, Germany: Hatje Cantz Verlag.

Le Corbusier. 2000. A Contemporary City. In *The City Reader*, ed. Richard T. LeGates and Frederic Stout, 2nd ed., 336–343. London: Routledge.

Lejano, Raul P. 2008. Technology and Institutions: A Critical Appraisal of GIS in the Planning Domain. *Science, Technology and Human Values* 33 (5): 653–678.

Leonard, Tom. 2009. US Cities May Have to Be Bulldozed in Order to Survive. *The Telegraph*, June 12. http://www.telegraph.co.uk/finance/financialcrisis/5516536/US-cities-may-have-to-be-bulldozed-in-order-to-survive.html.

Linkon, Sherry L., and John Russo. 2003. *Steeltown U.S.A.: Work and Memory in Youngstown*. Lawrence, KA: University Press of Kansas.

Lloyd, Christopher D., Ian G. Shuttleworth, and David W. Wong, eds. 2014. *Social-Spatial Segregation: Concepts, Processes and Outcomes*. Bristol, UK: Policy Press.

Lucy, William. 2010. *Foreclosing the Dream: How America's Housing Crisis is Reshaping our Cities and Suburbs*. Washington, DC: APA Planners Press.

Lucy, William H., and David L. Phillips. 2000. *Confronting Suburban Decline: Strategic Planning for Metropolitan Renewal*. Washington, DC: Island Press.

MacCallum, D. 2016. *Discourse Dynamics in Participatory Planning: Opening the Bureaucracy to Strangers*. Routledge.

Mace, Alan, Nick Gallent, Peter Hall, Lucas Porsch, Reiner Braun, and Ulrich Pfeiffer. 2004. *Shrinking to Grow: The Urban Regeneration Challenge in Leipzig and Manchester*. London: Institute of Community Studies.

Mallach, Alan. 2010. *Facing the Urban Challenge: Reimagining Land Use in America's Distressed Older Cities--The Federal Policy Role*. Washington, DC: Brookings Institution.

———. 2011. Comment on Hollander's 'The Bounds of Smart Decline: A Foundational Theory for Planning Shrinking Cities'. *Housing Policy Debate* 21 (3): 369–375.

Mallach, Alan, and Lavea Brachman. 2010. *Ohio Cities at a Turning Point: Finding the Way Forward*. Washington, DC: Brookings Institution Press.

Martin, Roger. 1965. South Terminal Project Given Highest Priority. *Standard-Times*, May 19.

Martinez-Fernandez, Cristina, Karina M. Pallagst, and Thorsten Wiechmann. 2015. *Shrinking Cities: International Perspectives and Policy Implications*.

Marx, Karl, and Friedrich Engels. 1951. *Selected Works*. New York, NY: International Publishers.

Massachusetts Executive Office of Transportation and Massachusetts Executive Office of Housing and Economic Development. 2009. *South Coast Rail Economic Development and Land Use Corridor Plan*. Boston, MA: Commonwealth of Massachusetts.

Massey, Douglas S., and Nancy A. Denton. 1993. *American Apartheid: Segregation and the Making of the Underclass*. Cambridge, MA: Harvard University Press.

Matthews, Anne. 1992. *Where the Buffalo Roam: Restoring America's Great Plains*. Chicago, IL: The University of Chicago Press.

Mayer, Henry J., and Michael R. Greenberg. 2001. Coming Back from Economic Despair: Case Studies of Small and Medium-size American Places. *Economic Development Quarterly* 15 (3): 205–216.

McAdam, Doug. 1982. *Political Process and the Development of Black Insurgency, 1930–1970*. Chicago, IL: University of Chicago Press.

McCabe, Marsha, and Joseph D. Thomas. 1995. *Not Just Anywhere: The Story of WHALE and the Rescue of New Bedford's Waterfront Historic District*. New Bedford, MA: Spinner Publications.

McConnell, Shean. 1995. Rawlsian Planning Theory. In *Planning Ethics: A Reader in Planning Theory, Practice and Education*, ed. Sue Hendler, 30–48. New Brunswick, NJ: Center for Urban Policy Research.

McDonald, John F. 2008. *Urban America: Growth, Crisis, and Rebirth*. Armonk, NY: M.E. Sharpe.

———. 2015. *Urban America: Growth, Crisis, and Rebirth*. Routledge.

Melville, Herman. 1988/1851. *Moby-Dick or, The Whale*. New York, NY: Penguin Books.

Metzger, John T. 2000. Planned Abandonment: The Neighborhood Life-Cycle Theory and National Urban Policy. *Housing Policy Debate* 11 (1): 7–40.

Millington, Nate. 2013. Post-industrial Imaginaries: Nature, Representation and Ruin in Detroit, Michigan. *International Journal of Urban and Regional Research* 37 (1): 279–296.

Mitchell, Timothy. 2002. *Rule of Experts: Egypt, Techno-Politics, Modernity*. Berkeley, CA: University of California Press.

Mitchell, Don. 2003. *The Right to the City: Social Justice and the Fight for Public Space*. New York, NY: Guilford Press.

Mouffe, Chantal. 1996. Democracy, Power and the Political. In *Democracy and Difference: Contesting the Boundaries of the Political*, ed. Seyla Benhabib, 245–256. Princeton, NJ: Princeton University Press.

Muro, Mark, John Schneider, David Warren, Eric McLean-Shinaman, Rebecca Sohmer, and Benjamin Forman. 2007. *Reconnecting Massachusetts Gateway Cities: Lessons Learned and an Agenda for Renewal*. Boston, MA: MassINC.

Nugent, Rory. 2009. *Down at the Docks*. New York, NY: Pantheon.

Oswalt, Philipp. 2006. *Shrinking Cities. Interventions.* Hatje Cantz Verlag.
Oswalt, Philipp, and Tim Rieniets. 2006. *Atlas of Shrinking Cities = Atlas der schrumpfenden Städte.* Ostfildern, Germany: Hatje Cantz.
Overmeyer, Klaus. 2006. Vacant Lots as Incubators? Interim Uses in Shrinking Cities. In *Shrinking Cities, Volume 2: Interventions,* ed. Philipp Oswalt, 324–329. Ostfildern, Germany: Hatje Cantz.
Pallagst, Karina M. 2008. Shrinking Cities: Planning Challenges from an International Perspective. Cities Growing Smaller. Accessed March 23, 2017. http://cudcserver2.cudc.kent.edu/publications/urban_infill/cities_growing_smaller/cities_growing_smaller_chapter _01_screen.pdf.
Pallagst, Karina, Thorsten Wiechmann, and Cristina Martinez-Fernandez. 2014. *Shrinking Cities: International Perspectives and Policy Implications.* Vol. 8. New York, NY: Routledge, Taylor & Francis Group.
Pallagst, Karina, et al. 2009. *The Future of Shrinking Cities—Problems, Patterns and Strategies of Urban Transformation in a Global Context.* Berkley, CA: Center for Global Metropolitan Studies, UC Berkeley, Monograph Series.
Pantalone, Stephen, and Justin B. Hollander. 2012. Relaxed Zoning Overlay. *Zoning Practice* 28 (9): 1–7.
Pattison, Gary. 2004. Planning for Decline: The "D"-Village Policy of County Durham, UK. *Planning Perspectives* 19 (3): 311–332.
Perloff, Harvey S. 1980. *Planning the Post-Industrial City.* Washington, DC: Planners Press.
Phillipps, Jeremy. 2008. Living on Past Glories and Future Dreams the Effects of Depopulation on Early Modern Urban Development in the Former Castle Town of Kanazawa. *European Journal of East Asian Studies* 7 (2): 263–294.
Popper, Deborah E., and Frank J. Popper. 1897. The Great Plains: From Dust to Dust. *Planning* 53: 12–18.
———. 1999. The Buffalo Commons: Metaphor as Method. *Geographical Review* 89 (4): 491–510.
———. 2002. Small Can Be Beautiful: Coming to Terms with Decline. *Planning* 68 (7): 20–23.
———. 2004. The Great Plains and the Buffalo Commons. *WorldMinds: Geographical Perspectives on 100 Problems*: 345–349. doi:10.1007/978-1-4020-2352-1_56.
Porter, L., and K. Shaw. 2013. *Whose Urban Renaissance?: An International Comparison of Urban Regeneration Strategies.* Routledge.
Purcell, Mark. 2008. *Recapturing Democracy: Neoliberalization and the Struggle for Alternative Urban Futures.* New York, NY: Routledge Chapman & Hall.
Putnam, Robert D. 2000. *Bowling Alone: The Collapse and Revival of American Community.* New York, NY: Simon & Schuster.
Rawls, John. 1971. *A Theory of Justice.* Cambridge, MA: Harvard University Press.

———. 1985. Justice as Fairness: Political not Metaphysical. *Philosophy & Public Affairs* 14 (3): 223–251.
Real Estate Research Corporation. 1975. *The Dynamics of Neighborhood Change.* Washington, DC: U.S. Department of Housing and Urban Development, Office of Policy Development and Research.
Reps, John W. 1992. *The Making of Urban America: A History of City Planning in the United States.* Princeton, NJ: Princeton University Press.
Rink, Dieter. 2009. Wilderness: The Nature of Urban Shrinkage? The Debate on Urban Restructuring and Restoration in Eastern Germany. *Nature & Culture* 4 (3): 275–292.
RKG Associates. 2007. *District Improvement Financing Plan for the Hicks Logan Sawyer Urban Revitalization Area in New Bedford, MA.* Durham, NH: RKG Associates.
Rodgriguez, Gregory. 2009. Bulldozing Our Cities May Wreck Our Future. *Los Angeles Times*, June 22.
Rosenfeld, Elske. 2006. What is Art Up to in Disused Buildings? In *Shrinking Cities, Volume 2: Interventions*, ed. Philip Oswalt, 355–361. Ostfildern, Germany: Hatje Cantz Verlag.
Rosenman, Emily, and Samuel Walker. 2015. Tearing Down the City to Save It? 'Back-Door Regionalism' and the Demolition Coalition in Cleveland, Ohio. *Environment and Planning A* 48 (2): 273–291.
Rugare, Steve, and Terry Schwarz. 2008. *Cities growing smaller.* Cleveland, OH: The Cleveland Urban Design Collaborative, College of Architecture and Environmental Design, Kent State University.
Rust, Edgar. 1975. *No Growth: Impacts on Metropolitan Areas.* Lexington, MA: Lexington Books.
Ryan, Brent D. 2012. *Design After Decline: How America Rebuilds Shrinking Cities.* 1st ed. Philadelphia: University of Pennsylvania Press.
Ryznar, Rhonda M., and Thomas W. Wagner. 2001. Using Remotely Sensed Imagery to Detect Urban Change. *Journal of the American Planning Association* 67 (3): 327–336.
Safford, Sean. 2009. *Why the Garden Club Couldn't Save Youngstown: The Transformation of the Rust Belt.* Cambridge, MA: Harvard University Press.
Salmon, Carole, and Dubois, Sylvie. 2014. À La Recherche Du Français En Nouvelle-Angleterre: Une Enquête De Terrain à Travers Six États. *Journal of French Language Studies.* MLA International Bibliography [ProQuest]. Web 11 Januaty 2017.
Saltzman, Avi, and Lauren Mansnerus. 2005. For Homeowners, Frustration and Anger at Court Ruling. *The New York Times.* The New York Times Company. Web.
Salzman, Avi, and Laura Mansneus. For Homeowners, Frustration and Anger at Court Ruling. *The New York Times*, June 24.

Sandercock, Leonie. 1998. *Towards Cosmopolis: Planning for Multicultural Cities*. New York, NY: John Wiley and Sons.
Sassen, Saskia. 1991. *The Global City: New York, London, Tokyo*. Princeton, NJ: Princeton University Press.
Schatz, Laura. 2010. What Helps or Hinders the Adoption of "Good Planning" Principles in Shrinking Cities? A Comparison of Recent Planning Exercises in Sudbury, Ontario and Youngstown, Ohio. Doctoral dissertation, University of Waterloo.
Schilling, Joseph, and Jonathan Logan. 2008. Greening the Rust Belt: A Green Infrastructure Model for Right Sizing America's Shrinking Cities. *Journal of the American Planning Association* 74 (4): 451–466.
Schmidt, Deanna H. 2011. Urban Triage: Saving the Savable Neighbourhoods in Milwaukee. *Planning Perspectives* 26 (4): 569–589. doi:10.1080/02665433.2011.601609.
Schneider, Paul. 2006. 36 Hours in New Bedford, Mass. *New York Times*, May 26.
Schumpeter, Joseph. 1942. *Capitalism, Socialism and Democracy*. New York, NY: Harper.
Schwarz, Terry. 2008. The Cleveland Land Lab Experiments for a City in Transition. In *Cities Growing Smaller*, ed. Cleveland Urban Design Collaborative, 72–84. Cleveland, OH: Kent State University.
Scott, James C. 1998. *Seeing Like a State: How Certain Schemes to Improve the Human Condition Have Failed*. New Haven, CT: Yale University Press.
Silverman, Robert Mark, Kelly L. Patterson, Li Yin, Molly Ranahan, and Wu. Laiyun. 2016. *Affordable Housing in US Shrinking Cities: From Neighborhoods of Despair to Neighborhoods of Opportunity?* Bristol, UK: Policy Press.
Sites, William. 2003. *Remaking New York: Primitive Globalization and the Politics of Urban Community*. Minneapolis, MN: University of Minnesota Press.
Soja, Edward W. 2010. *Seeking Spatial Justice*. Minneapolis, MN: University of Minnesota Press.
Sousa, Sílvia, and Paulo Pinho. 2015. Planning for Shrinkage: Paradox or Paradigm. *European Planning Studies* 23 (1): 12–32.
Southworth, M., and E. Ben-Joseph. 2013. *Streets and the Shaping of Towns and Cities*. Island Press.
Squires, Gregory D. 2002. *Urban Sprawl: Causes, Consequences and Policy Responses*. Washington: The Urban Institute Press.
Staeheli, Lynn, and Don Mitchell. 2008. *The People's Property? Power Politics and the Public*. New York, NY: Routledge.
Stoll, Michael A. 2005. Geographical Skills Mismatch, Job Search and Race. *Urban Studies* 42 (4): 695–717.
Streitfeld, David. 2009. An Effort to Save Flint, Mich. by Shrinking It. *New York Times*, April 21.

Sugrue, Thomas J. 1995. Crabgrass-Roots Politics: Race, Rights, and the Reaction Against Liberalism in the Urban North, 1940–1964. *Journal of American History* 82 (2): 551–578.

———. 1996. *The Origins of the Urban Crisis: Race and Inequality in Postwar Detroit*. Princeton, NJ: Princeton University Press.

Taylor, F.B., Jr. 1970a. New Bedford Neglects Housing for Poor and Blacks. *Boston Globe*, July 16.

———. 1970b. Not Much Evidence of Reconciliation in New Bedford. *Boston Globe*, August 16.

Teaford, Jon C. 1990. *The Rough Road to Renaissance: Urban Revitalization in America, 1940–1985*. Baltimore, MD: Johns Hopkins University Press.

———. 2000. Urban Renewal and its Aftermath. *Housing Policy Debate* 11 (2): 443–465.

Temkin, Kenneth, and William Rohe. 1996. Neighborhood Change and Urban Policy. *Journal of Planning Education and Research* 15 (3): 159–170.

Thomas, June Manning. 2013. *Redevelopment and Race: Planning a Finer City in Postwar Detroit*. Detroit: Wayne State University Press.

Tiebout, Charles M. 1956. A Pure Theory of Local Expenditures. *Journal of Political Economy* 64 (5).

United States Census Bureau. 2008. American FactFinder—Decennial Census. *United States Census Bureau*. Accessed December 10, 2008. http://factfinder2.census.gov/faces/nav/jsf/pages/searchresults.xhtml?refresh=t.

———. 2013. American FactFinder—Decennial Census. *United States Census Bureau*. Accessed June 6, 2013. http://factfinder2.census.gov/faces/nav/jsf/pages/searchresults.xhtml?refresh=t.

United States Federal Home Loan Bank Board. 1940. *Waverly: A study in Neighborhood Conservation*. United States Federal Home Loan Bank Board.

Urban Renewal. 1959. *Standard-Times*, May 6.

U.S. Census. 2014. Census Website. Accessed July 1, 2015.

Vale, Lawrence J., and Thomas J. Campanella. 2005. *The Resilient City: How Modern Cities Recover from Disaster*. New York, NY: Oxford University Press.

Vergara, Camilo J. 1999. *American Ruins*. New York, NY: Monacelli Press.

———. n.d. *The New American Ghetto*. New Brunswick, NJ: Rutgers University Press.

Voyer, Richard A., Carol Pesch, Jonathan Garber, Jane Copeland, and Randy Comeleo. 2000. New Bedford, Massachusetts: A Story of Urbanization and Ecological Connections. *Environmental History*. ProQuest SciTech Collection. Web 11 July 2017.

Wallace, R. 1989. 'Homelessness', Contagious Destruction of Housing, and Municipal Service Cuts in New York City: 1. Demographics of a Housing Deficit. *Environment and Planning A* 21 (12): 1585–1602.

Wallace, Deborah, and Rodrick Wallace. 1998. *A Plague on Your Houses: How New York was Burned Down and National Public Health Crumbled.* New York, NY: Verso.

Walzer, Michael. 1983. *Spheres of Justice: A Defense of Pluralism and Equality.* New York, NY: Basic Books.

Wiechmann, Thorsten. 2008. Errors Expected—Aligning Urban Strategy with Demographic Uncertainty in Shrinking Cities. *International Planning Studies* 13 (4): 431–446.

Wilson, William J. 1987. *The Truly Disadvantaged: The Inner City, the Underclass, and Public Policy.* Chicago, IL: The University of Chicago Press.

Wilson, D., and H. Margulis. 1994. Spatial Aspects of Housing Abandonment in the 1990s: The Cleveland Experience. *Housing Studies* 9 (4): 493–511.

Wilson, David, Harry Margulis, and James Ketchum. 1987. Spatial Aspects of Housing Abandonment in the 1990s: The Cleveland Experience. *Housing Studies* 9 (4): 493–510.

———. 2004. Spatial Aspects of Housing Abandonment in the 1990s: The Cleveland Experience. *Housing Studies* 9 (4): 493–510.

Wolfbein, Seymour L. 1944. *The Decline of a Cotton Textile City: A Study of New Bedford.* New York, NY: Columbia University Press.

Wolin, Sheldon. 1996. Fugitive Democracy. In *Democracy and Difference: Contesting the Boundaries of the Political,* ed. Seyla Benhabib, 31–45. Princeton, NJ: Princeton University Press.

Young, Iris M. 1990. *Justice and the Politics of Difference.* Princeton, NJ: Princeton University Press.

———. 2000. *Inclusion and Democracy.* Oxford, England: Oxford University Press.

Zodrow, George R., and Peter Mieszkowski. 1986. Pigou, Tiebout, Property Taxation, and the Underprovision of Local Public Goods. *Journal of Urban Economics* 19 (3).

Zumbrun, Joshua. 2008. America's Fastest-Dying Cities. *Forbes Magazine*, August 5.

Index

A
abandon, 21
absentee landlords, 88–92, 94
Acushnet River, 67, 107
affordable housing, 18, 23, 29, 30, 43, 55, 104
alternative neighborhood change theory, 41, 43, 93, 94
American cities, 12, 104
approaches, 6, 13, 16, 18, 22, 24–8, 30, 32, 41, 43, 44, 49–51, 56, 57, 83, 95, 97, 106, 124, 125, 127, 130, 133, 139, 143, 145, 146, 191
Atlanta, 3, 17, 18

B
Berlin Wall, 27
Boston, 1, 4, 8, 12, 15, 26, 31, 32, 41, 50, 88, 89, 92, 103, 143, 192
Brightmoor, 29, 30
Buffalo Commons, 25
Bullard Street, 65, 69, 70, 113–15, 119, 141, 152, 154

C
California, 3, 18, 27, 28
changes, 1, 2, 6, 7, 10, 12, 13, 16, 18, 20–2, 29, 39–42, 49, 56, 57, 63–85, 87–99, 101–3, 106, 107, 110, 113, 123–48, 151, 152, 179, 182, 189, 190, 192, 193, 195
Chicago, 26, 92, 130
cities, 1, 15, 18–27, 63, 87, 101, 123–42, 144, 147, 151, 189
community preservation, 30
consolidated plan, 29
Cove Street, 65, 67, 71, 72, 83, 84, 113–15, 117, 155–60, 175–81, 183–6
criminality, 2

D
Dartmouth, 63
de-annexation, 26, 27
decision theory, 23
decline, 1–4, 6, 7, 11–13, 39–44, 53, 56, 57n1, 64, 65, 68, 71, 83, 87, 92, 93, 96–9, 123–5, 127, 132,

135, 144, 146, 152, 157, 182, 190–2
declining neighborhoods, 24
defragmentation, 27
demand, 4, 20–2, 30, 48, 65, 67, 94, 97, 102, 106, 127, 129, 130, 142, 144, 145
demolition, 19, 29, 30, 44, 65, 67, 103, 105, 128, 132, 133, 144, 145, 177, 181, 182, 193, 194
density, 18, 25, 68, 81–4, 96–9, 104, 108, 112–14, 119, 144–7, 152
depopulation, 1, 3, 12, 13, 16–18, 22, 25, 28, 29, 31, 39–43, 56, 65, 68, 82, 85, 87–9, 91–9, 102, 104, 113, 114, 118, 123, 125, 127, 140, 143, 146, 147, 151, 181, 189, 192, 194
Detroit, 18, 19, 23, 25, 26, 29, 32, 147, 195
development, 1–3, 16–19, 22–6, 29, 41, 42, 45, 48, 52, 54–6, 65, 71, 93, 107, 111, 112, 114, 128, 131–3, 136, 140, 142, 143, 147, 189
discrimination, 20
disincorporation, 27
dissolution, 27
distress, 1, 133, 141
Down at the Docks, 10, 190
"Dying Cities", 28

E
ecozone, 71, 82–4
equilibrium, 29, 30
erosion, 21
expansion, 1, 17, 26, 41, 65, 107, 110, 111, 131, 178

F
Fastest Dying Cities, 28
fast growth (urbanization), 16–18

The Federal Reserve Bank (FRB), 29
filtering, 20
Forbes
    Forbes 10 Fastest Dying Cities Symposium and Art Exhibition, 28
Fresno, 27

G
gentrification, 3, 17, 18, 56, 93
Great American Cities, 99, 120
Great Recession, 2, 17, 71, 123, 141, 144
growth-decline, 2, 3, 12, 13, 39, 40, 42, 65, 71, 182, 194

H
headliner cities, 3
Hurricane of 1938
    Buffalo, 28, 132
    displacement, 104, 108, 114
    Erie-Niagara Framework for Regional Growth, 124
    GI Bill, 103
    Hicks-Logan-Sawyer Master Plan (2005), 128
    New England Council, 103
    open space, 112
    recreation, 103
    Sanborn Fire Insurance maps, 113, 151, 193
    United Front Homes, 110, 112, 113

I
income levels, 1, 27, 93, 94
incomes, 18, 29, 88, 92–4, 111

J
Jefferson Square, 25, 26
Johnson, Michael P., 17, 23, 26

L

land use, 26, 29, 44, 53, 107, 112, 131, 134, 147
land-use regulation, 2
locational advantage, 4, 6, 103
Low Income Housing Tax Credit Program, 23, 32

M

managing decline, 2, 21, 189, 190
managing growth, 2, 71, 129
market stagnation, 88, 91–4
Massachusetts, 13n2, 1, 4, 8, 13, 26, 49, 50, 63, 111, 126, 130, 194
megacities, 17
metro, 27, 81

N

neighborhood, 2, 16, 41, 56, 87, 104, 127, 151, 190
New Bedford, 1, 15, 39, 63, 87–9, 91–8, 101, 123, 151, 189
New England, 2–4, 7, 9, 12, 102, 103, 189
New Urbanism, 147n1
New York, 3, 4, 12, 17, 26, 43, 44, 55, 124, 130, 144, 145
non-residential investments, 26
Nugent, Rory, 10, 11, 89, 190

O

occupied housing unit density, 21, 68, 83, 84, 98, 99

P

partnerships, 23, 49, 64, 89, 103, 192
planned, 15, 43, 81
planned cities, 3, 12, 15, 16, 25, 28, 43–5, 112, 113, 118, 119, 124, 129, 130, 132, 139, 144, 147, 191, 193
policy, 2, 17, 18, 21, 24, 28, 29, 32, 39–43, 65, 94–9, 105, 107, 119, 123–47, 151, 181, 193, 194
population decline, 4, 18, 20, 22, 24, 32, 40, 71, 83, 87, 101–19, 190
Portland, 4, 27
post-industrial, 2, 4, 12, 18, 123, 130, 133, 189
postmodern planning, 16, 42, 44
poverty, 2, 10, 16, 68, 91
pre-modern planning, 15
problems, 3, 6, 7, 17, 19, 20, 23, 24, 28, 32, 39, 42, 50, 51, 89–92, 94–6, 101, 105, 111, 112, 127, 132, 139, 141, 145, 146, 194, 195
programming, 30, 193
prosperity, 7, 87, 123
public redevelopment, 22, 23

R

redevelopment, 22
regionalism, 27
relaxed zoning, 134
research, 1, 3, 4, 6, 13, 17, 19, 20, 24–7, 30, 31, 39, 43, 44, 51, 65, 71, 87, 88, 93, 96, 110, 113, 124–6, 129–33, 139, 142, 152, 155–7, 176, 177, 181, 187, 190–3
residential investments, 26, 142
Reverse Transect Model, 71, 83
Rust Belt, 4, 6, 18, 102

S

Section 8, 89–92
shrink, 1, 12, 17–30, 101, 114–19, 151

Shrinking Cities in a Global
    Perspective, 28
Shrinking Cities Project, 27, 28, 44, 132
side-yard acquisitions, 25
smart growth, 17–19, 22, 23, 39–57,
    130, 132, 139, 146, 147, 191,
    195
smart shrinkage, 12, 26, 28, 30,
    39–57, 94, 110, 112, 124, 125,
    127, 132–40, 144, 146, 147,
    189–91, 195
social change, 2
South Central, 65, 67, 113–15, 118,
    119, 152, 153, 156, 157,
    166–76, 180, 181
South Terminal Project, 107, 110–12
Sun Belt, 4, 18, 26, 71

U

U.S. Department of Housing and
    Urban Development (HUD), 29,
    104, 111, 112, 119
unemployment, 1, 8, 10, 23, 43
units, 4, 18, 20–3, 25, 29, 30, 32, 55,
    82, 83, 90, 98, 102, 106, 108,
    110–12, 114, 119, 144, 145, 156
urban agriculture, 25, 29, 133
urban change, 1

urban development, 2
urban planning, 2, 16, 17, 56, 97,
    123–7
urban renewal, 11, 41, 65, 67,
    104–15, 118, 119, 119n1, 123,
    144, 151, 152, 189, 191
urban studies, 1, 3, 24, 31, 39, 147

V

vacancy, 6, 12, 20, 26, 30, 67, 83, 98,
    129, 193

W

Wamsutta Mills, 65
Warren Buffet, 67
Waterfront Historic Area League
    (WHALE), 11, 112, 113
"weak market cities", 28
wealth, 1, 2, 7
Working Waterfronts Festival, 8, 12,
    13

Y

Yale Law Review, 27
Youngstown, 3, 7, 24, 28, 29, 44, 45,
    57n3, 87, 147

CPSIA information can be obtained
at www.ICGtesting.com
Printed in the USA
LVOW05*2038110817
544666LV00013B/249/P